THE WAY-BACK ROOM
A MEMOIR OF A DETROIT CHILDHOOD

Mary Minock

For Another Mary,
We have so much
in common. I am so glad
to have met you.
Mary

WORKING LIVES SERIES
BOTTOM DOG PRESS
HURON, OHIO

CREDITS:
General Editor: Larry Smith
Layout & Design: Susanna Sharp-Schwacke
Cover Design: Susanna Sharp-Schwacke and Larry Smith
Cover image of Detroit skyscape, Hiawatha Card Co., Ypsilanti,
Michigan, from the Collection of Steve Frenkel.

ACKNOWLEDGEMENTS

Publication Credits:
A slightly different version of the poem, "Freighter Horns, Southwest
Detroit," appeared in *Driftwood Review* 7 (2004): 95.
Excerpts from earlier versions of chapters appeared in issues of
Madonna Muse—"Saint Mary of Detroit," 3 (2009): 2-8; and "A
Chance to Win a New Mercury," 5 (2011): 8-13.

Sources:
Father Peter J. Forbes, "*Views from the Rectory*" (*Holy Redeemer Weekly*,
February 6, 1955).
"Elvis Presley fans—24,000 strong and all screaming…" (*Detroit News*,
April 1, 1957).

Photo Credits:
Cover photos of the following books:
John Carr, *Saint Maria Goretti: Martyr for Purity* (8th ed.; Fresno,
CA: Academy Library Guild, 1953; Dublin: Cahill, 1953).
Felix Sutton, *The Picture Story of Davy Crockett* (Illus. H. B. Vestal;
New York: Wonder Books, 1955).
Leo F. Griffin, *The Catholic Girl Examines Her Conscience* (29th ed.;
Huntington, IN: Our Sunday Visitor Press, 1953).
Photos of newspaper ads:
"Sorry, but I'm Staying!" (*Holy Redeemer Weekly*, May 15, 1955).
"Today Sunday Only! Elvis Presley" (*Detroit News*, March 31, 1957).
Photo of the 1955 Holy Redeemer faculty, and photos of the Holy
Redeemer complex, are generously provided courtesy of the Sisters,
Servants of the Immaculate Heart of Mary Archives, Monroe, MI.
Copy of my only surviving Elvis portrait, from 1956.

(Continued on page 213)

TABLE OF CONTENTS

FREIGHTER HORNS, SOUTHWEST DETROIT

Every country has its beauty.
In Iowa they stare into the irises
of sun flowers.
Here we listen
in the light after dawn
to freighter horns.
We cannot see the river.
The view is blocked
and has been all along.
Yet we cannot imagine
a country where there is no river
and there are no horns.
The logic of sound—
buoyant in belief
beyond the ground—
awakens us to morn:
against the horns
we invent ourselves.
From there we go on.

PRAISE FOR MARY MINOCK
AND *THE WAY-BACK ROOM:*

Mary Minock's memoir, *The Way-Back Room*, brings to life the sounds and smells—and the grit—of one fragmented family's home life in Detroit in the 50s and early 60s. Full of rich detail and texture, it offers keen insights into the subtle and unsubtle tensions in the life of a young woman coming of age in this era of change, trying to forge her own path to a clear view of her family history. Minock's sharp, vivid prose, and clear-eyed reflections on the past keep us with her all the way, cheering her on.

—Jim Daniels, author of *Trigger Man: More Tales of the Motor City*

The Way-Back Room is a lovely book: gentle, poetic and resonant. Mary Minock renders a vivid portrait of Detroit, the 1950s and her Catholic childhood, shadowed by the early death of her father and the mysteries of her mother. The characters you meet will live within you long after you close the back cover.

—Tom Stanton, author of *The Final Season*

Mary Minock's new book certainly evokes 1950's Detroit. Her father works for Cadillac, smells of "cigarettes and steel," and dies young of a brain tumor. The old neighborhood on Clark Street is working class, first and second generation immigrant families. Teenage Mary walks across the Ambassador Bridge to Windsor, as if that Canadian town were a suburb of Detroit. This book may derive its jibe from post-World War II Motown, but Minock's story is foremost an American memoir. Like millions of kids, Mary idolizes Davy Crockett, and later must choose between heartthrobs: Pat Boone or Elvis. At the heart of this memoir is a 1950's girl's sexual and intellectual awakening, the struggle against the guilt of a Catholic upbringing, but it's also the generational guilt that defined an era. Minock has written her story, and ours: the story of those men and women (especially women) who grew up back then, and a story for younger readers who always wanted the secret history that their own mothers and fathers would never share.

—Martin Lammon , editor of *Arts and Letters*

What a treasure Mary Minock has given us in *The Way-Back Room*. This memoir does what good memoir is meant to do: provide unexpected insights into the humanity we all share in a way that sometimes shames us, sometimes makes us laugh, sometimes hurts, sometimes makes us angry, and all too often breaks our heart—and she it does it beautifully. Young Mary Rhodes survives the death of her father, the neuroses of her mother, the cold shoulders of her classmates, the cruelty of the nuns at her Catholic school, an obsession with the martyred saints, and a crush on Elvis, sticking it out with bewildered determination, but determination nonetheless. And what a joy to see this portrait of a Detroit neighborhood in the 1950s, which Minock paints with such obvious love for the city. A rich and rewarding pleasure from start to finish.

—George Dila, author *of Nothing More to Tell*

BOTTOM DOG PRESS

HURON, OHIO

CHAPTER ONE
IN THE DAYS OF BECOMING LONELY

Mama could always tell the time of day by the smells of the neighborhood. In early morning, the pungent smell of damp tobacco drifted over Clark Park from the Scotten-Dillon cigar factory on Fort Street. By mid-morning, another smell replaced the tobacco, a mixture of grease and hot metal from the factories down toward the river on Clark Street, Fort Street and Jefferson Avenue. When the evening wind picked up, the air smelled of the river, with the sun going down on our back yard.

In those days, car carriers rolled up and down Clark Street all day, some empty, some loaded with big chassis from the Fleetwood plant on Fort Street lumbering north to the Cadillac plant to be fitted with engines. Others, packed with newly assembled cars from that plant, labored south toward the river to be loaded onto Great Lakes freighters, and then shipped across country. Empty carriers rattled. When full they shook the house.

In early fall, the cars were shrouded in canvas, so no one could peek at the new models before they hit the showrooms. Neighborhood boys and grown men who didn't work at Fleetwood or Cadillac pointed at the trucks, speculated, assessed and argued about the hidden designs. Nearly all the men in the neighborhood worked in the auto industry, loyal to Ford, or to Studebaker, or General Motors, or Chrysler.

Sounds floated through the air in counterpoint and harmony. In the fog around dawn, we heard the horns from freighters on the river. Later, they signaled to the mail boats when they passed. They moaned all day when it was rainy or foggy. Day and night steam whistles blew from the factories, announcing the ends of shifts. The sounds of freight trains and crossing bells rang out from the Wabash track between Fort Street and Jefferson. Sometimes at night, faster trains from the Michigan Central track went whizzing over the viaduct three blocks up past Toledo Street. We heard the hissing of molten metals being mixed, the pounding of tools, the stamping out of parts, the drumming and squeaking—the music of industry.

We were tenants, Mama and Daddy, my sister Betty and I, living in an upstairs flat on Clark Street, tied to the habits of our aging landlords, the Dixons, who lived in the flat below with their bachelor son. Each flat had its front porch, and Mr. Dixon's on the first floor featured a gray wicker rocker and a porch swing. "You girls should never sit on that," Mama said once after Betty took me down to try out the swing. Instead, we sat on a glider on our own porch above, shaded by a huge elm tree that branched so high above the house it never blocked our view of the lush park across the street.

The two-story gray clapboard house was old, even in 1950. Our landlord, Edgar Lee Dixon, who'd been a Detroit banker and real estate speculator, had the house built in 1910. He chose a lot that fronted the loveliest part of Clark Park—an elegant lake shaped like a kidney bean, with an open pavilion at one end, a smaller lake beyond it, and a tall band shell with Doric pillars at the other end. Mama told me there'd been a stone bridge arching over the smaller lake that was lined with lily pads.

Mama also told me stories of old man Dixon, who walked with a cane and smelled of pipe ashes. "Mr. Dixon was an important man. He ran the Detroit Convention and Tourist Bureau back in the Twenties." She told the story of how our upstairs flat came to be. Mrs. Dixon had run a boarding house for young men who came to work in the factories. "They lived in rooms upstairs here," she said, "and every morning and evening they used to go down the back stairway so Mrs. Dixon could serve them their breakfast and supper in her kitchen." In 1927, after the Western YMCA up the street opened, with four floors of sleeping rooms for single men, Mr. Dixon converted the upstairs into a rental flat for a family and added our little kitchen. "That was good for Mrs. Dixon," Mama said. "She was tired of all that cooking and cleaning."

Mr. Dixon created a private entrance by building a steep front stairway over a short side porch. He installed two matching side-by-side doors, one for the upper and one for the lower flat, each with rows of beveled windows. He then hammered separate address numbers next to each. The door on the left led to our flat at the top of the steep stairway.

As the story goes, Daddy spotted the "For-Rent" sign in one of the upstairs front windows, and told Mama, "Get there as early as you can in the morning." Those three big windows offered a grand view of the lake in the park. Mama and Daddy rented the flat for forty dollars a month in the winter of 1934. And in 1950 they were still living there.

I liked our house with its white Doric pillars—three on each side and one where the porch jutted out enough so you could see clear to the backyard. They made the house look like a temple.

Mrs. Dixon's bright yellow forsythia bushes grew tall on one side of the porch, so dense I could hide behind them. Once there, I could peer into the basement window where Daddy had built a room to store Mama's fruit jars and our old toys. Here I studied spiders that spun webs in the corners of the window. I imagined I surprised them, though I never hurt them.

The backyard was our orchard, with a mulberry tree, a pear tree, and an apple tree. Grape trellises bordered each side of the walkway from the house to the garage. One day Daddy made Betty and me a green enamel swing seat and strung it from the apple tree.

Once after it had rained, I wiped the beads of water from the swing seat and sat down, just as Mama was walking under the grapevines. I shook the rain from the apple tree, that fell on the grapevines, and then onto Mama.

"You're getting me wet!" Mama yelled as she started running and laughing.

I thought myself smart for knowing what the raindrops on the leaves would do.

Like the moon that rose over the park and flooded through our upstairs windows, water floated in and out of my earliest memories. There was the lake Mama talked so much about, and there was the lagoon that replaced it sometime in the late 1940s.

Mama used to sit on the porch glider in the late afternoon with me, slowly rocking, looking out over the park, telling stories, keeping alive a picture of the lake. She told of how she and Daddy used to sit on the same glider and watch the large Japanese goldfish as the sun glinted off their backs when they floated toward the surface. Boys would sail their model boats on the lake with white swans floating across. One cold winter night she and Daddy watched beyond to the old Western High School building as it burned down—the entire building engulfed in flames in the snow. "In the morning it was completely covered in icicles," she said, nodding, "All that water the firemen sprayed."

As I listened to Mama's story, I squinted through the trees to Scotten Street. The long, rose-red brick Western High School built in its place didn't look new to me, though it was made of bricks—too strong to burn or blow down.

Mostly I remember the lagoon that replaced the lake. Lined with concrete, the lagoon had a rounded lip and gently sloping sides that descended five feet underground. In the spring, lines of black tar, which marked where the huge chunks of concrete had been fitted together, softened or hardened depending on the air temperature and the amount of sunshine.

When the City filled it with water in the summer, we waded in the shallows or sat on the rim and splashed. As summer grew older, I walked farther and farther out into the cooler water away from the rim. There was a point, and I remember it, where even on tiptoes I could walk no farther. I bounced myself off from the concrete and learned to swim to my older sister Betty. Some summers when the City didn't fill the lagoon, but only a wading pool farther south in the park, the lagoon became quieter, lonelier, more given to wind and beauty.

For six years I drank in the sounds and scenes and smells of the house and park and neighborhood, learning their rhythms and rituals. I was a beloved happy child, born at the start of my parents' middle age into a small family. I absorbed a strong and lasting sense that underlying all the things that were modern were the things that were old.

*   *   *

"Sit there, Honey, so you'll be out of the way," Mama said. She'd led me out of the hallway into the front of the house directing me to the horsehair sofa near the archway that divided our living and dining rooms. My six-year-old feet dangled over the edge, and the backs of my knees rubbed against the scratchy fabric. Usually I avoided sitting on the sofa unless I had one of Mama's quilts underneath me—smooth, cool and comforting. This afternoon, though, I sensed the crisis and didn't complain. I did what I was told.

There stood two ambulance men in white uniforms at the end of the crooked hallway near the back bedroom where Daddy lay in bed. They talked as though they were trying to solve a puzzle, pointing at the turns in the walls.

The day before, Dr. Agnew had made a house call, and I overheard him say to Mama, "He's a very sick man." I couldn't contemplate Daddy being sick. Mama always told people, "He's never been sick a day in his life," and that seemed right to me. Grownups in general, and Daddy in particular, didn't get sick; they took care of sick children. When I had measles, Daddy walked up to Cook's Drug Store and brought back for me a stack of seven tiny books that fit into a pretty flowered box.

I sat on the sofa alone and waited. The ambulance men had brought a curious object into the house. The folded chrome frame of a gurney sat propped against the opposite wall next to the piano. The couch's horsehair scratched my legs that had gone to sleep. I wanted to get down. I wanted to know what was going on, but I couldn't hear what they were saying in the back of the house. I wanted to see Daddy.

I waited a long time, until finally I saw the ambulance men emerge from the hallway into the dining room. They held him up, one on each side. Daddy was dressed in pajamas. I'd only seen Daddy in pajamas twice, and both times I thought he looked funny. Now it wasn't funny. Daddy was dressed in his pajamas, and it was way past morning.

He leaned heavily on the men, first rocking toward one who braced himself, then swaying toward the other, staggering, as though he'd fall, as though they all might fall. Inch by inch they guided him into the dining room, continuing to the living room. I was afraid to breathe for fear they all would topple. They stopped directly in front of me.

"I'll need my pants if I'm going out," Daddy said. Mama rushed back to the bedroom to grab his pants, the ones he wore around the house with the frayed hole on the side near the front pocket, the blue pants he wore on Saturdays, the ones he changed into after work. I liked when he wore them and I sat on his lap—they were soft. One time I sat on his lap when we were visiting at Aunt Dee's house. He was dressed in his navy blue suit, and it was scratchy, scratchy like the coat he wore when it snowed and he hugged me. But it wasn't as scratchy as the whiskers he had sometimes, when he teased me by rubbing his face down my cheek until I begged him to stop. And then, a minute later, I begged him to do it again. He laughed and I leaned into him, and then I took in his smell—cigarettes and steel.

The men stood in the archway, working to steady him. Both were stouter and taller than Daddy, who was now bent over. Each man held a corner of the top of his pants, and one of them told him, "Please, Mr. Rhodes, lean on me," while the other stooped and Daddy's leg came up, searching for the hole of the pant leg. I looked at his face, frowning. I never saw him look like that. His nose was red, the bridge of it swollen, his brow so twisted I could hardly see his eyes. He winced and looked down. Was he embarrassed…was I? These men were, after all, putting his pants on over his pajamas. He looked at me (I needed to believe he did) and then he glanced away, as though he didn't want me to see him like that.

Finally each of his legs found the pant holes. The men helped him draw up the trousers, which they buttoned but didn't belt. They talked more. One of the men moved to the open stairway door. He looked down and talked about the curve and the steepness of the stairs. The men looked at each other and then one said to Daddy, "We're going to carry you down on the stretcher."

One of them opened the gurney while the other steadied Daddy. The gurney clanked and then clicked as it changed into a cart with wheels. They strapped Daddy to a contraption that looked like Mama's ironing board, smooth and white on one side. One man stooped at Daddy's feet while the other stood at Daddy's head. They looked in each other's eyes for a long second, and then in unison lifted the board and Daddy as though he was light as a baby. As they placed the board on the gurney, I heard another clink. They adjusted the straps. I couldn't see Daddy's face anymore. I longed to go to him, kiss him and say "Goodbye," but I was told not to get off the sofa, to stay out of the way. I needed to do what I was told, that maybe I could help by being good.

Fighting back tears, Mama said to Daddy: "I'm coming right after you." Her face was red and swollen; her upper lip quivered, but she didn't cry. She was also trying hard to help by being good.

"We're going down, now," one of them said. "We'll make sure you're okay." They picked Daddy up again, rounded the corner and went down the stairs, out of my sight. That was the last time I saw Daddy alive.

In the lobby at Harper Hospital, green leather couches, end tables, floor lamps and ashtrays rested on a parquet floor that looked like it had been scuffed up and waxed many times. When I had stared at the floor long enough, I saw complicated patterns. Children under twelve were not permitted to go upstairs to visit patients. Betty was twelve and I was six, so she and Mama got to see Daddy. Every day I sat in the lobby and waited through the evening visiting hours and waited through the afternoon visiting hours on the weekends. Sometimes on the weekends, my Aunt Bea or my Aunt Dee came and waited awhile with me, but mostly I waited alone.

At first I just sat on one or another of the cold couches. But then I found something to comfort me—the deep red velvet ropes that draped between iron dividing pillars—like the ropes and pillars in the bank. In the hospital nobody was looking. I wrapped my hands around the velvet and slid my hands up and down the rope. The velvet was cool.

I waited every day for a month, out of the way, vaguely aware of what was going on, all the while aching to see Daddy. I kept my mind open, expecting he'd come home soon. Hospitals were where sick people went to get better. I balanced my hope and my wish to help by being good against my rage. I never got to see him. I never got to say goodbye.

I had a hard time believing Daddy was dead. Soon I'd have a hard time negotiating the terms between death and memory; death sets in motion the need for memory, the only way to make a dead person come alive. But one memory would lead to more and more memories, and before I knew it I would remember the intricate fabric of my life with him and then I'd be angry or I'd want to cry. I didn't cry. It was Betty who was angry. It was Mama who cried.

The dead man at the funeral home, whose head had been shaved in the hospital operating room, wore a wig. They couldn't find a red-haired wig, so the Daddy with gray hair lying in the casket, the one they encouraged me to talk to, to kneel before, to pray and mourn for, was an imposter. Mama sobbed and threw herself into the lap of this stranger's corpse. The relatives with their ashen faces grieved over nothing. Daddy would come back. He'd be there when we got home.

Besides, I found better things to do. Even though I'd been to Hackett's Funeral Home on Vernor and Junction before, for the wake of a neighbor, I never knew the basement stairway led to a large happy knotty-pine-paneled room with a shiny checkered linoleum floor. My cousins Jeff and Bobby and I ran and slid, played tag, gobbled up nuts and potato chips from the little bowls on the end tables, and laughed so loudly we got in trouble. Aunt Mag was the meanest. "How can you behave like this when your father is dead?" She hurt my feelings, and besides, my Daddy wasn't dead.

All Mama ever said to me about Daddy's death was that even-toned sentence that seemed to embarrass her, "Your Daddy's gone to live in heaven." She brought home some of the floral arrangements from the funeral.

I rubbed my hands up the stalks of the gladiolas and asked Mama, "Why do they call them gladiolas when nobody is glad?"

"I don't know," she said.

As the flowers died, I gathered all the cheap fat ribbons that had been affixed to them and made a ribbon bouquet. For a few days I enjoyed the silence in the house. I didn't know what death was. Could it be a good thing because now Mama and Daddy wouldn't fight anymore?

The evidence mounted every day when nothing changed: no matter how long I waited, I never heard Daddy unlock the door downstairs, cough in the stairway, tread up the steep stairs with his heavy tired feet, and open the upstairs door. Perhaps they were right, and Daddy was dead. Shame washed over me as I recalled the fun I'd had in the basement of the funeral parlor. As I was to believe many times over the next years, I thought maybe it was I who'd made him die. I hadn't prayed enough in the waiting room of the hospital. I hadn't paid enough careful attention. It would take years for me to stop punishing myself or to stop listening for him to come home.

Mama repeated the explanation of how Daddy died to all who asked. She learned to tell it as a fast story, strangely, to me, using fruits and vegetables as metaphors. In the months that followed I'd hear the story become more and more succinct. I memorized it.

"When they did the exploratories the first week he went in, the tumor was the size of a lemon. By the time they did the autopsy a month later, it was the size of a grapefruit. They couldn't operate. It was growing in the center of his brain. He'd have been a vegetable." She would say it like that, evenly, and look away. It was an explanation that saved a lot of further questions.

The memory of the sound of his voice started to drift away. Except for the last time I saw him in agony, so did the memory of his face. The other memories came in fragments, delicate and airy, elusive, always in danger of being lost, ready to disperse into dust, yet these memories I reached for, sought after as treasures to be kept hidden and guarded. They needed to be hidden, for any talk of Daddy, of Daddy and me, had ceased. I guessed that if I shared my memories they too would be wrenched from me. Whenever the memories brought me too close to the precipice, I pushed them away rather than cry. If I remembered, I wouldn't be able to bear it. I'd be all alone and I would cry, and if I cried I'd make Mama cry. Mama's tears were a flood; the power of them would wash mine away. It became harder and harder to believe I was his. Harder and harder to believe he was mine.

No one spoke about him. At least no one spoke to me about his having anything to do with me. No one spoke. When no one spoke to me about him, and when I knew that anything I spoke of would be wrenched away, the fragments caused me shame. The echo of the hospital regulation haunted me. *Children under twelve are not permitted.* Maybe it was so. When I remembered, I believed I was encroaching, sneaking, bad, a thief. And yet I remembered fragments, some from my earliest consciousness, some from just before he got sick and died:

Daddy, quiet and still, working on something at the dining room table, the top of which I couldn't see. It was at a time when I reached for grownups often and curled my arms around them as they picked me up and clutched me to their chests. Standing below table level, I saw Daddy as only a motionless bent leg in soft blue cotton sitting on the chair. But then I called to him and reached for him, and he lifted me onto his lap. It was a different world up there. A large object of light brown leather sat in front of him, little iron tools scattered across the surface of the oil-clothed table. Daddy was carving patterns on a leather saddle. It smelled of saddle soap. Sitting on his lap awhile…and when I got restless, his gently setting me down.

Daddy and I played car. "Mama, bring us a plate," Daddy said, and Mama brought one of the white ones with little waves in it. The plate was the steering wheel, and I was in Daddy's lap being the driver. He was the car, and he kept making rumbling noises. When I turned the plate back and forth fast, I was driving fast. He started bumping me around on his lap, and his rumbling got louder. "There's a car up ahead of you," Daddy said. And when I stuck out my foot, he screeched and stopped like I was putting on the brake. Sometimes I stuck my foot out only a little to see if he was paying attention. He always screeched and stopped. Every time.

At first Mama wouldn't let Betty and me cross Vernor Highway, so we waited for Daddy outside Pete's Barber Shop on the corner. Over time Betty cajoled Mama into letting us go farther, crossing at the light while Betty held my hand. We skipped to Toledo Street to wait for Daddy, who was working then at Cadillac as a plant policeman.

So many men marched away from Cadillac at four o'clock that I couldn't see Daddy. Betty spotted him sooner than I could, and when she pointed him out, I could see him too. He was taller than most of the others and smiling. He held his lunch box in one hand, and waved to me with the other. I hopped on one leg and the other, waiting for the traffic to clear so he could cross, pick me up and kiss me, then set me down, as we all walked home. Sometimes he let me carry his lunch box and pretend that I too was walking home from work.

One morning Mama noticed that Daddy had forgotten his lunch box. We set out in the car to take it to him while he was on duty at the Gate. The factory noises scared me, so that I always covered my ears when we drove by. Mama didn't seem to be afraid. She knew just where to find Daddy, handsome in his uniform with the blue policeman's cap. He sat alone in the tower behind the glass, with telephones and papers and pencils and keys on the little counter. Mama tapped on the glass at the side door, then she gave him the lunch box, and kissed him on the cheek. It only took a minute. We couldn't stay because Daddy was at work. He smiled and waved at me through the glass, and in the uniform he looked so different. But I knew it was him.

Mama and Daddy were fighting—something Mama promised to do. They stood in the tiny kitchen while Mama washed dishes at the sink. Daddy shouted and Mama cried. I stood in the doorway, hoping they'd notice me and stop fighting. But Daddy passed by me as if he didn't see me. Mama stopped washing dishes and went to the bathroom. I went to find Daddy. He was sitting in his red chair with his head in his hands. I didn't know what to do.

"I bought us a surprise," Daddy said. It looked like a big ball wrapped in brown paper. After he unwrapped the paper, we saw that the ball was blue like water in a painting

with big orange patches all over it. An extra metal ring with numbers and inch marks encircled the ball. He unwrapped a shiny dark wooden four-legged stand with fancy scrolls and designs on it. At the top of the stand a metal post stuck up where he inserted a metal arc with a groove along its length. He finally slid the ball with its metal ring into the groove on top of the stand.

Mama and Betty and I crowded around. When it was assembled in the middle of the living room floor, it stood exactly at my height—as though the ball was me with a big head, and the stand was me with a skinny body. Daddy stood back a minute and looked at it. "It has to be tilted on its axis," he said, so he slid the ball until the extra plate with numbers and "Noon" and "Mid-night" written on, tilted a little to the side.

"It's the world," he said, "and we're on it." He showed me where I was, in Detroit, standing in this living room. He showed me where Tennessee was, because that's where Daddy came from before he moved to Detroit. "Tennessee," he said. I liked when he said Tennessee. It was a funny word. Tennessee.

"See, Michigan is a mitten," Mama said. She pointed to the tiny jagged glove hand that framed Detroit. Daddy turned the globe around to the other side and searched its surface, trailing his finger across the ocean. "See," he said. "Italy across the ocean is a boot."

The blue was water: the rivers and lakes and seas and oceans. "See how it spins?" Daddy said. He gently twirled it. "The world turns around," he said. "That's what makes day and night. Night is when it turns away from the sun."

I wanted to believe that Daddy was the person who introduced me to the moon. *I was three weeks old and had just left Harper Hospital. It was the first day I would enter the upper flat, the first time I came home. On that day, released from hospital regulations, Daddy greeted me and held me for the first time. Mama was resting. It was evening. He saw me stir. He picked me up and swaddled me in a thin blanket. He took me to the front porch door. The sky was clear although a few hard snowflakes swirled earthward. He held me up. He raised his head to gesture. He said, "There is the moon."*

I saw it. I wobbled my head, held in the palm of his hand.

CHAPTER TWO
MAMA GOES TO WORK

I stooped at the kitchen screen door performing my chore of swatting flies, and listening intently to the talk between Mama and her good friend Evelyn Smith, who Mama called simply Smitty. They sat at Smitty's kitchen table in one of the row houses on Christiancy Street. I came as Mama's sole tag-along, for Mama had sent my sister Betty down to Tennessee on the train to spend the summer with our uncles, Daddy's closest brothers, Odell and Odo.

"It'll be good for you," I heard Smitty say to Mama. "It'll get your mind off your troubles. You might as well give it a try." Smitty was the only person who could lighten Mama's heavy tone of voice that summer.

Mama probably wouldn't have taken on the job if it hadn't been for Smitty. And she probably wouldn't have done it if she hadn't decided to do it soon after the funeral—before the numbness wore off and the paralysis set in. Mama signed up to become an Avon Lady.

Soon after she enrolled in the training program, the fragrance of Avon breezed into our down-turned lives, tilting our heads up a little so we could smell the sample vials of perfume from Mama's kit: Cotillion, Quaintance, Golden Promise, Forever Spring, and To a Wild Rose.

After the first week of training, Mama took me along to the sessions, held in the Lafayette Building in downtown Detroit. I was the only kid there; I felt important and enjoyed the meetings, especially the performance and pep talk of the gesturing lady running the program, who whipped us all up into a fervor.

I learned a surprising number of tips for selling, as the process of suggestive selling rested on the simple premise that one sale leads to another, a concept even a six-year-old could understand. If the customer buys a Spark of Fire lipstick, for example, she'll want to do something about her too-pale cheeks, maybe something complementing the lipstick. And how could she put Pink Tinge rouge on her cheeks over the wrong foundation? Before you knew it, the customer would buy Avon products to care for her entire beautiful body, from her hair to the tips of her lacquered fingers and toes. The trainees were told to repeat: "Avon sells itself. Yes, Avon sells itself." Mama looked over at me and smiled, as I joined in.

After the second week, Mama brought home her kit, a stylish dark green leather, over-the-shoulder bag, rectangular with burgundy suede lining.

Empty, it smelled like new leather. The big front pocket was divided into two sections, one to tuck brochures, and the other to store the free lipstick and cream sachet samples. The trainer explained: "If the lady of the house is not at home, the Representative leaves her brochure with her name and telephone number and a sample lipstick."

If the lady of the house were home, the Representative could politely persuade her to invite her in. Once in, she opened the larger part of the kit by flipping over the hinged top. Inside the kit was a world of wondrously fragrant balms, emollients and essences—so many that if the Representative worked slowly, she could keep pulling out more and more of them, spellbinding her customers like a genie or a magician while the kitchen clock ticked. The kit contained sample vials and tubes of practically everything in the entire Avon Catalog, all neatly organized in smaller containers. At home, I abandoned my toys to play with Mama's kit.

I loved the kit. When I promised to be careful, Mama let me look at everything, the vials of perfumes and foundations, the palettes of rouges and eye shadows, everything except the leather crescent containing standard-sized tubes of lipsticks. I sat on our dirty gray living room rug and took everything out, looked it over, twisted off caps, smelled everything, carefully repackaged it all, and closed the kit. Then I took everything out again. The samples were like dollhouse furniture, just my size. Everything smelled new, a thousand bouquets.

I also enjoyed arranging the tiny sample tubes of lipstick that Mama distributed to customers. I never wanted to put them on. I only wanted to line them up by the most beautiful to the least beautiful colors in that order. I liked the rosy ones. I also liked to line them up by hues. They came in subtly gradated colors with evocative names, from the lightest pink—Plum Pink and Pink Rose, to pink orange—Solo in the Sun, Silver Trill, and Orange Chiffon, to red—Clear Red, to redder red—Magic Red, Spark of Fire, Ripe Cherry, to the dark and darker maroons—Crimson Beauty, Blue Jewel, Burnt Sugar, and Blue Flame. Blue Flame was almost blue, named I was sure after the gas flame on the stove.

In order to compare them, I had to open them, and I found it difficult to get the caps back on the tiny tubes without smudging the lipstick. Mama solved the problem by selling me the whole line of samples. They cost the Representatives two cents each, so she sold all thirteen of them to me at cost, gave me a penny discount so I only had to pay a quarter, and took it out of my allowance. Then I had my own collection of samples that I could arrange anyway I wanted to. Mama had plenty more.

Mama would use me as a "customer" so she could practice her sales pitch. She turned my wrists over to show the veiny side and dabbed Cotillion on the left wrist and Quaintance on the right. "Which do you prefer?" she asked politely.

I sniffed each wrist. "Cotillion," I answered.

Mama made eye contact. "We have Cotillion in perfume, cologne, toilet water, cream sachet, Beauty Dust and talc. You may want to buy our perfume and perhaps supplement that with cologne for after your bath. And...you just might want to use a little toilet water in your hair."

When Mama said the words, she didn't sound like Mama. She sounded haughtier, a little like a thin lady in high heeled shoes. It didn't matter. She was trying to get it right. Sitting kitty corner from me at the table, she leaned back, looked deeply into my eyes and studied me. Smiling faintly, she said, "Let me see. I think green eye shadow would look best with your eye color and your hair." I loved it when she looked at me like that.

On September 18, 1951, exactly four months after Daddy died, Mama received her signed Certificate of Selection to sell Avon. She was given a territory of 120 customers in the area north of Toledo Street between Junction and Livernois Avenues, a not-very-wealthy neighborhood that abutted the raised viaduct of the Grand Trunk Railroad. The neighborhood was home to a mix of Southerners, Mexicans, Maltese, but mostly Polish who spilled over from St. Hedwig's Parish. Her territory was a little more than a half mile away from home.

Even though Mama didn't smoke, she started using Avon's Smoker's Toothpaste. Her teeth gleamed. It was remarkably good stuff. She set off with white-toothed optimism just as I went back to school after lunch. It was the first time I saw her smile broadly since before Daddy got sick, even if the smile came from Avon.

Like her friend Smitty, I wanted her to do well. The trouble, as I saw it from looking at the training manual and the brochures she got for each campaign, was that Mama just didn't look the part. The Avon ladies in the pictures were young and thin and wore up-to-date hair-dos. Mama was not so young, was getting noticeably fatter, her hair was graying, and she still wore it in a 1940s style with a big puff of it rolled straight back from her forehead and with French braids in the back. And she wouldn't wear the Avon hat, which looked similar to one of those elongated Boy Scout caps, the folded-flat kind you opened to put on your head. The hat didn't work, so the green leather kit would have to be the only Avon mark.

During the first few weeks, when I got home from school, Mama was usually back from working her territory, already discouraged. Her feet hurt, or something came up, or it got cold, or she didn't get very far. "I was only able to do one block of Brandon," she said slowly. She wasn't smiling.

When I went with her on Saturday to deliver her orders and, supposedly, to sell more, I saw her mistakes. She never wore much makeup herself, mostly just Avon's Powder-Pak foundation. She wore lipstick and a little rouge, but never applied eye makeup. In fact, Mama held a fairly rigid, old-fashioned idea of how painted a woman's face ought to be.

When Mrs. Alcanter wanted to try the line of eye shadows, Mama said, "I don't think you need to wear eye makeup. You look just fine without it. And what if that stuff gets in your eye?"

If Mrs. Caruana said she wanted three lipsticks, Mama said, "Do you really need three? You know you might want to just stick with the Pink Rose and Crimson Beauty for now. That should be enough."

If Mrs. Czarnecki's order cost too much in Mama's mind, Mama went over it again with Mrs. Czarnecki. "You know, Helen, that's all going to amount to $9.92, and I haven't even added the sales tax. Are you sure you don't want to skip the Beauty Dust?" Mama's fear of spending money was projected onto everyone.

Although discouraged at first, a few months later Mama began returning home a little later and a little brighter. She'd been talking to Mrs. Vella on Hammond Street. Then it was Mrs. Lopez on Manson, or Mrs. Ference on Federal, or Mrs. Eplett on Plumer. She couldn't cover two houses in her territory without being invited in for tea. Or pie, coffee, scones, potato salad, or *pierogis*.

"Mrs. Gasiorek makes *real pierogis*," she told me. "You should taste them."

At Mrs. Vella's she tried Maltese squid, and I heard her telling my Aunt Kay about it on the phone. "It was good. Not rubbery like I thought it would be."

At Mrs. Hernandez's house she tried authentic Mexican enchiladas. "They were good, and they're really not all that spicy."

She made it to the sixth house on Federal and got invited in just to talk.

The friendly women in her territory enjoyed consoling the new widow with the beautiful smile and lovely skin. She met so many people who wished her well. She experienced the insides of so many houses that wore their culture like a badge on their sleeves. She started learning the census of nationalities on each block—three houses Polish, then one Italian, one Maltese, one Southern, two Mexican, two Polish again, one Irish, and again two Maltese. She ate her way to a kind of international awareness. And sometimes her hostesses bought Avon.

Many weeks Mama spent so much time talking to some of her customers that she didn't find time to deliver her orders to the rest of them. That meant long Saturday afternoons when she dragged me along. She had no one to leave me with, as my sister Betty had now been invited to live at my Aunt Marie's to help care for my dying grandmother. Betty attended eighth grade in the suburb of River Rouge and rarely came home on weekends.

Going along with Mama on the Avon deliveries turned out to be a torment, the only thing I hated about her selling Avon. The deliveries must have signaled to me my rapidly evolving role in the few short months after the funeral: with Betty gone, I was becoming an only child. With Daddy gone, and with her sadness deepening, Mama relied on me more and more. I was turning into her companion. My grief at losing myself as a happy younger child felt strangely like shame. I didn't want to go. I didn't want to be seen.

"I'm just going to run in and deliver this to Dorothy," Mama said. "It'll only take a minute. Stay here." I waited more than an hour in the car.

At another house, she said, "Come on in with me. Mrs. Ochoa will be glad to see you." I was paraded and expected to behave exactly like whatever ethnic version of a well-behaved child should be. As I tagged around with Mama from door to door, I got so I could sense the differences in expectations as easily as my nose could identify the different foods cooking in the kitchens, and my eyes could notice the different decors and different saints hanging on the walls. Sometimes they gave me cookies and a Faygo orange pop and let me sit with them at the table. Other times they made me wait silently on the edge of a living room chair. And I learned in the Maltese and Mexican homes they are kinder, and in the Italian homes, where they always give me candy, they are the kindest.

Still they really didn't know me. When they were kind, they cooed at me and asked me simple questions, treating me like I was a little doll—"Are you getting new clothes for Easter?" "Are you glad that school's out?" "What grade are you in now?" "My, you're getting big!" And it was Mama pushing me to answer, talking to me in a way totally different from the way she talked when we were alone, or worse, talking about me, which I hated most of all.

I never could decide whether I liked attention better than being ignored. Being ignored usually had its advantages. But not always. One time I was forced to sit on a hassock in Mrs. Kowalczyk's living room facing her husband and two sons, all in pajamas, sitting on a couch watching something boring on TV. For almost an hour I watched them sit there gazing at the television in absolute stony silence. Every time we heard the strains of Mama's fake cheerful agreement from the kitchen, "Yes, Sophie," "You're right, Sophie," Mr. Kowalczyk shot a murderous glance at me. He wanted us out of there, and I couldn't help wondering were Mr. Kowalczyk and his sons like that all the time, or only because I was there?

When Mama eventually breezed through, she seemed to assess the scene as something cozy. She smiled generously and said, "Well, Mr. Kowalczyk, it looks like you and your boys are having a relaxing day." She then stopped to collect me on her way to the door, as though I were a sweater or a light jacket. I trailed along, limp with embarrassment.

Often I sat there visible but silent, especially if left alone, and waited through conversations that always took a lot longer than Mama promised, "We'll just be there five minutes." The long talks covered many topics before, during, and after they focused on Avon. Thus I could never predict when, if ever, they were going to end. It was torture.

Although I behaved most of the time, I sometimes blew the whole thing apart, deliberately acting like a brat. I usually did this in the kid-friendly homes where it felt safer to act out.

"I think you need the astringent rather than the freshener," Mama said to Mrs. Caruana. "Isn't your skin a little oily rather than dry?"

Mrs. Caruana rubbed her own cheek, a little tentatively. "I suppose it's oily," she said.

"Let's go," I said. "You promised."

Mama stared at me across the shiny enamel tabletop.

"Would you like another pop, honey?" Mrs. Caruana said. "I can get you one." She pointed to my empty bottle of raspberry Faygo and started to rise.

"No, I don't want it."

"Would you like me to show you a sample?" Mama said. "I've got some astringent in my kit."

"Let's go," I said. "You promised. You said we'd only be five minutes." Once into brat mode, I was systematic and relentless, interrupting every exchange until we were out of there and in the car.

Our conversation in the car revealed our evolving relationship, not a chastisement from Mama for behaving like a brat, but an excuse. "I didn't know she was going to want to order something. I just thought I was going to deliver the order and collect. You know her husband got called to work a second shift, so I guess she's got some extra money." We never talked about whether a six-, or seven-, or eight-year-old might find it frustrating to be there in the first place. Mama took me almost everywhere she went.

Sometimes, during the weeks when Mama's sadness got in the way of her responsibilities selling Avon, I worried. During those weeks she sat in Daddy's old chair by the living-room front windows in the gray light. "I've got to fill out my order," she said. She didn't move a muscle. "It's got to be there by Thursday." But she still didn't move. She got a call from Mrs. Kowalczyk wondering about her delivery. "It's here, Sophie. I should be able to swing by there later this afternoon." She went back to the chair and sat back down. During these times, I regretted being a brat. I didn't know what to do. One time, only one time, she got a polite letter from headquarters inquiring about why she was slowing down. That alarmed her.

Though I hated going with her on most deliveries, I enjoyed going to the sales meetings downtown. The sales meetings, like Sunday Mass at Holy Redeemer, had a predictable beginning, middle, and end. I got to observe the career Representatives, the ones with pencil-thin eyebrows, Avon pancake makeup thick enough to peel, and their sharp way of talking that told you they wanted to get to the point. I couldn't figure out what was wrong with these ambitious Representatives after Mama told me they had husbands. They acted as though they enjoyed working. They carried pointed pencils, took notes while listening to the managers, asked elaborate questions, and always won the three-week campaign sales awards.

Mama sat through the spiels from the managers, clapped as they gave out the sales awards, listened to the announcements of the next round of prizes and campaign goals, and jotted down a few notes about what would be going on special and what to sell. On the way home, though, her polite silence changed to laughter about the drama of the managers, and she gossiped about Lucille Nichols, the recurring champ seller for the district in almost every campaign. Lucille lived in Saint Gabriel's Parish on Cadet, but she covered a prized territory in our parish, the rich Irish neighbors on Campbell and Cavalry, right behind Holy Redeemer. "You know she's got others selling for her. If she gives away ten percent of her forty percent commission, she'll still be doing OK. Even if it's against the policy." Mama went on to give me a math lesson that was way beyond me. I listened to the excitement in her voice. This was the Mama I loved, glad to be alone with me. She loved math.

Mama sold Avon for a long time, through bad years and good. She never sold a lot, and sometimes only enough to keep her territory. She never once worked fast enough to cover all the customers in her territory during a campaign. She wasn't able to "saturate" it, as they suggested at the sales meeting. In fact, two or three blocks of her territory were never once visited. They remained like virgin timber.

Still, Mama eventually hit her stride, and Avon brought us a regular supply of unexpected blessings which we would have found difficult to do without. Every three weeks the order arrived in heavy cardboard boxes with the green Avon logo. I wanted to be there for each ceremonial opening, so if the mailman came while I was at school, Mama always waited until I came home. After a year, Mama made me the official opener of boxes.

Once I opened the boxes, flowers blossomed everywhere. Frigid dry boxes in winter, softer warm boxes in summer. Sometimes I imagined the smell of Avon battling the sadness. In winter it countered the smell of the coal furnace and the diagonal streak of soot that soiled the wall above the living-room heat register. In summer it tackled the smell of hot sunshine through the dirty front windows settling with the dust on the gray rug. When I opened the box, something happy emerged, something good and sweet.

The products were packed in shiny embossed boxes that my fingers skated across like reading Braille. When I first saw the beautiful lady with the frilly pink long skirt on the box of Quaintance, and then saw the rosebud cap on all the bottles, I took back what I'd said to Mama about liking Cotillion better. I became a devotee of Quaintance and the letter "Q." The gift boxes came with ribbons on them. Flamboyant bows. I loved them. The deluxe gift tube of Burnt Sugar lipstick that Mrs. Algeier bought for her sister's birthday was topped with a pearl surrounded by diamonds. Packed in a gold box with raised cardboard covered in white satin, it nestled in a cozy little bed. I imagined myself resting in such a bed.

After I opened the boxes and spread all the products on the floor, Mama did an inventory from a checklist. I worked along with her, carefully opening the little boxes, looking at everything, holding each item up to my nose, before she took the products from me to put them in white paper bags for individual customers. I sat in a fragrant space of delight on our gray rug in the center of the living room, enveloped in the colors, the patterns, the cleanness, and the feel of all the boxed treasures. I helped her find what she needed—two tubes of Smoker's Toothpaste, one bottle of Sunny Rachel Color Pick-Up, a jar of Golden Promise Cream Sachet, all for Mrs. Ochoa. One bottle of Avon Astringent, one jar of Avon Cleansing Cream, two Color-Last Lipsticks, one in Pink Rose and the other in Crimson Beauty, all for Mrs. Caruana. One Deluxe Burnt Sugar Color-Last Lipstick in gold Gift Packaging, for Mrs. Algeier. Once everything was sorted, which sometimes took hours depending on Mama's mood, she repacked the big boxes with the bags to be delivered and set them in a corner of the living room. The fragrance never completely left the room. By the time she made her last delivery, the next order would arrive.

The emptied Avon boxes came in handy. They held the newspapers and other junk Mama wasn't able to throw out. They proved especially useful when the doorbell rang and someone arrived. We scooped up everything that cluttered the two front rooms, threw it all into Avon boxes, and carted them to the back hallway. We later retrieved them, or didn't, depending on whether we remembered what was in them or not.

As the decade progressed, the number of Avon products doubled, and the names and packages got more and more daring. Most of Mama's customers couldn't afford the fancy deluxe bottles and gift boxes, but they could afford the new fragrances in their standard new packaging. The five fragrances Mama had started with became seven, and then more. On one of the bright red boxes I saw a gold tree blowing in a breeze. Inside was a bright red oriental genie bottle of Persian Wood. Persian meant "passion," I thought, but Mama let me know it was more exotic than that. She described Persia, the land of Aladdin and his magic lamp, of Ali Baba and his forty thieves, of Scheherazade and the thousand and one Arabian nights. The words of Avon floated in the air like distant strains of seductive music. No matter how sad Mama got, she never failed to explain the words to me when I asked, sometimes with wry humor. "Quaintance. That's like 'acquaintance.' I guess it means that if you wear it you'll meet somebody."

Although Mama could not have foreseen the blessings Avon would bring, she did follow a shrewd plan when she first began selling it. The week after Daddy died she went downtown and applied for Social Security benefits. Beginning in June my sister Betty and I would get a check each month until we reached eighteen, and Mama would get a check each month as long as she didn't earn too much money, and as long as she didn't remarry. She wouldn't be making enough money at Avon with her forty percent commission to jeopardize her monthly checks from Social Security—unless she got awfully good at it, and Mama wasn't in much danger of that, even if the mantra was correct, "Avon sells itself."

To other families, the monthly Social Security checks would have kept them just above the poverty line. To Mama the checks were fortune enough—slightly more than half of what Daddy had earned at Cadillac. She thus felt no need to work hard at Avon for the money. Given Mama's frugal ways, we were getting by well enough to satisfy our needs. We just weren't saving so much.

For me, Mama's frugal ways made me aware of the stream that had dried up—the stream of carefully chosen surprises that Daddy used to bring home to delight us so much. The Avon boxes full of beauty proved some ritual payback: the mailman ringing the doorbell, understanding that the answering sound of our shrill upstairs buzzer meant "Press the door," thumping up the stairs with the heavy boxes, waiting only for Mama's signature, sliding the boxes into the flat, not entering, not seeing the clutter. The Avon delivery often marked the only time the doorbell rang in a given month, the boxes often the only brand new objects to come into the house. Given Mama's way of keeping everything that came—the mail, the newspapers, and the empty mayonnaise jars—the Avon products, belonging as they did to other people, were often the only things to go out again. Only Daddy seemed to bring us treasures.

Eventually I began to search for Daddy in all that he left, turning his objects over and over, looking at them from different angles. What did they mean to him, this fifth and youngest son of a Tennessee farmer who fell in love with the big northern city? The box of leather-working tools, hidden on the high shelf of the front closet, the globe of the world, the 1949 Unabridged Webster's *Second International Dictionary*, the 78 recordings of Rachmaninoff, Beethoven, Bizet and Marion Anderson, the volumes of the *Britannica* set he'd carefully covered in brown paper and labeled with fountain pen in his hand.

What did they mean to me? I handled his objects until I could find the messages Daddy had left for me, and it took me years to figure. The toolbox meant care and precision. The globe meant knowing the world and my place in it. The dictionary, the encyclopedia, the music: it took me years, but I came to think that maybe he wanted me to be smart.

The Tex Ritter children's songs, the Golden Records of classical music themes, the Hopalong Cassidy thermos and lunchbox—those I didn't need to ponder. After all, he brought those things home just for me.

Mama continued to sell Avon through the 1950s, along with taking other part-time jobs for far shorter periods. In April of 1956, she placed third in the Detroit Board of Education's civil service test for a job as a handicapped children's bus attendant. She was to assist and ride with handicapped children who were picked up from home and bussed to special schools. She subbed at that job until it became permanent in February of 1958. It was her first full-time job since Daddy's death, one that she held until she retired.

And so in January of 1961 Mama finally gave up her Avon territory. Officially quitting didn't stop her from continuing to sell Avon to her relatives and pack of loyal customers. She contracted herself out to Lucille for ten percent, and then, when Lucille moved to Florida, to a woman named Sally. As the neighborhood changed, her customers recommended her to new neighbors, and she kept pace with the ethnic migrations in the neighborhood, making new Latina friends. Mama bought and sold Avon until three or four years before her death, Avon the glue that provided regular visits to her old and new friends.

CHAPTER THREE
LEFT TO TAKE CARE OF MAMA

After Daddy died we continued as upstairs tenants in the house on Clark Street. Nine months later, death struck again when Mama's mother died. My grandmother, who wore black clothes, carried a black purse with her everywhere, even to dinner, often poked aggressively with her cane, never addressed me, never smiled at me and never referred to me by name—was no more. Death also struck our downstairs landlords, leading me to believe, among other things, that the house was haunted. Death, and its companion, sickness, hovered over the house and over our lives.

Even before Daddy died, old man Dixon and his wife became incapable of caring for themselves and so were sent by their children to separate rest homes. The separation seemed strange to me, but the story Mama told was that they didn't get along anyway because Mr. Dixon was in love with his secretary. Their younger son, Merville, became the sole occupant of the downstairs flat.

While old man Dixon died soon after entering his rest home, Mrs. Dixon lingered on in hers—beyond Daddy's death—for more than another year. The old woman was senile, toothless, hard-of-hearing, bedridden, and unable to recognize Mama when she came to visit. None of this, though, stopped Mama from visiting and bringing me along.

It wasn't easy for me. In fact, visiting Mrs. Dixon terrified me: the powerful smell of urine as we entered the nursing home, the old folks in their wheelchairs throwing out their arms to embrace me, calling to me with words I couldn't understand, their dusty smell, the unwanted attention, and Mama's coaching me not to be shy. I may have represented life to them—a child, a pretty little girl, yet they only signified more death to me, and I feared their clutching at me would pull me under.

Standing in front of Mrs. Dixon's bed, Mama gently pushed me toward her, saying, "This is Mary." When the response of the bewhiskered, dozing woman was only a moan and a flickering eyelid, Mama repeated herself, more loudly. "This is Mary." The old woman's recognition of me would have been a miracle—a cure for which I think Mama wanted to be responsible. I knew it was a tall order. Mrs. Dixon hardly knew me when she lived downstairs from us. Like my grandmother, she gave me the impression that I'd been born too late. Besides, if anyone was going to be difficult to recognize, it would be me, the growing girl. Almost all the adults who did know me but hadn't seen me in a few months remarked on how tall, or big, or different I'd become.

If ever there was a wrong place for me to be, it was that nursing home. I knew it at the time, but I had become Mama's prop as she performed the role of widow in public. When we showed up at places where no other adults brought their children, and where no child would want to be brought, Mama batted her green eyes and said, "I didn't have anywhere to leave her." Truth is, she needed me for companionship. At the same time, she used me as proof of her heroic struggles. All anyone had to do was look at me—a living testament of her burden. She dutifully visited Mrs. Dixon every month, each time dragging me along, coaching me in the car to be gracious.

One day I'd had enough. "I'm not going," I said.

"Then you'll have to wait in the car."

"I'm not going. You can go while I'm at school."

"We can stop and get ice cream."

"I'm not going. You can go while I'm in school."

Mama reluctantly backed down, grumbling about my "obstinacy," as she called it. Still, that day I learned I had the power to say "No."

Sickness was epidemic. While Mrs. Dixon lingered on in her rest home, Merville, her bachelor son in his fifties, started failing—shuffling as he walked to the YMCA four doors up the street to buy his newspapers, shaking and stumbling in a way that made me worry that he'd fall on the sidewalk. He probably suffered from Parkinson's disease.

Doris, the Dixons' daughter, invited Lois Farrell, a chain-smoking woman from Georgia, to move in as a roomer and to keep an eye on Merville. Shortly after Mrs. Dixon died, Merville took a slide downhill, falling one day in the downstairs flat and cutting open his head. He was sent to yet another nursing home, and Doris offered to sell the house to Mama. Doris held no sentimental attachment to it and no interest in cleaning out old man Dixon's office. Mama sensed there might be value in old man Dixon's documents and antiques.

Mr. Dixon had kept an office of old books and various mementos in a back room at the farthest recess of our upstairs floor. Old man Dixon's locked office was the spookiest destination at the end our spooky dark hallway, beyond our back entrance hall. Once, when I was very young, I remember Mama hurrying to the back stairway to ask Mr. Dixon something when she heard him stumbling with his cane up the stairs. I peeked from around her skirt to see his office door open, a dusty sun-beamed room smelling of newspapers, with curious objects, figurines, clocks, books and bookcases, all on top of a swirling deep-red wine-colored oriental rug.

Should she buy the house? Mama whipped herself into an agony of indecision over several days. I heard her talking on the phone to several of her sisters, mentioning new words like "mortgage" and "interest" and $8,000.

She consulted my sister, who'd come back home for the second half of ninth grade. I heard Mama in the hallway talking to Betty who was grabbing underwear out of the dresser in the front bedroom. Betty was on her way out to Aunt Marie's to spend the weekend. In fact, Aunt Marie, who'd taken Betty downtown somewhere, was waiting in the car.

"What do you think I should do?" Mama said.

"Do what you want," Betty said. "But if you buy it, Aunt Marie says you should move downstairs." She brushed past Mama on her way out to the living room. "I got to go. Marie's waiting."

After Betty said her goodbyes, rushed down the front stairway and slammed the door, Mama came to find me where I'd been eavesdropping from my place at the dining room table. She sat down wearily at her own usual place where she could get a straight but distant view of the park, kitty-corner from me. Slowly she propped her chin into her palms and sighed. Her voice dragged with that heavy quality of worry that always made me worry.

"What do you think?" she asked. "Should I buy it? If Doris sells it to someone else we may have to move."

She didn't mention moving downstairs, where the flat was much nicer, laid out in a reasonable way, with oak trim and pillars, a livable kitchen and a normal-sized bathroom. Had she contemplated that possibility, our lives would have been different. At a time when pressure was put on everyone to be "normal," we would have at least been spared some of the accommodations we had to make to the strange layout upstairs.

When old man Dixon converted the upstairs into our rental flat in 1927, he cobbled out a curious arrangement—the steep front stairway leading to an attractive living room with a brass chandelier, grand windows and an upstairs porch overlooking the park, and an attractive dining room off the living room, with a matching chandelier. Beyond that a strange assortment of rooms extended back—a tiny kitchen, a huge bathroom larger than a bedroom, a back bedroom with a closet cut into the middle of it, and a crooked hallway that got darker and spookier the more it traveled away from the front of the house toward the back stairway. The hallway was rendered even more depressing because something appeared to be wrong. It was subtle: two of the walls weren't plumb. Beyond the back stairway was old man Dixon's office.

Mama pressed. "I don't know what to do. Should I buy it?"

I got up and took a slow walk into the crooked hallway. I couldn't imagine any other option. Looking around at the Avon boxes full of all the things that had come into the house in a given week or day—S&H green stamps, junk mail, school papers, rubber bands, trinkets of all sorts, keys, pillows, packets of plant food, rubbing alcohol, dental floss—all scooped off the dining room table that had gotten too cluttered for us to eat on—even after we'd shifted the junk aside, I knew moving wouldn't be easy. The boxes piled along the back stairway wall already blocked the hallway. I came back and sat down again.

Given Mama's inability to put her things in order, it was no wonder she couldn't contemplate moving downstairs. Mama didn't want change. Change scared me, too…. more than the haunted house. Incredulously, she left the decision up to me. At eight years old, I felt the weight of the responsibility like a block of iron.

"Do you want to stay here?" she said.

I gazed at the latest installment of papers and playing cards, shoe horns and shoulder pads that were piled high on what had been Daddy's place and chair at the dining room table. I turned around to see the mounds of mail and magazines on the buffet. I knew what I decided would have consequences. I felt queasy. In an instinct to build support for the decision, I also tried to ferret out what I thought she wanted me to say, what she wanted to hear.

I thought about it, not able to envision any other place or any other life than the one we were surviving. I didn't know the process. I didn't know how long it took or how easy or difficult it would be to move. "Yes. Go ahead, buy it," I finally said.

In the end, Mama took the $8,000 out of her savings. Fundamentally opposed to paying interest, she thus avoided the need to take out a mortgage. Shortly after the transaction, Merville died.

Lois Farrell settled in as the downstairs tenant, inviting her fat grown son, Jack Ramsey, who worked at Turnstead's, to join her. Mama bought or was given many of old man Dixon's antiques and as many of the leftover documents and books as she could manage. The Dixon children wanted nothing that would remind them of the man who'd been so unkind to their mother. Eventually, a little of that lode passed to me.

A week after Mama bought the house, the drain in the kitchen stopped up. She plunged and plunged, but the water wouldn't go down. She called Mr. Yost, an old classmate of hers from Saint Patrick's High School in Wyandotte. He worked at Copp's Hardware on Vernor in the neighborhood. Mr. Yost wasn't a plumber, but he was cheaper than Gambling Plumbing, and he was sympathetic toward Mama and her plight.

I started to regret my decision to buy the house, hearing Mama lamenting, then flirting, then raising her voice in alarm, as she listened to Mr. Yost. Mr. Yost, who'd lost one eye in a BB gun accident long ago, stood there winking like Popeye, filling the tiny kitchen with his presence and tools, scratching his head and listing all the things he might do: "I can knock out a wall downstairs." "Maybe I can get a longer snake, but honestly I'm not sure." "We can start by tearing out these cabinets to get behind the floor boards."

It didn't take long before I started to believe that anything that went wrong with the house—small or large—was my fault. After all, I'd made the decision. I would gradually take more and more responsibility for the house, in part to ease my guilt.

*   *   *

Betty at fourteen was already taller than Mama, and her weight was substantial. She looked and behaved far older than fourteen. She liked it better living at my Aunt Marie's because she liked Aunt Marie far more than Mama.

In fact, by the time we bought the house in July of 1953, the struggle for Mama to keep Betty home, and secondarily for me to keep my sister, became a losing battle. Betty had only come back home and enrolled at Holy Redeemer for the second half of ninth grade. She was to stay home for five days of the school week, with the understanding that for the weekend and during summer vacation she could flee to Aunt Marie's again. She often got angry at Mama and took the bus earlier—Thursday, or even Wednesday, taking the same bus she took out to "the Rouge," as River Rouge residents called their city, to get off at Fort Street and Junction and walk to school at Redeemer.

With public transportation so convenient and running well, we couldn't keep her. Strangely, Mama would not forbid her to leave. I even hoped she'd bar the door, but Mama would not put her foot down. And my Aunt Marie, who had no children and was slightly older than Mama, was perfectly capable of offering a haven to Betty any time she wanted, and without Mama's permission.

Yet after buying the house, Mama was up for doing anything to keep Betty home. She even offered Betty Mr. Dixon's old office as a bedroom of her own. That was when we started calling his office "the way-back room," to distinguish it from the back bedroom we'd already named the "back room." "Come home, Betty," I heard Mama on the phone. "We can fix up the way-back room. I'll buy Venetian blinds, and it can be your bedroom." The offer appealed to Betty since the generous room stretched across the entire width of the house and included a walk-in closet and a large leaded-glass picture window. Besides, it was situated beyond the back stairway leading downstairs to the backyard, so Betty could use a private entrance if she wanted. The down side was that there was no heat in the way-back room, and the winters were bitter.

When Daddy was alive, Betty and I had shared the front bedroom. But shortly after Daddy's death, and with Betty gone, Mama pulled me in to sleep with her in the back room, where her snoring made it difficult for me to stay asleep. If Betty took the way-back room, I reasoned, the front bedroom would be open, and I might find my chance to escape from Mama.

Mama next hired a team of soft-spoken brothers, who'd just come up from Kentucky, to paint the way-back room green and sand the attractive pine floor. She crammed more of old man Dixon's junk into the walk-in closet and dispersed some of it to other rooms. She made good on her promise to install Venetian blinds, big fat metal ones that cut your fingers. By January 1954, the way-back room was ready.

Betty moved the maple bedroom furniture, lace doilies, milk glass lamps, perfume bottles, and her vanity mirror from the front bedroom to her new space in the way-back-room. She set everything up in symmetry, added a chenille bedspread and scatter rugs. The floor gleamed. With Betty in charge, the room was neat and orderly.

Even though the room came with old man Dixon's green asbestos space heater shaped like a seashell, it wasn't enough to keep it warm. Mama and Betty bickered incessantly about it.

"Turn that heater off when you leave!" Mama called in her fearful tone almost every time Betty emerged. "My light bill's going to be outrageous."

Betty hated Mama's stinginess. And she hated the inevitability of what followed: "Turn that light off when you leave that room." Like me, she hoped that just once she could leave in stillness without hearing that anxious command. It was Mama's doggedness, and it encouraged us to sneak.

In the weeks after Daddy's funeral, with Betty in Tennessee, I'd felt my first relief from Mama and Daddy's fighting. But then, the more I missed Daddy, the more I interpreted my relief to mean I'd caused his death. I deserved the punishment. Now I was doubly punished, for the fighting between Mama and Betty was even more vicious.

Mama and Daddy had fought about things that baffled me. Mama didn't keep the house clean and that was supposed to be her job. Every Sunday without fail they fought over her taking Betty and me to church, sometimes so long and hard that we missed the last twelve-thirty Mass at Redeemer and had to attend the one o'clock Mass at Sainte Anne. Mama told Daddy we didn't need what he bought whenever he spent money. And she kept things that were supposed to be thrown out. It seemed to me they fought over who should win the argument. It scared me. When they fought they forgot about me, and I drifted to the bathroom where it was warm and I could lean against the heat register. Still, there were times when they smiled together and touched each other's arm. When they weren't fighting, they both always smiled at me.

With Mama and Betty, the fighting was endless, and Betty held the trump card. After all, she had a place to go to, away from us—my Aunt Marie's reasonable house, with its freezer door above the fridge, its gleaming white porcelain enamel set of cabinets above and below a spotless dual sink, its kitchen big enough to eat in with a clean checkered linoleum floor, its new stove, and its bathroom with a shower. "Aunt Marie is modern," Betty pronounced.

Since Betty had been taken into confidence with Mama's three most powerful sisters when she had helped with our grandmother in the Rouge, she also became the conveyer of family judgments, taunting Mama with what they said about her. "Aunt Mag says your house looks like a cyclone hit it." "Aunt Marie says she can't believe you're so stingy with money." "Aunt Dee says she tried to get you to buy something pretty instead of those old lady shoes. She told you your feet looked too big in them." Mama's friends, Mama's habit of being late, Mama's slow ways and stocky body all came under fire. The consensus, which Betty was fond of reporting: Mama was a mess.

The splitting of my grandmother's fortune made things worse. My powerful trio of aunts—the ones I'd later dub the Triumvirate—who inherited my grandmother's "Big House" on the Detroit River in Wyandotte, determined that a rental property Mama got from the estate was worth a little more than each of their shares. They claimed Mama should pay them $200 each, for a total of $600.

"Pay them, you owe it to them," Betty admonished. Mama was indulgent, not much on authority, and not good at making decisions. But when it came to money, real dollars and cents, she was decisive enough. She wasn't about to allow anybody, especially her daughter, to tell her what to do with money. She responded with her usual eye darting and declined an answer.

"Don't pay them. You don't owe it to them," my Uncle Pete said. "Don't pay them," my Aunt Bea said. "Take the money and buy yourself a brand new wardrobe."

Once Aunt Bea explained to me what the word "wardrobe" meant, I, too, thought it would be a nice idea for Mama to get all new clothes. Of course, I couldn't picture her spending the money on clothes she thought she didn't need.

My cousins and I endured mind-numbing—sometimes tearful—debates around the table, around several tables, as the question was posed to all of Mama's siblings. In the end, Mama paid her sisters.

Then there was the main thing that Mama and Betty fought about— my dead father. If it wasn't Betty screaming, "Daddy was right about you," or "Daddy told me he was going to divorce you and live at the Y," then it was Betty shouting, "Daddy loved me more than you. He did. He did. He told me so." One time she drew the color out of Mama's face by declaring with quiet fury, "I wish it had been you instead of him!" The words were blasphemy to me, and I expected the walls to fall down. These were the days when I was learning the commandments from Sister Florita, examining my conscience about honoring my father and mother.

The situation spun totally out of control, and at nine years old, I had no perspective to see my towering angry, grief-stricken teenaged sister as a troubled child. I also had no concept yet of rightful ownership. I wasn't aware enough to tell them, "My Daddy also belongs to me. He's my Daddy, too." Instead, I accepted the fact that I was unentitled, especially as it seemed they had each grabbed and were pulling on one of his two arms. The fights between Mama and Betty left Mama defensive, something she continued with me. She rarely spoke of Daddy to me. And when events or situations demanded at least some mention, she always carefully presented him as her husband, as though I were a new friend who'd just come on the scene. Consequently I had to look for him only in the things he'd left behind. And keep it a secret.

Mama, of course, was difficult to deal with—it was almost impossible to honor her in any conventional way. She was childish, eccentric, stubborn, insensitive, compulsive, fearful, old-fashioned, and deliberately naïve—living as though innocence would ultimately make the world a better place, guilelessly showing her neck to predators and often getting us in a heap of trouble. And then looking to someone else to get her out of it. Still, she always came out on the short end of Betty's anger, for even though she wasn't much for empathy, and incapable of establishing any authority, she was well-mannered and kind. She loved Betty even when Betty would leave in a huff to catch the last bus to the Rouge at 9 PM. Mama would sit there like a wounded child, whimpering. It was left to me to make things better. I developed a fierce loyalty and protectiveness of Mama, and I suppose it's the basis of my defense of the underdog.

Yet I was incapable of any advocacy for myself. In my own home it was as though I didn't exist.

The bad decision I made to buy the house crystallized on a February Sunday night in 1954 with Betty there. Not only was the way-back room cold, with no tentacles from the old coal furnace stretched to heat it, but the whole house was cold, and drafty. We had never put up the storm windows after Daddy died, and the wind whipped across the park and in through the gaps around the big front room windows and the upstairs porch door. The curtains inside the closed windows quivered with each blast.

The park at twilight was at its winter loveliest—white snow, dark trees silhouetted against a deep purple sky, the lights from the Ambassador Bridge beyond, and the day-long snow continuing to fall into the night, the frenzy of the flakes illuminated by the street light.

As usual, Mama made a big to-do over shoveling. Now that we owned the house, and with Lois Farrell's grown up son, Jack Ramsey, unwilling to volunteer, it fell to Mama to shovel. Several times a week, I felt the stab of regret, for had I not decided to buy the house, someone else would be out there shoveling. Someone else would be responsible for all the other things that went wrong as well. Mama always lectured Betty and me about the responsibilities of landlords, always trying to make us feel guilty enough to help her. I'm sure she longed for a family of cheerful, supportive daughters.

"I wish we had someone to do the man's work. You know, you girls could pitch in." The trouble was that, once she described it as man's work, we felt ashamed to do it. Besides, we didn't want to be pitied by our neighbors. We'd rather hide, or at least I'd rather hide. Mama shoveled the walk herself.

Around seven in the evening, with the snow having stopped, we were startled by a sound—a steady, aggressive thump, thump, thump. All three of us got up to look out the front windows. Four boys were throwing snowballs at the house.

Mama immediately hit upon a strategy: "Just ignore them." Her eyes darted in fear, or embarrassment, but she calculated right—they made a racket out there but carefully aimed at the clapboards that would not give way.

Betty, seeing Mama's retreat, became annoyed with her submissive strategy. Moving past her, she stepped into the male role and marched to the window.

Mama pleaded, "Don't engage them! Ignore them!"

Betty raised the window.

"Ignore them," Mama said.

"Get the hell away, you punks!" Betty called, leaning her head out the window.

As soon as she leaned back in, lowered the sash, and turned to us triumphant, a snowball shattered the glass. It was thrown with such force that the glass didn't slow it down. It landed near my feet on the other side of the room. Wind immediately poured in, penetrating the entire house, even wending its way down the twisted angles of the long hallway.

All hell broke loose.

Betty started to curse, while Mama started to cry.

The recrimination.

"I told you to ignore them! Now you've made it so they'll come back and break more."

The lamentations.

"It's Sunday night. I can't call Mr. Yost until morning."

The warnings.

"Don't touch that glass with your hands. Get the broom and dust pan."

Somehow, after what seemed an eternity, Mama, or Betty, started to sweep it up. Mama reasoned that a cut-up Avon box would supply enough of a cardboard barrier that some of the force of the blowing wind could be stopped. She finally got the wherewithal to tape it into the window frame.

As soon as that snowball came to a stop in front of my feet, I retreated to the sink in the bathroom and leaned against the heat register. It was warm there, the force of the furnace at that register strong enough to drug me drowsy. I always hid there when people were yelling. At least the screaming voices and the sobs and tears were kept a little distance away. It was there that I consciously tried to enter a twilight world where I could numb myself to pain.

Why had I told her to buy the house? Now she was crying, the boys would come back and break all the windows, and there was nothing I could do. What might I have done if there had been someone to comfort me, to treat me like a child, to say, "There, there. The window will be fixed tomorrow. Don't worry. Don't cry"?

The episode of the broken window hastened my sister's final departure, one of the last times I remember her being part of our household. Later in the spring Mama got Mr. Yost to help her haul the maple bedroom suite out of the way-back room and put it back into the front bedroom. Thus I saw my opportunity to get away from sleeping with Mama. The way-back room became the repository of the junk. The front bedroom became mine.

Betty left to live with Aunt Marie for good. And I was left to take care of Mama.

CHAPTER FOUR
THAT HABIT

As fall passed into the winter of Mama and Betty's most bitter quarrels, pop singer Eddie Fisher sang "Oh My Papa." Every week the song remained at the top of the charts, the cast of *Your Hit Parade* acted it out in different scenarios. Each week I watched the scenarios—always a grownup missing his elderly deceased father and remembering his father's devotion to him during his childhood. But never as the most shameful scenario of all—a child with a father already dead. Worse, Mama hummed along in her lovely alto voice as though there couldn't possibly be a person in the house with a dead father, who had been brought to the brink of her grief through the song and was finding warm places in the house where she could stand and cry and hide. *Gone are the days when he would take me on his knee, / and with a smile, he'd turn my tears to laughter.* And so it was that in our house I took the role of observer, never expected to be affected or involved. If I was affected and it happened to me, then it was just too shameful to consider. There was no one to turn to.

That was also the winter of my fourth grade, under the rule of Sister Florita. Whenever I was at school, I also stood outside myself, as an observer, gathering clear memories, but memories shrouded in a haze of sepia hue. I was too afraid to be involved. On the inside I only had my grief and "that habit." And I was in trouble because of "that habit."

When it started the summer after Daddy died, I didn't have the name "that habit." I didn't have any name for it until Mama later gave it one. But I remember the day it started. I even remember that empty car carriers were rattling by on Clark Street when it happened. As I'd done a hundred times before, I slid down the pipe railing next to the four steps leading from the front porch. On this particular day, though, I felt intense pleasure as I did so. The moment my feet hit the ground, I ran upstairs to tell Mama.

"I slid down the railing and it felt funny and good…'down there.'"

"Well, don't do it again," Mama said. "You might injure yourself 'down there.'" Her words were matter of fact, but the tone of them let me know we weren't supposed to talk about it. I knew what the word "injure" meant, but I wondered why she hadn't used the word "hurt" instead. Yet it seemed to go along with the vague words we both used for that region of my body—"down there."

In the next weeks and months, I discovered how to control the pleasurable feeling from funny and good to climax. Sitting sideways on a hard chair, I rubbed my legs together while swaying and rocking. I closed my eyes or trained them not to focus. It wasn't long before I also discovered what I thought was the most appropriate place and time to do it—during those long, boring, painful, lonely hours when I was forced to sit at a desk in school.

Daddy had insisted we attend Maybury Elementary rather than Holy Redeemer. After all, he'd conceded our deliverance into the hands of the priests at Baptism; and Sunday mornings, following the weekly argument about it, he gave in to Mama's taking us to Mass. He would not, however, bow to her desire to send us to Catholic school.

In second grade at Maybury, in the year following Daddy's death, a school psychologist took me out of class, walking me to a private room. She let me play at a table-high sandbox while she asked me questions. I sensed I'd been called to see her because of my behavior. We didn't talk about it specifically though, and she never once even hinted that I was being "bad." I talked to her about my imaginary friends, Berker and Brown. She asked me what they did, and I told her, "Sometimes they play dolls with me and sometimes they go along with me to the store. Berker is nicer than Brown." I related a couple of our adventures where we invented funny words nobody else knew, and she laughed. She didn't mention Daddy, and I didn't tell her I missed him. I didn't tell her it must have been my fault he died.

One day in Aunt Mag's kitchen I overheard Mama and Aunt Mag talking. Sitting at the table with the checkered yellow oil cloth, Aunt Mag shouted at Mama who sat there taking it the way she always did, hardly speaking, about to cry. Her eyes darted around the room. Aunt Mag scolded, "You're committing a mortal sin by not giving those girls a Catholic education."

"But I sent Betty to Catechism," Mama said. "She made her First Communion."

"That's not enough," Aunt Mag insisted. She rose to stir something on the stove. Then to drive her point home, she turned to Mama with the spoon in her hand. "Don't you read the *Michigan Catholic*? You're supposed to have those girls in parochial school." Aunt Mag was the oldest and the family boss.

Mama said she'd think about it, but she didn't think about it for long. I'm still not sure whether her decision to put me in Holy Redeemer was because Aunt Mag said to, or because Mama thought the nuns might make me a better-behaved child.

Shortly before my eighth birthday, starting in third grade, I was enrolled at Holy Redeemer. The week before, Mama and I stopped by Kopecky's Children's Store on Fort Street to buy my uniform, a navy blue gabardine jumper, a white blouse with a Peter Pan collar, and a navy blue beanie. The jumper came with a monogram on the right vest—the Holy Redeemer crest in the background and the raised gold letters "HRS" for Holy Redeemer

School. I liked the uniform, and I especially liked that the blouse and the beanie came in cellophane wrap. The blouse, folded and pinned, needed to be ironed, and I knew nobody else but I had ever even tried it on. I seldom got brand new clothes, as I stood next in line for the outgrown clothes of my cousin, Mary Magdalene.

Mama and I arrived at school a day early for an orientation, found the assigned room, and were welcomed by Sister Elizabeth Ann, a kind young nun in a navy blue gown. She smiled and shook my hand.

I couldn't see Sister Elizabeth Ann's entire face, but I could tell by her mouth that she smiled at me. She wore what looked to me like a white bathing cap pulled down over the top of her forehead so I couldn't see any hair. A strip of what looked like snow-white cardboard curved around the entire top of her head in an upside down U from chin to chin. The arc over her head was like the arc of a stained glass window. Attached to the cardboard, a long black veil flowed like hair down her back. Since the cardboard extended an inch or so in front of her face all around, I wondered if she had any peripheral vision. She wore a collar of more snow-white cardboard around her neck that came down in a circle in the front and extended to the end of her shoulders. A crucifix fell in the same little valley all grownup women had in the middle of their chests. When she rose to retrieve something from her desk, two long sets of beads hanging from her belt rattled against her navy blue gown.

From the way she moved, nonchalantly yet with energy, I could tell she was accustomed to sitting, walking and talking in this costume. I liked that and thought I would like Sister Elizabeth Ann. I also thought I would like Holy Redeemer because Sister Elizabeth Ann gave us a box of weekly church collection envelopes that came with my enrollment. She also gave me a copy of *Mine Magazine*, with games and stories in it, along with pictures of other sisters dressed similarly to Sister Elizabeth Ann, only they wore black.

Unlike at Maybury, where each student sat at an individual seat with a platform desk attached, at Holy Redeemer the seat of one desk connected to the writing platform of the desk behind. The rows of desks were screwed to wooden runners. It was as though the entire row of students sat in single file on a sleigh.

As I'd done at Maybury in my move toward orgasm, I rocked my desk. Only this time I disrupted the entire row.

"Stop shaking," said the girl behind me.

"Yeah, stop shaking," said the girl in the seat behind her.

I couldn't. And when I couldn't, they knew something was wrong.

Ann Bresnahan in front of me turned around and tried reason. "Would you please stop shaking? I can't write when you're shaking. You see, I've blurred my paper?" She held up a sheet of scored paper with her single row of black wavy cursive capital M's in fountain pen. She was so pretty, so neat, so sure, one of Sister Elizabeth Ann's pets. I didn't want her to blur her paper, but I couldn't stop it. After that, she ignored me and didn't speak to me again until years later. In no time, I became "that girl," an outcast. No one spoke to me. They made a show of moving away from me whenever we stood in line at recess or side by side to sing.

I withdrew more and more, prompting me to engage in "that habit" more often. The school day was long and had to be endured. Some of it reached me—the stories of the saints, but most of the time I didn't pay attention to anything going on around me. Although I read at home, I didn't read in school. I didn't stand and answer questions. I couldn't be pried from my own little world where I could escape being a girl with a dead father she could never see. I daydreamed about soft beds, about being alone in a tower, about hiding in a forest of jade plants, about being somewhere else, perhaps the park in a time long ago, some place with lapping water or falling crystals of snow. I daydreamed, rocking and swaying, experiencing sexual pleasure throughout the day.

Sister Elizabeth Ann stopped smiling. Several times I saw her face appraising me and slowly registering alarm. I knew I was a bad girl, a problem child. Soon Mama was called to school. Before Mama left, she said to me, "I'm going up to school because Sister Elizabeth Ann wants to see me about you." Her eyes were so sad, as though this burden might be the last that she could bear.

Later, I heard Mama coming up the stairs. Slowly, the way she always did. Gray afternoon light seeped through the front windows. The sky verged on twilight. I was watching *Kukla, Fran and Ollie* on TV when she opened the door, took off her coat, laid it on the chair, and walked past me to the kitchen to make a sandwich. When my show was over, she sat down beside me.

"The reason I had to go to school was because of you and 'that habit.'" She looked at me long enough for me to know what she was talking about. Then she turned away.

That was the first time I had a name for it, a name I hadn't needed, and one I hated: "that habit." Her eyes told me I'd made it hard for her, that I'd embarrassed her, that the weight of her sadness, at least most of it, was me. We never spoke about it again.

At school the next day, Sister Elizabeth Ann asked me to stay after.

"I talked to your mother yesterday," she said. "I thought you helped her around the house. She says you don't help her with the dishes." She looked at me with disappointment.

I knew she was referring to the Fourth Commandment. She didn't think I honored my mother.

"You know she's a widow, and she needs all your help." A look crossed Sister Elizabeth Ann's face that seemed to be remembering the poor besieged widow.

I knew exactly how Mama had presented herself, and I wanted to cry. I neither had the words nor the charm to get anybody to pay attention to or feel sorry for me. All I had that I could count on for comfort was "that habit."

*   *   *

Mama talked with Dr. Himmelhoch, our pediatrician. With his office
door open and me in the waiting room where I could see them but couldn't
hear, I'm sure they talked about "that habit." Every time she looked out at me
she appeared sad and tortured. He didn't appear that way. In fact, he smiled
reassuringly when he responded to her and glanced out at me. She might
have told him only half of it; she was so embarrassed. He might have told
her to ignore it, him being secular and Jewish with no concept that what I was
doing was a mortal sin which would doom me to hell. Of course, I too was
unaware that what I was doing was sinful. I knew I was shameful, disgusting,
an outcast, a disappointment, in trouble, a bad girl, a burden and an
embarrassment. I knew that most of the time I was lonely and sad. Despite
all that, I never imagined I was committing any sin.

Although I worried and disappointed poor Sister Elizabeth through
third grade, in fourth grade, I enraged Sister Florita.

"Mary Rhodes!" Sister Florita shouted my name at the very moment
I shook most at my desk. The other kids looked toward me. She reeled back
a step, standing silent at the front of the room. Her face reddened as she
waited—maybe counting, maybe praying. Then she lost control. She tore
down my row, picked me up from my seat, dragged me to the front of the
room, shook me ragged, then stood me in the corner. The kids in seats not
attached to my seat followed the drama dumbfounded. Mary Rhodes, thrown
into the corner. Again.

I don't remember Sister Florita's face, but I do remember her voice
and sudden movements, the blue swirl of her fury. I remember the loathing
in her voice as she called my name. I remember it also as a loud, violating
interruption. People told me later that she was a small woman, short in stature,
but that description doesn't help me visualize her face. As short as she might
have been, she was taller than I. And angrier.

The kids took to imitating Sister Florita, and, in an instinct for what
would hurt the worst, taunted me with my name—whenever opportunity
arose, whenever Sister Florita happened to be called out of the room. "Mary
Rhodes!" one of the boys called, trying to make his voice sound as disgusted
as Sister Florita's.

"Mary Rhodes, Mary Rhodes, Mary Rhodes," another said.

"Mary Rhodes, Mary Rhodes, Mary Rhodes, Mary Rhodes," a third
boy called, sing-songing it faster and faster as though it were a tongue twister.

Each time someone said it I felt stabbed by Sister Florita again. I sat
there wishing they'd call me stupid, or ugly, or even smelly. I had no defense.
I could say, "I'm not stupid," "I'm not ugly," but I couldn't say I wasn't
Mary Rhodes. I was Mary Rhodes, and that was worse than anything. To
this day, I find it hard to hear that simple formal version of my birth name
without cringing.

*   *   *

It was a long cruel winter, and I descended into a blur of warmth and cold, of gray and brown colors. The sky beyond the windows was gray. The air smelled of the huge furnace and boiler room, of hot water through layers of old paint. The radiators hissed. Too hot to touch. Everything in the classroom was a shade of brown—the bleached maple floors, the dark rows of desks with their black cast-iron framing. The brown desktops with faded varnish toward the center, thick and darkened on the edges.

I made friends with my desktop. I knew its contours, the place where the shine became the rub of use in a pattern where I saw varnished continents and islands. I longed to live on the islands. Sometimes I studied the ancient newness of the edges and imagined a frozen pond that would shine like that across its surface, where little people of my island skated freely in the cold winter.

The silence was most acute when the other kids came in from lunch. They talked and giggled, wisecracked and teased, chafing against my silence.

What if a stranger came in who didn't know me? Would he deem me bad? Would he know immediately? I sat rocking at my desk in silence while the others talked about television shows of the night before.

Sometimes I listened to the normal talk. They'd all seen Ricky Ricardo taking care of Little Ricky on *I Love Lucy*. I'd seen that show, too. I wanted to join in. I crossed the boundary of my desk, broke in. "I saw that."

They stopped a second, surprised to hear me. "No you didn't," Michael O'Connor snapped.

The desks had holes in the right upper corners for inkbottles. We were told they'd been used before they invented fountain pens. I played a game. I stuck a pencil in the hole and twirled it around the circle—fast, stopping at the point when I could no longer sustain the centrifugal force to keep it going. At what point would I feel my arm weaken and the circle stop? Would it stop at the same place each time? Or was I making it stop because I knew where it had stopped before? I wasn't sure I trusted the game any more.

The minutes after lunch before Sister Florita arrived were fierce. The boys smelled of asphalt, the girls of their mothers. I was supposed to stay for lunch because my home was peculiar—on Mondays, Wednesdays and Fridays Mama worked at the American Brass cafeteria. I feared the old nun who kept the lunchroom and made us eat everything on our plates, even the powdered eggs on Friday. So sometimes in the fall I snuck out and wandered around the dime store across the street, past the smell of the fertilizer for the house plants, exploring the toy aisles, stopping at the lunch counter to order a barbecued beef sandwich and a root beer with the quarter Mama had given me to buy lunch at school.

Not long after, around my birthday in November, I got caught. That day at Kresge's, instead of buying a sandwich with my lunch money, I bought a globe bank with the quarter. The lunchroom nun waited in the playground. She grabbed the bag from me, looked inside to see the globe, knocked it onto the asphalt. The insulted tin rang and dented.

"You're supposed to stay here for lunch. You are stealing from your mother."

What would a stranger seeing this say about me? Would he know the joy I felt seeing the continents stamped on the tin, the seam at the equator forming a little ridge of overlap—the place where the circle stopped?

The old nun pushed me against the brick wall—the boys snickered. When the bell rang and the arch of tears had been suppressed, I got my globe back. The boys and the lunchroom nun marched inside. Clutching the bag, arriving a moment late, I stuffed it into my desk. Sister Florita didn't know, but the boys watched my aching face.

Mama had cried and told them of her struggle with me. They monitored me now. I was allowed to sit at my desk instead of going to the lunchroom. I ate a cheese sandwich, cut awkwardly by Mama. Once in awhile, Sister Patricia Anne, the second grade teacher, thought to bring me a bottle of warm milk. I remember her lone smile.

The winter grew in silence, as "Oh My Papa" ran through my mind— most often as a tune now, the words no longer causing me to cry. One day Sister Florita was angrier than usual. Lunging down the aisle, she shouted, "Mary Rhodes!" She slapped me across the face, as she often did, yanked me up from my seat, again dragged me to the front of the room. Instead of shaking me and standing me up in the corner, this time she threw me against the blackboard. My body hit the chalk ledge and slid to the floor. The skirt of my uniform flew up, exposing my underpants to the class. Sister Florita picked me up and carried me out of the room, plunked me down in the corridor.

"Stay here until you can sit still at your desk," she said. I cried.

I sat on the freezing cold floor for a long time, my feet tucked up under me, staring at the boot puddles on the wood floor. I whimpered awhile, shivering and sniveling, wiping the snot off my face with the back of my hand. Then the whimpering got useless. There was no one.

When I listened hard I could hear different teachers in the classrooms up and down the hall. Some teachers droned on; others talked enthusiastically. Maybe you could be in any classroom lost in a dream world of your own, I thought, and not be missed. Which class would I want to be in? The one where none of the other kids knew me.

Unsure of how long I sat, growing colder and colder, wishing I wasn't there—I considered getting up, sneaking into the cloakroom, getting my coat and going home. But I knew I'd be caught and, probably, slapped again. Whatever Sister Florita did she'd do it in public where I couldn't hide.

The custodian came along. A dark-skinned stout man of around fifty with crooked white teeth, he didn't have a name like white men did, not Mr. This or Mr. That. He had only one name, a single given name, "Jim." He was the only black person in my world, aside from the beautiful elevator operators at Hudson's department store. His slow movements, his strength, and his quietness differed from other men. Certainly unlike the priests for whom we stood when they entered the room, Jim was simply there. But like all males, particularly grown men, he scared me. Strange. Unreachable.

Jim ambled by when all seemed hopeless, as I sat in the hall—through Religion, Reading, and Spelling. My feet and legs fell asleep; they tingled, and my butt ached. He looked down at me with soft eyes, the hint of a smile around his closed fat lips. In a gentle voice, full of his unfamiliar dialect, he asked me, "Are you a bad girl?"

"Yes," I said, though I felt a little warmer. I knew he was trying to comfort me. He went away and came back with a paper towel so I could blow my nose.

Sister Florita finally came out of the classroom. She seemed startled to see me sitting there, as though she'd forgotten about me.

"You can get your coat now, Mary Rhodes," she said. "It's time for you to go home."

The winter plodded on. The sounds of the furnace and boiler room, the hiss of the radiator, the buzz of the overhead fluorescents, and the puddles from the boots in the cloakroom. The catechisms were gray, but in them was certainty. The class studied for the Sacrament of Confirmation. The Bishop would come in the spring.

Q. "Why did God make me?"

A. "God made me to show forth His goodness and to share with Him His everlasting happiness in heaven."

Each page memorized.

Sister Florita walked down the rows, firing questions. Each kid stood straight to answer, answering in a complete sentence. I was hopeless, so I wasn't asked to answer. I sat rocking at my desk, contemplating the fresh scratch in the pale enamel at the edge of it, rocking, rocking, while the Irish boys answered more staunchly, while the Polish and Lithuanian girls recited the most difficult ones. They ignored me. It was better that way. In the seat ahead, Ann Bresnahan's black ponytail wagged. She swung to stand and answered crisply, the smell of her mother released in the warmth of a sun-glint on the hair brushed at lunchtime. Then Marianne Volskis, behind me, took her turn.

I pretended in that space of time to be at my worst, rocking feverishly, even drooling, making it convenient for them to leave me alone. Sister Florita's eyes darted hate. They could be avoided.

The Bishop was coming. The weather was warming. He would come from Lansing. Bishop Zaleski.

"He is young," Sister Florita told us. She almost giggled.

She showed a photo that she passed up and down the aisles—waxed black hair, high forehead, and deep Slavic eyes in bishop crimson cassock.

"The Bishop is coming," Sister Florita said. "We will practice in the church. We must be at our best."

A rustling of boots and raincoats and talking in the cloakroom, then across the sea of asphalt we stumbled, even Sister Florita did not keep silence. In the church the boys tramped too loudly and startled the few old ladies praying with sad faces. But Sister Florita pushed us to perfection. For days we practiced until the genuflections synchronized.

The Bishop was coming. Would he know I was bad? In the church I practiced with the rest and perfected the arch of my praying hands until I was sure the angle pointed straight to heaven. My thumbs crossed, I never trembled as my back stayed ramrod straight throughout the genuflection. No stooping.

Back in the room, it was time to recite the answers, this time out of order. Sister Florita, more at ease now, toyed with the pages of the catechism, proud, smiling, no one sure which question she'd pick.

"Who is God?"

The Irish boys squirmed in their seats, their hands waving flags to answer. "Me, Sister. Me, Sister!"

"James Casey?"

"God is the Supreme Being who made all things."

"Where is God?" she said.

It was the easiest question. The Irish boys went wild. "Me, Sister. Me, Sister!" they shouted.

The Lithuanian and Polish girls raised their arms. They waved furtively, reigning in their desire to shout like the boys. The Italian boys, the Mexican boy, the Maltese girls, the boy from the Army base, all raised their arms, and Sister Florita stepped back to see her work, proud, toying with the fervor.

The joyful fervor awakened me. Of course I knew the answer. Finally I too raised my hand, as the Irish boys became impatient and the "Me, Sisters" grew aggressive.

"Mary Rhodes?"

"God is in heaven."

Wrong. I knew it. Why had I said the wrong answer? "God is everywhere," was the correct answer, and I knew it.

The winter of 1954 ended with a March blizzard, one that shut down the school for a day, and then gave over to a glorious spring. I was a girl with two sides to me, one the lonely, grieving and traumatized girl living in a private world that nobody wanted to reach—the bad girl who was bad because they said she was bad.

And then there was the other side of me. I crouched behind a pile of dirty melting snow at the side of our house next to Mrs. Dragon's house, thrilled to be smelling the rich earth, thrilled to be hearing Bobby Gardner count and shout, "Ready or not, here I come."

CHAPTER FIVE
THE AGNES OF THE TWENTIETH CENTURY

During the winter of fourth grade, I started floating over to the holy store after school as the place where I could transcend the suffering I endured each day under the rule of Sister Florita. Ironically, I came armed with the very stories and the doctrines I had learned from Sister Florita. During the weeks just before my Confirmation in May, I stumbled upon a little 75-cent paperback along the back wall that was to have a profound influence on me.

Rossman's Religious Store, which everybody referred to as "the holy store," stood directly across from Holy Redeemer Church on Junction Avenue. The tiny store housed everything you would ever need to buy to be holy, from infant Baptismal gowns to sick-call crucifixes that stored the oil and beeswax candles the priest would need to administer the Last Rites when you were dying. Rosaries, relics, incense, Marian Missals and Douay Bibles, portraits of Jesus and Mary, statues of saints, vials of holy water from Lourdes and elsewhere, priestly vestments, holy cards and scapulars: the holy store was a treasure house of the fragrant, tactile, sacred, and mystical.

Saint Maria Goretti: Martyr for Purity was written by an Irish priest, a Redemptorist with a "C.Ss.R." after his name, just like our own Redemptorist priests at Holy Redeemer. The author's name was John Carr, which rhymed with C.Ss.R. The book contained a *Nihil Obstat* and an *Imprimatur* on the back of the title page, which Sister Florita had told us meant the Church approved of its content.

A forward to the book was written by the Bishop of Kerry, and I read it over and over again, along with the text, until I had it almost memorized. The Bishop writes: *I should like to see this little book in the hands of every girl of to-day.* He also writes that the book *should get a warm welcome from Catholics in these lands.*

Saint Maria Goretti, a genuine virgin martyr, was only a little older than I when she died at eleven, and like me she had lost her father at a young age and was being raised by a distracted mother. She was stabbed to death in July 1902, which meant she lived in the same century as me, *the Agnes of the twentieth century*, the book said. Like Saint Agnes in the third century, who was beheaded at age twelve rather than commit a mortal sin with a Roman soldier and worship the goddess Minerva, Maria too died rather than commit a mortal sin against purity. Her life could teach me about what I'd have to do myself to become a saint. Eagerly I read the book.

Written in a way that I couldn't doubt the author was talking right to me, the book provided a sly way of pointing out my imperfections. *Maria loved the Mass...*, the author writes. *She never looked about her, as children commonly do, but remained motionless, her head bowed low....She loved listening to sermons and greedily drank in the truths of faith....* I resolved to pay better attention to Sunday sermons and not daydream through them waiting for the holier part of Mass after the collection.

The book also made clear that sainthood was not an easy thing to achieve, that you had to go beyond being good to seek perfection. *Maria Goretti was not merely a pious little girl who said her prayers well. Many pious little girls and boys go thus far and no further, and had Maria done nothing more than this, we are not so sure that we should be writing these pages.* So far, then, they wouldn't be writing about me. I'd have to go further to become Saint Mary of Detroit. *Child as she was, she practiced virtues of a very solid kind. She was obedience itself, to her mother to the end and to her father while he lived.... Every order she was given was carried out with promptitude and exactness, and when little brothers would raise the flag of revolt, she would.... insist on respect for their mother and her bidding....* I had to stop and think about this because already I saw a big problem: Mama never asked me to do her bidding. How was I to solidify my virtues if everything was mushy? How was I going to be obedience itself if never given orders?

Now, Nancy Markowitz's father, he gave orders. He kept a belt hanging around the doorknob of the closet door off the living room, and he'd just look at it if his kids didn't immediately do what he said. How I envied them. They never had to be confused by all the things they might possibly do. They didn't have to worry about it. They were given orders. And they might even get a whipping with a belt.

I wrote a little book of my own on parenting. First, the rules: "Number 1: Give Orders," and then I drew the obedient children in cartoon frames with great smiles and with great security running to do exactly what they were told. When I had my own ten children, I'd give them orders and I'd expect them done. "Wash the dishes." "Vacuum the rugs." "Go to the store." "Feed the dog"—we'd have a dog. And my children would obey me with promptitude and exactness. I wouldn't nag like Mama did, with that little sad reverent begging tone, with something in the pauses in the question to make you think she was expecting you'd say "No"—"Mary, honey ... Would you... please... help me with... the dishes?"

Maria Goretti was a hard study, but on the next score I got a few ideas about how I might apply the lesson of Maria to my own quest for sainthood. *Now even all these very good and definite points in Maria might have come to very little but for something else: her devotion to duty and her love for work.* I liked to work. *The running of the house—the washing, dressing, cleaning, cooking, mending—fell almost entirely on Maria's two small shoulders.* Mama wasn't very good at cleaning and running the house. Now there was some work I could do. *Without demur, with never a murmur of rebellion at her lot, the little girl took it on and gave her goodwill and bent all her child's energies to the task, though it meant enjoying few of childhood's pleasures…. There was always plenty to do and she was never seen idle.* Maria's parish priest claimed *"The home was her passion,"* and the author tags on his own observation, *A rare passion nowadays.*

I could imitate Maria's virtue in my own situation through housework. I could also make the home my own passion. It wouldn't be a rare passion nowadays. In fact, the author's words puzzled me, for the home was *the* passion of every other mother on our block except mine. Making their homes neat, clean and gleaming, and getting supper on the table was what they did all day. Our home was the exception.

Through housework I too could be dutiful and never idle, even if I was never given orders. It wasn't long before I sought out the vacuum cleaner camouflaged among the clutter in the front closet. The humble unpainted metal hood of the heavy old-fashioned Hoover looked exactly like Mama's beat-up spaghetti pot. Its black detachable bag required you to stand over a section of the newspaper to empty it. You had to hold your feet on the metal lip and shake the bag, careful to keep holding your feet on the lip so as not to let the dust escape into the air. The elastic cord, meant to hold the bag upright and attach it to the handle, had long since broken, replaced by two interlocking large safety pins. The black rubbery casing on the handle had started to disintegrate so that the handle was sticky, unpleasant to touch, and if gripped too tightly left a black residue on your hands. Mama and Daddy bought this Hoover when they moved into the flat, the same year they bought the gray wool living room rug with swirling tufts, and the three red patterned fringed throw rugs that went under the legs of the sofa and two upholstered chairs. The Hoover could be set to Medium or High.

The first time I vacuumed, and subsequently after that, Mama worked herself into a fit. Her eyes darted hither and yon in alarm. "You'll ruin that rug if you sweep it on 'high.'"

I set the vacuum to "medium."

"Be careful of that fringe. You'll get it caught in the sweeper. It's going to tear."

I tried to lift the vacuum when I rolled over the fringes of the throw rugs, but occasionally it caught anyway. I broke into a sweat, turned the vacuum off, and worked like crazy to release the fringes before she noticed.

"Don't move that! It's too heavy," Mama warned when I started to move furniture. When I stopped lifting and started pushing, she said, "Don't scoot it. You're going to break the legs." I quickly learned how to use my hips to push the furniture. In no time I could move everything except the piano.

The Stanley furniture polish and the dust rag were also tools of my new trade. I took all the vases and knick-knacks off the tables and piano, dusted them, and set them in the chairs. I then poured a white pool of Stanley's into the rag. I swirled the polish around on the mahogany piano, the maple dresser and chest of drawers in my room, the walnut buffet and china cabinet, the oak side tables, all the wooden surfaces of the house, except for in the back room where Mama slept. (In that room there were too many boxes.) I admired the dry wood soaking up the polish, and I enjoyed inhaling the fumes. I shined nearly every surface in the house, while Mama, whenever she caught sight of me, lamented in agony.

"Did you shake that before you poured it?"

"Yes," I said, whether I had or hadn't.

Mama's voice got higher. "You're using too much!"

I put clean runners on the furniture and threw the dusty ones in the hamper for Mama to wash.

Eventually, Mama found them when she went to the hamper. "I just washed doilies last week," she said. "They wear out faster if you wash them too much."

I used the same method Mama used to deal with the clutter on the floors and on the tables and the chairs. I scooped it up, put it all into Avon boxes, and carted them to the back hallway in front of the way-back room. However, I did it more frequently than Mama did.

"Where's my girdle?" called Mama. "Where's my checkbook?" "Where's that letter from the City?" Ah, at long last, I could do her bidding.

I got good at cleaning, and I got even better at it when I waited for Mama to go downstairs and do the wash on Saturday mornings. That way I could clean without having to hear her bothering me at every step. What could she do when she finally came upstairs and saw that everything was lovely? It was too late to stop it. And I was becoming a saint.

I sought in all ways to make the same progress as Saint Maria Goretti. *Maria Goretti, at the age of ten,* the author writes, *was something more than a little girl who said her prayers and was never naughty.... In the footprints of Maria's childhood we recognize the footprints of the childhood of many a canonised saint.* How fervently I wanted to be a canonized saint.

On the next virtue, purity, I had to submit to confusion. I didn't know what *purity* was. I didn't have a clue. The author, swinging into the goriest part of his story, starts a new section and makes a grand transition, with the style that by now I really liked and was thoroughly used to. I read carefully:

But there is one virtue which flowered early and with a particular loveliness in the soul of Maria Goretti and on which her short career on this earth hinged. We must speak of it now.

"Please do," I said to the page.

What struck all those most who came in contact with her was her purity. Its peace was in her limpid eyes. Its brightness shown about her. Its fragrance clung to her. It was to be her undoing in this world, her making in the next. It was to put an undying lily, together with a martyr's palm, into her child's arms and give her entrance into that high company in heaven of those who follow the Lamb withersoever He goeth.

The writing left me breathless. I loved it. Especially as I learned where to pause, for dramatic effect, while reading it out loud. Still the mystery—what exactly was *purity*? The more I read, the more confusing it became. Examples of purity: limpid eyes? In the following pages were more examples and explanations. The priest who gave Maria her First Communion, the author writes, taught his *little band of First Communicants… a love for purity "at all costs" and watchfulness in guarding it. Maria's modesty struck everybody,* the author writes. *She hurried along the country roads and through the streets of Nettuno almost with the shrinking of one who clasps a treasure, though she scarcely knew what that treasure was. She never loitered or gazed about her.… She always longed to be home again.* I didn't know what the treasure was either. *Following in the steps of her mother, she was modest, wore a long frock, and even in the hottest days of summer never allowed herself any latitude in this matter.* The author tells that she also had a twinge of sadness in her eye. I tried to imagine that. Her eyes were limpid and clear and a little sad.

Of course I knew what modesty was. It was all about clothes and not letting boys see your underwear. It was also about not wearing clothes that were "too loud," as Mama would say, or too low cut. I wondered why the author suggested that a long dress on a hot day was necessary. I decided that was an olden-day custom I could ignore. Still I couldn't quite understand about purity—how it could be a flower in your soul, shine like a light, seem to be solid like a treasure to be guarded, and then become undone like a scarf or a bow.

Perhaps it had to do with boys and girls, with men and women. It was something girls and women had that men and boys would ask for. It made me feel a little excited in a funny way. And giving it away was a mortal sin. Still it wasn't clear. I'd have to study further.

If I had to study further to understand purity, I had no trouble with the murder, the murder the author described in thrilling gory detail. Maria was murdered by Alessandro, a twenty-year-old who, along with his father, shared the house of the Goretti family. The author tells us why Alessandro did it, even before he describes the events leading up to the murder. *Through the constant reading of papers containing detailed descriptions of sex crimes, and of lives of notorious murderers—which unfortunately at the time could be procured in plenty for a few pence, and which were procured by Alessandro without the knowledge or with the connivance of an indifferent father—his mind had become perverted and his heart had become a sink. He was thoroughly brutalized, and he now drew Maria into the unclean world of his thoughts and longings.*

Even though a word I'd heard but didn't exactly understand—*sex,* and *sex* combined with *crime*—deterred me a little, the rest was perfectly clear to me. Such a crying shame. Alessandro's father should have monitored Alessandro's reading. There shouldn't have been "dirty newspapers" around for Alessandro to get so cheaply. And if there were, they should have had the Legion of Decency like we did in our time in America. The Legion of Decency viewed every movie and then told you in the *Michigan Catholic* whether it was a sin to see it. Parents made sure their children didn't see any AII or AIII movies, not to mention the B or C movies that no one should see. The Catholic Legion of Decency didn't put out a list of all the bad books like they did for the movies, but they published guidelines for parents to follow.

By now I also understood that Alessandro was a filthy dangerous man. His heart had become a sink. Probably a dirty sink like the one I envisioned—the one down by Stony Pointe on Lake Erie where we swam with my Aunt Kay and cousin Bobby, with lots of flies and stray cats around it, where fishermen gutted their fish. The sides of it were scummy, and scraps of pink ugly stuff clogged the drain. Even though I knew where the story was going, especially as I read it again and again, I prayed each time that Maria's mother would wake up and intervene, that Maria wouldn't end up in the house alone with Alessandro. So why did I feel a small thrill when I read that Alessandro *drew Maria into the unclean world of his thoughts and longings?* It was the *drawing in.* It seemed romantic to be drawn in to someone's longing.

The murder scene was one I couldn't help reading again and again—even when I felt like skipping some parts of the book that bored me after a couple of times, like all the tests for Maria to become Venerable, then Blessed, and then canonized a Saint. The murder scene went on for several pages:

Alessandro and Maria were now alone: the hawk with the dove, the wolf with the lamb, the brutal boy of twenty and the gentle girl not yet twelve. The struggle for mastery was to begin. What chance had she? Physically, none. Physically he could have bent her to his will with ease. Why the thrill, reading the words *bent her to his will?* I imagined her body bending gracefully like a dancer. And the concept of mastery: to be mastered by a male, a father, a head of household, a leader, a boss, all of that which was missing in my life, all of which was something I secretly longed for.

But virtue... has that in it, even when exercised by a child, that can cow the beast in a man and turn the edge of his unruly appetite. This alone can explain why Alessandro did not take what Maria would not give. What was it he would not take? And why did the words *take what Maria would not give* thrill me so?

The author stops the action to ruminate over the theological question, claiming that Maria *knew enough theology to get to heaven,* knowing that she would rather die than commit a mortal sin. And when he resumes the action he draws the scene out with so much dialogue that it seems to last as long as the scene would take in reality: *"No, no, no. What are you doing, Alessandro? Don't touch me! 'Tis a sin!"* She protests and protests, and when Alessandro threatens death if she will not yield, she thinks of the consequences of the sin on Alessandro's soul. *"No, no, no! God does not wish it. If you do that you'll commit a sin, you'll go to hell."* But she was reasoning with a wild beast. He then gagged her with the handkerchief he had brought for the purpose, to keep her from calling for help. The author makes it clear again that Maria is not giving in, forcing Alessandro to choose a better course of action over the mortal sin that would involve them both. For as bad as it was, the better course is only one mortal sin, and that is murder. It's clear that Maria is charitable. She's thinking of Alessandro's soul as well as her own.

And then the author finally gets to the stabbing, the goriest part of the book: *Maria chose and Alessandro struck. He struck with all the savagery of his baffled lust and his pride humiliated by the unyielding obstinacy of a little child. He struck so fiercely and repeatedly that when he plucked away the reeking weapon, her very entrails followed it. With a groan of agony, but gathering her garments, which had been torn by the dagger, modestly about her, she sank to the floor a bleeding little heap.* The scene was horrible, and so gory that any of the strange good feelings I'd felt about whatever gross immodesty it were were now gone. Poor Maria.

The effect of the scene was ultimately confusing. Not confusing of course in terms of what happened. That Maria was hacked to death was patently clear. But confusing in that the barbarous deed is described in thrilling detail. What I knew at age nine was a primal feeling, a feeling of arousal tinged with pain and masochism, for even as Maria is hacked to death, the thrill still seems to be that she was wanted by a man.

Maria lived another day, and on that day she received her last Holy Communion, called a *Viaticum*. She explained what had happened to her, why Alessandro had stabbed her, because that was the grounds for her becoming a martyr. *Because he wanted me to commit a horrible sin, and I said to him: No! No! No!* She formally forgives Alessandro, promises to pray for his soul and others when she got to heaven. The author points out that her surviving as long as she did—more than twenty hours—can only be explained as a miracle. To be a saint you needed at least two miracles. And Alessandro, after spending a long time in jail, went to Confession and asked God and Maria's mother to forgive him—another miracle.

A blue-tinged portrait of Maria Goretti graced the cover of the book. The same portrait painted in sepia was on the inside. I studied it over and over again. Her light hair seemed to have a reddish cast like mine, although hers was curlier, as it flowed down into the single braid that started at her neck. The portrait was a profile, and she held a white dove in her hand, a dove that stood for purity. She wore a long-sleeved tunic over a flowered blouse, but you could see only the collar of the blouse at the neck. Over the tunic she wore a fringed shawl. I felt so sorry for her, and I knew she was like Agnes, the Roman Christian martyr who also died to keep her treasure.

I couldn't take the Confirmation name Maria because Maria was just Mary in Italian and Latin. So I took Agnes, in honor of both saints, Saint Agnes and Saint Maria Goretti. Sister Florita had told us, "You'll have to have your minds made up by next week when I pass out the forms. And then you won't be able to change your minds." When the time came to write it, I wrote Agnes. The holy card of Agnes showed her with a lamb. Agnes meant lamb in Latin. *Agnus dei* was another name for Jesus, the Lamb of God. Agnes in Latin also meant *victim*.

The next week I knelt with the others at the Communion rail. Bishop Zaleski from Lansing anointed me with *chrism*, rubbing the Sign of the Cross with it into my forehead, uttered my name in Latin, *Aaagh*-Noose, and administered the gentle ritual slap on the cheek. I was on my way to sainthood.

CHAPTER SIX
SAINT MARY OF DETROIT

In third grade, I listened to Sister Elizabeth Ann's gentle stories of the saints. In fourth grade, I listened to Sister Florita's gorier stories of the saints and learned what I thought was all the rules for avoiding sin. I longed for someone to tell me what to do and punish me if I did wrong. I longed for brothers and sisters, to become a secure and loyal child in a large family. Our Lord and Our Blessed Mother, and all that sprang from Our Lord's Church, provided an elaborate hierarchy of authority and the largest family imaginable, with hundreds of heroic saints to emulate. If I became a saint, that would make the saints my sisters and brothers. I would stand beside them in heaven: Saint Mary of Detroit.

On earth I would follow the saints' examples, the saints who found a reason for their suffering, who turned it into deliberate acts of devotion, who found joy in their devotion. I wanted, like Saint Rose of Lima, to sleep on broken glass. I wanted the sense of humor and sharp wit of Saint Lawrence who suggested to his tormentors burning him on a pyre, "Turn me over. I'm done on that side." I wanted to be an early Christian martyr.

I loved the homelands of saints, Italy especially, where I might go to see the Holy Father, or, better still, the catacombs and Coliseum, where so much was risked for Christ and where so much sacrificial blood was shed. When Frank LaSalle, the corner grocer from Naples, gave me a package of almond nougat candy labeled "Imported from Italy," I turned it over and over again for weeks before I opened it. It had touched the holy land of stories I wanted to inhabit, stories of purpose with a place for me, stories of human connection.

I also set about to raise the consciousness of my peers. After school and during summer vacations on Clark Street, we played a game I invented called "Christian Martyr." Bobby Gardner, a year younger than I, made a perfect Roman soldier with his Mohawk helmet. With one of his mother's old broaches, he pinned his cape to his tee shirt at his right shoulder. He fashioned a whip from six sections of clothesline, taped them together on one end to form a handle, and knotted the end of each rope. He scourged us with the whip, chasing us down into the catacombs at the bottom of the basement stairway leading from the Markowicz's backyard.

Bobby spit, hurled insults and shouted, "We'll rid the empire of you, Christians."

Our role, me and mostly the younger kids, was to run, but once overpowered, to smile beatifically, roll our eyes toward Heaven, and let him herd us up the stairs, where we marched and submitted to the next segment of the drama, being tied together to a tree in Mrs. Dittmer's front yard to await—the lions. Then, as we were being eaten, we uttered prayers and lolled our heads. To be chased, to be scourged, to be overpowered, to be eaten—all of it thrilled us.

We played our roles to the hilt. We'd all seen *Quo Vadis*. We'd all seen *The Robe*. And we continued to play through the release of *Demetrius and the Gladiators* (1954).

Suffering was the thing; we suffered for our Faith. Suffering was the measure of our Faith. When it got too cold to play outside, we suffered as much as we could inside. My girlfriend Randy Lambert and I took turns tying each other up to the Doric pillar in the archway of her dining room, scratching each other's arms with a toothless comb until they streaked red and our heads flopped like Jesus on the cross. Our devotion and our play took a turn toward apparitions after we'd watched the reruns of the *Song of Bernadette* and the *Miracle of Our Lady of Fatima* at the Saturday matinee at the Stratford Theater. Then we imagined She appeared to us—Our Lady in the backyard in the snow, or near the frozen lagoon in the park.

One time we were cutting through the alley, on the way to Frank LaSalle's store on Christiancy and McKinstry, when I bent down to tie my shoe. Glancing up the alley past the tennis courts of the YMCA, almost up to Vernor, I saw Our Lady in the Saturday morning mist. The telephone poles planted at wide intervals on the left side of the alley gleamed darkly, the wires dripping with fog. The April air blotted our skin cool and wet. Somewhere down the alley in a garage, somebody sawed through wood with a power saw. Centered in an oval, slightly raised above the ground, She appeared shivery silver, exactly like the Mother of Perpetual Help medal Father Forbes had given each person in the school.

"Look, Randy, look there, up the alley!" I said. "I see Our Blessed Mother. Can you see her?"

Randy stepped toward the center of the alley and squinted in the direction I pointed. At first she just gazed.

"See her? There in the mist. She looks like a Perpetual Help medal."

Randy squinted again. And then, "I see her! I see her!"

We both dropped to our knees, right there in the wet gritty, glass-strewn alley. We knelt silently for a couple minutes until somebody walked by on Christiancy and we felt a little foolish. Besides, the apparition was fading. Although I suspected I'd imagined it, I also knew it could have been true—Our Lady ready to trust us with a message, perhaps distracted by the buzz saw. Why not? And who better than us? We were just ordinary girls like Bernadette at Lourdes, ordinary children like Lucia, Francisco and Jacinta at Fatima.

*   *   *

The first statue I bought from the holy store was Saint Theresa, the Little Flower. I was taken by the bouquet of pink and yellow roses cushioning the crucifix she carried in her arms. The bouquet cascaded over her cream-and-brown tunic in the most graceful arching way. She was a Carmelite nun. Unlike some other saints, who rolled their eyes toward heaven, Theresa smiled in her portraits, always appearing happy, kind and pretty. Since she was modern, dying in 1897, a real photograph of her existed, and even in the photograph she smiled. She smiled, despite coughing up blood at a young age. Her life story revealed hidden suffering, and because of that, she seemed simpatico. Besides, I loved the name Thérèse, Thérèse Lisieux, which included funny silent letters, and I vowed to name the first of my ten children Thérèse, complete with the French accent marks.

For a gang of pious girls from the other fourth grade classes, the holy store was the after-school hot spot. What drew them in as regular customers was something amidst the hoard of gorgeous priceless artifacts that we all could afford. For slightly more than two-cent lunchroom milk, and slightly less than a five-cent Snickers bar, the holy cards called out to us from their wooden stepladder boxes where they were arranged like greeting cards on the right as we walked in.

Three or four of us could browse them at a time, and we collected and traded them. Like boys who learned from trading baseball cards, we learned the art of paying close attention, and the basics of buying, selling and negotiation. If we didn't learn much math from calculating lifetime batting averages, we absorbed the rudiments of Western art history and the practice of art appreciation, even if we lacked the vocabularies.

I stood enraptured by more than a hundred holy cards. "You can look at them without touching them," the store lady said, more than once.

But I couldn't make a decision without touching them, without taking them from their boxes and holding them up to the light.

The Crucifixion cards moved me the most—Our Lord so vulnerable, so dying, so dead. Some with the thieves alongside Him. Some with Our Lord alone. One disturbing one that showed them all nailed up haphazardly, their poor arms and legs falling into weird angles. It made me realize that the body wouldn't have stayed straight. Our Lord must have suffered horribly for our sins.

One time Marie Ritterbeck pointed to one and said, "Look, His loincloth is drooping."

The three of us in front of the row of cards giggled. Later, when I examined my conscience, I felt guilty. Later, I decided that since I wasn't the one who pointed it out, I hadn't committed a mortal sin against purity. But I did commit a venial sin, one of omission, because I failed to set her right. Instead of giggling I should have told her to be more respectful. I confessed it, and even limited my association with Marie for a while. She was an occasion of sin.

*   *   *

So many cards to buy and to organize and so many ways to interpret them. Since our perspective and opinions about them changed from day to day, we had good reason to trade them.

The first step was to arrange them. I spent hours and hours gazing at them and sorting them, sitting in silence on the dirty living room rug at home. I usually organized the cards thematically, starting with Our Lord—His life from the Nativity to the Ascension, then going to Mary, and then the rest of the saints in alphabetical order. Organizing them by theme allowed for the most comparison. One Madonna and Child showed a cute chubby Infant. An Infant even cuter went ahead of the first one. An Infant with a cute face, but boldly and immodestly showing his "boy-thing" might be a candidate to trade with Kathleen Antononi. He went to the back of the pack. In one the Infant appeared too old to be a newborn, definitely a candidate for trade. Several showed the Infant stylized, acting God-like, sitting up straight with his hand raised in blessing. There were several in this style of other scenes, for instance Our Lady of Perpetual Help—the cards greener and flatter than the others, with more elaborate halos. I later learned the style was Byzantine.

Sometimes I brought the stack to the dining room table where more of the overhead bulbs were working and I could examine them more closely. The longer I gazed at them the more I noticed. I noticed that several of the paintings revealed the source of light—I could imagine where it came from even if it wasn't in the picture. I saw depth in others—how far the angel stood in front, how far the garden receded into the background.

When, as an adult, I finally made it to the Louvre in Paris and stood in a gallery drinking in the Titians, Raphaels and Botticellis, I was struck by a sudden bolt of lightning: these were some of the paintings I'd studied and admired for hours as a child, in our humble Detroit neighborhood, printed on three-cent holy cards!

Pat Proctor, Marie Ritterbeck, and Kathleen Antononi were steady holy card buffs, but my most frequent trading partner was Marie Polanski. Marie was an attractive person to trade with because she frequented the holy stores farther up on Junction near Saint Hedwig's when she visited her grandmother. Her collection included cards I'd never seen, and she acquired more all the time.

One Saturday morning I took my stack to her house. Marie owned a card I wanted, a gold leaf picture of a Guardian Angel with white wings protecting a brown-haired hapless-looking boy crossing a mountain canyon on a plank bridge toward a coiled snake in the foreground on the other side. What made the card particularly attractive was that it was mounted on and bordered by a lace fringe.

Before I entered the negotiations, I contemplated what I'd trade. I suspected she'd require two of mine for her one. Perhaps that was fair. None of mine were framed in lace. I decided I'd barter some of my Madonna and Childs, which were easy to garner, and almost all of my Nativity scenes, which were even easier to get, since you could even cut them out of Christmas cards.

Marie didn't gush or exude exuberance about the cards like most of the other girls, and so she proved to be a hard bargainer. She wore a placid expression on her pink face that appraised her clean well-cared-for collection in relative silence and then laid each card, one atop the other, on the table facing me. She seemed almost bored when I laid mine out, never letting on if or how much she coveted any of my cards.

"Would you like to trade the angel with the lace border?" I asked, trying to make my voice nonchalant.

"I don't know. What will you give me for it?"

"I don't know. What do you want?"

"Well, you're going to have to give me at least five of your cards for the angel," she said. "You know he's got a lace border."

"Five seems like a lot. What if I gave you four?" I knew I was already bargaining beyond my budget. I'd let her start the bidding, and she'd started so high.

"No. You'll have to give me five."

I thought about what I could part with. If she wanted five, I'd give her the worst ones, the ones without gold leaf, the ones on thinner paper. Maybe I could clean my collection of ones that weren't very nice. I wanted the angel with the border.

I thumbed through my collection, disregarding what I'd said to myself beforehand about trading the Madonna and Childs and Nativity scenes. This time I plucked out anything that looked mass produced and fuzzy, anything cheap. I laid a small stack of about ten cards face down on the table. "OK," I said. "You can pick out five from this pile." I turned the cards over so she could select.

"These aren't as nice as the other ones you've got," she pouted.

"But you wanted five for one," I said. "I can't give you the best ones."

"OK, four then," she insisted.

We continued dickering until I had the Guardian Angel with the lace fringe. Four of my best—a nice Saint Ann and Mary with gold leaf ringed halos, a gaudy Nativity scene with a trace of glitter, and two of my better Madonna and Childs—were passed.

In fifth grade I grew more fervent in my quest for sainthood, as Catholic rituals gave me more and more to learn and know about. The high point of the winter came when I said Mass in the "catacombs," the ones located in our living room. We were hiding from the Roman soldiers overhead. I draped one of Mama's long linen furniture spreads over the closed piano keys, and with the mahogany scrolls and mother-of-pearl inlays on the front of the big upright piano, it looked exactly like an altar. I brought a crystal chalice out of the china cabinet and dropped a few Necco wafers into it. I filled half a cream pitcher from the kitchen with grape juice. I dragged a linen napkin out of the buffet drawer to wipe the vessel that would hold the Body and then the Blood of Our Precious Savior. I placed all these things on the keyboard altar.

Nancy Markowicz played the part of altar boy, engaging a little press bell Daddy had bought for me to play office. It wasn't a gold bell you shook like the ones used in church, but it sounded the same if pressed repeatedly. She would ring the bell when I elevated the Host and the Chalice of Our Lord's blood. I set candles on each side of the keyboard that Nancy would light before Mass. I turned off the overhead light so it looked more like church. I practiced the Latin with my Marian Missal, nailing the most important parts, and the easy parts, the stuff I already knew, like *"Kyrie Eleison, Christe Eleison,"* (*Lord have mercy on us, Christ have mercy on us*) and *"Agnus Dei, qui tolis peccata mundi, Miserere nobis,* (*Lamb of God, who takes away the sins of the world, pray for us*) and, of course, the last time you say the *"Agnus Dei"* you end it with *"Dona nobis pacem"* (*Lord grant us peace*) instead of *"Miserere nobis."*

At the appointed time, five of the kids from Markowicz's four-family flat showed up at the door—Randy Lambert, Bobby Gardner, Nancy Markowitz, and her little sister, Patricia, who tagged along. They also brought Jerry Ashe, a Protestant kid from Georgia, who shouldn't have been there. Would the Mass keep his attention and would he know what to do?

Sure enough. At the most sacred part of the Mass, as I raised a Necco wafer and recited in my priestly tones, *"Hoc est enim corpus meum,"* (*This is My Body*) and Nancy pressed the bell as loudly and as many times as she could, and all the others, heads bowed, were kneeling and beating their breasts, Jerry Ashe interrupted. "When are we going to get done with this?"

My smiling statue of Saint Theresa cheered me, but she looked a little lonely sitting on the dresser by herself, and so I saved my allowance to buy a statue of Our Lady to keep her company. It was the statue of Our Lady dressed in blue and white and slightly stooped with her arms outspread. She smiled a demure smile as she crushed the head of the snake of Eden under Her left foot. Only Our Lady could stomp on Satan like that, since she was born without Original Sin, which is what Sister Florita meant when she talked about Our Lady's Immaculate Conception. At the holy store they stocked several identical Our Ladys in three sizes. I chose the medium-sized statue I could afford, pointed to it through the case, and the holy store lady retrieved it, wrapped it in brown paper, and put it in a bag for me to take home.

I tried putting the statue in various places in my bedroom. Somehow Our Lady didn't look right next to Saint Theresa on the dresser since Theresa was taller. Theresa looked just fine at eye level, but Our Lady did not. I discovered that Our Lady looked much better, not so stooped, if I put Her on top of the bookcase in the hall where She could gaze downward and I could gaze upward. But since I didn't want Her to be anywhere outside my room, I made a platform out of a couple of the old cigar boxes Mama had saved and covered them with a linen dresser scarf. On top of my dresser, standing on the platform, Our Lady then appeared at Her best, and I could turn Saint Theresa so she'd be standing in attendance. Theresa too gazed up at Our Lady.

When spring came, I made a glorious May Altar with all the lilacs and lilies of the valley I could find in the yard, arranged them in all the vases we owned, and placed them symmetrically around the platform on my dresser.

"Mama, you kneel down for the Procession," I said. I ran downstairs so I could start from downstairs at the front door. I carried the statue of Our Lady up the stairs while singing *Oh Mary, we crown thee with blossoms today, queen of the angels, queen of the May.*

When I came through the living room with the statue, Mama was kneeling, just like I told her to, and when I passed her with the statue, she bowed her head and made the Sign of the Cross. She got up and followed me as I solemnly moved through the dining room and through the hall to my bedroom where the glorious altar awaited—with the real flowers and streams of pink and red crepe paper roses I'd made to hang on ribbons draped around the mirror, all of it reflected again. There were lit candles, six on each side, even though Mama wouldn't let me use the real beeswax altar candles she'd saved from Daddy's funeral. The breeze billowed the curtains, and the fresh May air poured in, stirring up the fragrance of God's lilies and lilacs. By then I'd progressed to singing "*Salve Regina*," and Mama joined in, both of us singing "*Salve Regina, Mater misericordiae, vita dulcedo et spes nostra, salve. . . .*" I sang the Latin songs last as the most serious. I placed the statue of Mary on the platform in the center of the dresser, this time the cigar boxes covered with blue satin. And then on Her head I placed the crown, a wonder of tiny paper roses attached to a circled braid of pipe cleaners, with satin ribbons twirled around and around. As I placed it on Her head, She almost moved Her arms to bless us.

We waited a significant moment, made the Sign of the Cross again, and then sat on the bed and said a Rosary.

Rosaries. To become a saint, I'd have to say a lot of them. Saying them by myself earned me Partial Indulgences, which helped reduce any time I'd have to spend in Purgatory after I died. If I said them in the right place, in Church or with the family and others, or at the right time, during the nine-week Novenas to Our Mother of Perpetual Help, I received extra grace in Heaven. I could earn a Plenary Indulgence, which would get me out of having to go to Purgatory at all.

I recited Rosaries on my way to school. If I said them fast, I could complete two of them. If I said them even faster, and with some practice, I could get up to four. So I prayed the Rosary—trudging up Christiancy, past Frank LaSalle's Market at McKinstry where we shopped and where Mama said they had the best meat. I glanced at Ernie Piper's Protestant Lutheran corner store across the street and continued to Lansing Street, where Pete Peterson, the kind English man, ran the store with all the cats winding around the barrels and vegetable bins, the grocer who also offered the most conversation and the very best candy. I marched past Ferdinand, where the mysterious man who didn't speak English ran the spooky corner store. Being on the lookout, I passed the corner house on Morrell that I could see from Christiancy. A sickle hung from a hook on the back door, probably a sign that the occupants were Communist. Arriving at Junction, I made the sharp right turn and kept marching to school.

When I prayed fast all the words ran together, and I didn't even need to finger the beads in my pocket—I could count ten by turning fingers, and then I got so good at the rhythm of prayers and feet on pavement that I didn't even need to do that.

"HailMaryfullofgracetheLordiswiththeeblessedartthouamongwomen …. GlorybetotheFathertheSontheHolyGhostasitwasinthebeginning..."

It wasn't hard once you got used to it. I earned so many Partial Indulgences that I couldn't even count them. And I wondered, although I never asked, whether I could give any away.

This was the time of Rosaries, including the Radio Rosary Crusade, sponsored by the Archdiocese of Detroit, to stop the spread of Communism. Each night at 7:15, Catholics of the Archdiocese could turn on their radios, kneel down and pray. Praying along with the radio counted as praying the Rosary with others, so it carried along with it a Plenary Indulgence. Everybody in the parish talked about it—what a good idea.

One time I got Mama to do it. She didn't believe you could really hear the Rosary on the radio, but when I turned it on and tuned it in, she shook her head a little and reluctantly pulled out her rosary from the buffet drawer and knelt down.

The next evening she got stubborn. "My knees hurt," she declared.

I knew what she said was final. I wasn't going to get her to budge off the chair where she was reading the *Detroit News* in her systematic get-her-money's-worth way. Admittedly, it had been a little embarrassing—kneeling down with only Mama and looking at nothing but the dust under the furniture, hearing Mr. Dixon's clock tick-tocking on the buffet and the same old words coming out of the radio over and over again from the mouth of a person we couldn't see.

Besides, in the Archdiocese campaign they stressed "The Family." "The family that prays together, stays together," said *The Michigan Catholic*, and I had trouble thinking of Mama and me as a family. We just didn't seem to have the necessary prerequisites, the first one being a father who knew best. While other Catholics in the Archdiocese kept tuning in to the Radio Rosary Crusade, Mama and I gave it up after one try. Of course, that didn't mean I stopped praying the Rosary—at novenas, at funeral homes, and on my way to school.

I couldn't stop praying to stop the spread of Communism, for Sister Callistus, my fifth grade teacher, kept us ever vigilant about the threat. Sister Callistus often stood in front of the classroom and wept. She was extremely unhappy about the Communists. The unconfirmed rumor circulated that she had family left in Eastern Europe under the repression of the Communists.

"This is the Iron Curtain," she said, tracing a line with her pointer on the pull-down map at the front of the room, cutting smack dab through Germany on down to the Mediterranean, stopping to dwell on the good Catholic countries shrouded from Western light. Tears rolled down her rosy cheeks. "Look at the Baltic Sea," she said. "Do you see that, it's Our Lady praying over Russia?"

With her rubber-tipped pointer, she outlined the body of water: Our Lady on bended knees facing east, Stockholm on Her back at Her waist, Her head sticking up above Finland, and sure enough, Her praying hands pointed right toward Communist Leningrad, which used to be named for Saint Peter. Sister Callistus' observations were compelling, and once you looked at it her way, you could never mistake the Baltic. Never mind that the Baltic existed long before the Communists. That was easy to resolve. Our Lady knew that eventually the Communists would be there, so She started praying in advance. Through her tears, Sister Callistus interrupted the geography lesson so we could pray together to stop the Communists. We knelt down next to our desks.

Sister Callistus saw Communism as a big conspiracy, and she made sure we were alerted to it. The conspiracy extended into areas that seemed to go beyond politics and reached closer to home. She told us it would be a sin to watch the television program, *I Led Three Lives*, because it portrayed Communism. She even directed us away from Milton Berle because he was non-Christian. In fact, he didn't believe in Our Savior, Our Lady, and the Resurrection because he was Jewish. With tears streaming down her face, she made us rise and recite the Legion of Decency's Pledge. We stood beside our desks, made the Sign of the Cross, then raised our right hands. *I acknowledge my obligation to form a right conscience about pictures that are dangerous to my moral life. As a member of the Legion of Decency, I pledge myself to remain away from them. I promise, further, to stay away altogether from places of amusement which show them as a matter of policy.*

We all promised we would never in our lives see a "C" movie. For Sister Callistus, the implication was that "C" movies were full of Communism. Her logic was such: indecent immodest content in films was a ploy to hook you in. Once you responded to the immodesty, you were fair game to be converted to Communism.

Communism did not provide the only reason for Sister Callistus's tears. There was the problem of me and "that habit," for even though I had my aspirations to become Saint Mary of Detroit, I still had my moral blind spot.

My picture of Sister Callistus is clearer than my picture of Sister Florita. But I have a less clear picture of myself and "that habit" at this time. Was it less or more? Was my situation in her class better or worse? Sister Callistus never slapped me or pulled me from my seat, and so I remember fewer scenes.

Unlike Sister Florita who moved like a fury, Sister Callistus stood stone still. She gazed at me across the classroom, trying to engage my eyes. When unsuccessful, her already pink face grew pinker, tears welled up, overflowed, and ran down her red cheeks. I sensed her crying as a variation of Mama's sadness over me and "that habit." Could Sister Callistus teach me to stop by showing me the distress I brought to others? I'm not sure whether she thought I'd stop through her efforts, or whether she considered me a cross for her to bear. Whichever it was, I didn't feel welcome.

One day, after I'd returned from being sick the day before, Janet Mooney, who sat behind me, tapped me on the shoulder. "Sister Callistus told us yesterday that we shouldn't play with you. You're an occasion of sin."

My mind raced. Why would Sister Callistus say a thing like that? It must be "that habit." But my thinking didn't get me to the occasion of the correct sin. I reasoned "that habit" made me an outcast, and an outcast can be an occasion of sin, a bad companion. A bad companion is one who doesn't reinforce a person's resolve to walk in the correct ways. That made some sense to me.

"Did she tell the whole class?" I said.

"Yeah, she told everybody. You're an occasion of sin." Although fond of tattling, Janet's voice wasn't taunting. In telling me she gave me a gift of knowledge.

One sign that things were getting better for me was that what Sister Callistus said about me didn't make me feel that bad. It was so obvious, and I had no need to respond. Nobody's playing with me. Can't Sister Callistus see that? Nobody plays with Mary Rhodes. But then I remembered those who did play with me—all the kids on Clark Street, who were either Protestant or in different grades or rooms, most of them admittedly a few years younger. And a few girls in other fifth grade rooms associated with me after school at the holy store. These kids didn't know about me. But even a girl or two from our class talked to me, a girl or two also on the fringe. In fact, Janet Mooney had just talked to me, and she wasn't on the fringe. I liked her for that.

Although the frequency of my habit may have been waning, and Sister Callistus never slapped me, one time she hurt me as badly as Sister Florita, but in a different way. It happened in spring, with the year nearly over, around the time of the city primary elections. The nuns voted at the fire station on Junction Avenue. They may have taken a walk afterward. At any rate, Sister Callistus must have seen the bar that stood farther down the block on Junction with the slick white marble-looking front and big green neon hand-written signature across the entire building, saying "Eddie Rhodes Tavern." Mama and I used to drive by there all the time, and we noted the sign of a Rhodes person proud enough to spread his name in neon on a wall and wealthy enough to own a bar. I liked the sign, the way "Rhodes" was written with an upward tilt.

"Mama," I said, "Do you think he might be a relation?"

Mama knew about Daddy's family, even his cousins. Daddy was the only one who'd stayed up North. "Don't I wish," she said, "but, no, I'm sure he's not any relation."

So that day in spring following the election, when I started rocking at my desk, Sister Callistus began to cry and pointed toward me, her eyes welling. Then she pointed her finger again and said to the class, "Look at the behavior of this girl—whose father owns a bar."

I was flabbergasted. She hadn't called for a response, but I knew this time I had the right to speak, to defend myself against a lie. She thought I had a father in a sinful business. But I couldn't speak. I couldn't say, "No, that's not my father. My Daddy doesn't own a bar. My Daddy has no business now. He doesn't go to work. He doesn't come home. My Daddy is dead."

I sat there dazed, descending into my interior world of shame, but I still hadn't exhausted trying to figure out what to say. Sister Callistus had told a lie about me to the entire class. Yet I couldn't bring myself to say my father was dead. That was the biggest shame. Everybody had a father. Fathers were everywhere, and every night there were wonderful fathers on TV. *Leave it to Beaver, Father Knows Best, The William Bendix Show*, everywhere there were fathers—funny, adorable, loving, strong, protective, resourceful fathers. Fathers were necessary to make a family, to make things normal. I didn't have one, and that was what made me abnormal and forlorn. I didn't have a father, and Sister Callistus was making me aware that I missed my father. I missed Daddy. How could I possibly tell that to the class?

I thought of telling a half-truth. "My father works in Plant Protection at Cadillac. Eddie Rhodes is no relation." What was the lie? Only in one letter—"works" instead of "worked." I couldn't do that either. It was still a lie. I couldn't answer a lie with a lie.

I felt ashamed. Yet I would have been proud to have a father who owned a bar. I felt ashamed because I couldn't defend myself without shaming myself further. There was a lake full of tears in me that wanted to spill out. I suppressed them. Not one of them dropped on the worksheet on my desk.

Within an hour I started recalling all the forms I'd filled out since second grade. Mama had taught me how to spell it correctly, and on all the forms where it asked, "Father's name?" I always wrote "Omer (Deceased)." The word "deceased." I hated the word. If I could have stomped on it I would have. It made me feel so ashamed. I was sure I had had to fill out forms in Sister Callistus's class. Sister Callistus thought I was a bad girl, an occasion of sin for the others, a troublemaker, and her cross to bear. Yet she didn't know the first thing she should have known to know me. My father was deceased.

At that moment my mind moved to bracket her. It helped that she was odd, eccentric, and that some of the bolder kids laughed at her behind her back. Something about my faith in her started to shift. Unlike Sister Florita, who I always believed in and even loved, Sister Callistus had crossed a line in my mind. She had lied, and I didn't believe in her or her authority anymore. As much as she hurt me, I didn't need to find the way to defend myself. She didn't know what she was talking about.

Sister Callistus could hurt me, and yet, from shards of evidence, I also think I was emerging from "that habit." Things were getting better for me. At age ten, I'd become alert to the world in that fall of 1954 and spring of 1955—the world of saints and rituals, the world of books and television, and the world of other children. Despite many disappointments, I was starting to act on my longing for a normal family, for community, for ideals, for something to believe in and die for.

CHAPTER SEVEN
FINDING CUMBERLAND GAP

By December 1954, I had my panoply of saints and martyrs, my ambition toward sainthood, and my fifth-grade troubles with weeping Sister Callistus to occupy my heart and mind. I didn't know it at the time, but I needed more. What I needed most in the entire world to flourish was a lucky break.

The luckiest of breaks occurred when the first TV episode of *Davy Crockett* aired on the *Disneyland* program on Wednesday, December 15. Along with most of the other kids in the country, I watched in rapt attention.

Davy came along at the perfect time for all of us, just a week or so after anti-Communist Senator Joe McCarthy had finally been censured by the Senate leaving Sister Callistus to weep even harder. Davy Crockett didn't accuse, or defend, or insinuate, or outline conspiracies, or become sarcastic, or rap a gavel on a table, like the real people on TV who so fascinated the grownups. He provided the antidote to the grim black-and-white grownup talk. Though we viewed him on our Admiral 7" black-and-white screen, he seemed a bona fide hero in living color. And he was just as real as the senators on TV, a real historical person.

Davy answered my need and longing for connections, and I knew that right away. Like Daddy, he was born in Tennessee, the greenest, smokiest, most whimsical, mystical, and elusive state in the land of the free. He even talked with that slow, mild, gentle mid-Southern accent, like all the loved ones I knew from the state of Tennessee, like my Uncle Odo looking out over his pasture, "I reckon it'll rain 'fore dark." Calm, resourceful, courageous, handsome and romantic, Davy knew how to make up his mind, and mountain pride spilled out in his boastful sense of humor. I knew he really hadn't "killed a b'ar" when he was only three, but I thrilled to the flight of fantasy in the tall tale. Though the memory of Daddy was receding—Daddy a tall red-haired figure down a tunnel I couldn't enter—Davy seemed to bring my Daddy back.

Davy really lived. Walt Disney told us that in the introduction to the first episode which showed Davy as a boy, and when Davy's father chases him through the woods to beat him, Davy runs away rather than submit. He hides under the cover of a wagon bound for Virginia, and when he is discovered, he apprentices himself to the wagon master. They cross the mountains at a place called Cumberland Gap. I loved that Davy got away, that he protected himself. I loved his flight to freedom, and I loved the sound of "Cumberland Gap."

I looked for it on Daddy's globe, but I couldn't find it. I found Tennessee and then Virginia, but I wasn't sure where to look for Cumberland Gap. I figured the globe was too small to show everything, and if the story of Davy Crockett were true, I might be able to find Cumberland Gap on a map. So after school one day I didn't turn on Clark Street to go home, but continued on Vernor to the library, stumbling over the ridges of ice in front of Royal Welding and Dix Auto Electric, the only businesses on the strip that didn't bother to shovel their sidewalks. I guess they thought that since they fixed cars, everybody would just drive in.

Of all the grand buildings in the neighborhood, I considered the Bowen Branch of the Detroit Public Library the most welcoming—not an inch of it spooky. Up until age seven or so, I walked there with Mama or Betty, or sometimes stopped with Daddy in the car on our way home from studying trains at the Depot. Through the rooms' open alcoves, I could spot Daddy in the Adult Room, or Mama in the Arts and Crafts Room, or Betty in the small Young Adult Room, while I picked out my books in the Children's Room. With one or more of them visible, I felt safe, and I could concentrate on choosing the two books Mama said I could bring home from all the ones I wanted.

I liked that everybody in the family radiated toward different rooms, and I liked being alone and busy, doing my own serious work. The public library itself represented unusual license and liberty—a store where all the books were free as long as you brought them back.

The low-slung building sprawled on one floor, but its ceiling vaulted high enough to accommodate a small interior balcony centered behind the circulation desk. The librarians took their coffee breaks there. I could smell their percolated coffee from the desk. In the alcoves I smelled the books. The smell got drier in the Arts and Crafts Room where they also kept the newspapers. High windows over oak bookcases in every alcove drew in lots of natural light. A fireplace stood on the far side in two of the alcoves, the one in the Adult Room decorated with that thick blue-green tile I saw in many of the important buildings around Detroit. The tile on the fireplace in the Children's Room was red, but featured the same matte glaze that made me want to spit on it and rub it to make it shine. In spring and summer the moment I came in the door, I felt the cool breeze from the huge ceiling fan and open windows. I could stand in the small vestibule and read the announcements for story hour on the wall while I cooled myself off and adjusted my eyes to the softer light.

Located only five blocks from home, I walked there by myself from age seven. But until the day I went in search of Cumberland Gap, I hadn't been going often. Now in winter I looked forward to standing in the same vestibule to feel the gust of heat. The wind blasted more fiercely around the islands on

Grand Boulevard than it did at the smaller more sheltered street corners on Vernor. By the time I crossed the Boulevard, crossed Vernor, and opened the door, my ears hurt, my cheeks burned, my nose ran, and a few tears came out of my eyes. Winter or summer, I always stood in that vestibule for a while to get adjusted. I flicked away the tears and rubbed my nose with my mitten, snorting up the remaining snot before proceeding to the Children's Room.

The Children's Room stood on the right beyond the vestibule. I put my school bag on a table, took off my coat and draped it on a chair, sat down and settled in. I saw the tree limbs waving beyond the high windows and a fire flickering in the fireplace. The discomfort in my ears and on my cheeks melted away.

The children's librarian sat at the desk set back from the middle of the room, turned so she could see the fireplace, see the babies looking at board and picture books sometimes pulling them from shelves, and see the older kids browsing for the chapter books. Behind her, a tall shelf contained reference books, and to the right of her an extra wide book case housed the map books, all stacked horizontally. To the right of that were two globes, one midnight blue and white, that might have been the sky, and the other with oceans and continents, similar to, but bigger than, Daddy's. The bare top of the map case allowed space for the map books to be opened and viewed without needing to carry them far.

I felt relatively comfortable in libraries since I'd gone with my family to other libraries, the Main Library on Woodward, and the Business Library downtown, where we'd leave Daddy poring over stock reports while the rest of us went shopping at Hudson's. I'd already observed Mama, Daddy and Betty asking questions of librarians many times, and so that helped me work up the nerve.

I was powerfully motivated to ask whomever I needed to ask. I wanted to know everything real about Davy Crockett. I knew that Daddy's family migrated from North Carolina to Tennessee around the same time as Davy Crockett. Could they have gone anywhere near Cumberland Gap?

"Do you have a map of Tennessee that shows Cumberland Gap?" I said, careful not to reveal why I wanted it.

I'm sure the librarian had a name, but I never remembered names. I wasn't even good at faces, since I was too shy to look at them. Still, I think the librarian was aware of me in an insightful way. "I think so," she said.

She rose from her chair, bent at the waist to look in the case, and then reached in, pulling out a big blue book that she opened on top of the case. She thumbed through it until she got to the right map. A map of mountains, with greens and yellows, and various shades of orange, some of them so hot they seemed to want to be red. "Here it is," she said.

And then she became curious herself, it seemed. "It looks like this is the best way to get to Virginia." She explained the colors, how the oranger the color the higher the altitude. We both pored over the map. With her finger she traced the path, the narrow jagged sideways slide, along the ridges of the smaller mountains nestled between the taller peaks, how one could pass between the high mountains, the only reasonable way one could journey from Tennessee to Virginia, from Virginia back to Tennessee and then Kentucky. Right before my eyes, she showed me the way to negotiate Cumberland Gap.

My heart started beating faster as I visualized the hotter and hotter colors at higher and higher ranges. I saw them on my right and left as I wheeled along in that wagon with Davy. "Around there, that way, we'll swing a little that way. If we make good time, by nightfall we'll camp at Cumberland Gap. The oxen'll go over easy in the morning if we give 'em a good rest." I couldn't believe that a hero so lovable and exciting on television could be real. The Lone Ranger and the Cisco Kid had adventures, but they weren't real. Roy Rogers and Gene Autry were real, but not adventurous. All they did was sing.

Davy, my hero from Tennessee, made Daddy real. I became secretly proud of my redheaded rough-and-ready mountain heritage. My Daddy's family had been in Tennessee since 1794. Maybe Daddy's father's father's father's father passed by Davy and spoke to him. "How do you do, sir? The weather holdin' on the other side?" Maybe they passed each other or walked along together, singing the same songs, as they climbed up to the gentle ridge and trekked through that green tunnel in the high mountains where a team of oxen and a wagon could pass into that greenest state of Tennessee, or back to blue Virginia, through Cumberland Gap. Maybe they couldn't resist shouting down into the valleys and hearing the echoing, "Ho, hello." How I would sing if I were there, "Down in the valley," and how it would echo, down into the valleys on either side below. How joyous I would be, finding a way around obstacles, traveling through Cumberland Gap.

The librarian taught like a master. If she'd lectured like a classroom teacher even once, I would have retreated back into my shadow world. After looking at Cumberland Gap, just looking at it long and hard, sharing the wonder of it without speaking, she seemed to get another idea. "You know, there may be a couple books for you to read about Tennessee. Let's go see."

She plucked some from one shelf, walked to another section, pulled out a few more, then moved to a third section—geography—where she found even more. To my amazement she found pictures of the mountains, books about my hidden passion, frontier history. At each step she only gently brushed against my privacy and freedom with the lightness of a feather. "You might want to just look at this one. You can put it on the table. See if you like it. It doesn't matter how many you take home."

By the time the books were all stamped with due dates and I prepared to stomp home in the crunchier colder snow, I'd filled my plaid schoolbag so full of books, the brown tabs wouldn't close. The lady at the circulation desk gave me a big brown paper grocery bag to carry the rest of them. I left with thirteen books, some of them containing the knowledge I most longed to know. The librarian helped me find them. And she never once mentioned Davy Crockett.

I had to walk slower than usual. The schoolbag hung over my shoulder, but the extra bag I balanced around my midriff got pretty heavy after a block or two. I set it down a couple times to give my arms a rest, and I avoided that long stretch of unshoveled sidewalk in front of Dix Auto Electric by turning down Vinewood, then turning on Baker and cutting across the park. The park wasn't shoveled, of course, but I found it a lot easier plodding through the snow than balancing on the rippled ice that had been last week's slushy footprints. And in winter in the blue twilight, the park was always so quiet. Even when skaters laughed on the lagoon and skate blades clinked on the ice.

I couldn't wait to get home. I wanted to start reading the books, and it was always warm around this time, after Mama had stoked the furnace. From the park I could see our windows and the chandelier on our ceiling with its soft yellowish light.

Mama was in the kitchen peeling potatoes when I got home. Still, she came out to the dining room to greet me. I told her I'd gone to the library. Her eyes fell to the extra bag of books in my arms.

"How many books did you get?" she said.

"Thirteen," I said. I started pulling them from the paper bag and out of my schoolbag and stacking them up on the clean spot on the table. They were cold, as though they needed to be warmed by eyes.

"Thirteen books!" she exclaimed. "You can't read all of them. You're going to have to take some of them back."

"I can read them," I said.

"Who let you take so many?" Her eyes looked alarmed.

"The librarian," I said. "She said I could take home as many as I wanted."

"But there won't be any left up there for the other little girls to read."

I hadn't thought of that. I didn't want to think of any other girls but me. There were so many books in the Children's Room. I instinctively moved to trump her with the higher authority. "She said I could take home as many as I wanted," I repeated. Since she'd mentioned all the other little girls waiting like me to read the cold books begging for warm hands and eyes, I felt a little shaky.

"Well, you're going to have to take some of them back tomorrow," she said. "I'm not paying the overdue fines." She was so worked up, with her voice so firm, she was behaving like the rest of the parents in the neighborhood, giving me an order. "You're going to have to take some of them back."

I tried to ignore her, although she went on fuming for the rest of the evening, erupting every once in awhile. "Thirteen books! You can't read them all on time. They'll be overdue. I'm not paying the fines."

I hoped that by the next day she'd return to her lethargic self. If I resisted then, she probably wouldn't have enough energy to find her shoes, put on her strange black floppy rubbers over them, and take the books back herself.

I was right. She forgot about the books so they stayed with us, and I made sure I read them all. Of course I wasn't going to tell her if she checked to see. My reading fed my deep longing for privacy, for something of mine that couldn't be observed, guided, or taken away. What I read was my business.

By the next episode of *Davy Crockett*, I'd learned as much about Davy as I could. But also about Jim Bowie, Daniel Boone, and as many other frontiersmen as I could read about, including the French voyageurs, and the early settlers in Virginia and the Carolinas. I also learned about the unfair campaigns against the Cree and Cherokee tribes during the Andrew Jackson administration. TV Davy had actually pointed me in that direction, because toward the end of the first episode he lamented about the broken treaties. It was one thing to fight Indians in a fair fight, but to lie and cheat was another. I started reading more about Indians. I also learned more than Smoky Mountain and Tennessee geography. With the help of the librarian, I had developed a program of reading.

The next episode of *Davy Crockett* detailed Davy's middle years, when he served in Congress. It aired on January 26, 1955. I eagerly waited to see what I'd want to learn more about next. I was already entrenched in a habit of reading that would extend through my high school years.

By the time I followed Davy through the last of the original episodes of *Davy Crockett*, which aired on February 23, 1955, where he, Jim Bowie, Sam Houston and others die heroically fighting nasty Santa Ana at the Alamo, I was deeply involved in the migrations of American history. The restless Davy in his travels—Tennessee, Virginia, Tennessee, Washington, Tennessee and Texas—gave me the foundation. It was geography, movement across the land, following the lakes and rivers, building and navigating the canals, portaging around the waterfalls, finding the gaps in ranges, swimming in the prairie grasses, and finding the Indian trails. The settlers, frontiersmen, the farmers, pioneers, soldiers of fortune, spilling into territories, buying land, seeking gold, seeking elbow room—elbow room like the repeated line in a poem I'd read about Daniel Boone, *Of streams unstained and woods unhewn! "Elbow room," laughed Daniel Boone.*

In our school textbooks we learned one version of the push toward the West. In the books I read I learned another version of the story that told about the deceit and greed—from the delicate prairie land plowed up for crops to the broken treaties and the killing of the buffalo. The globe, the one Daddy gave us and the ones I saw flattened out in books, took me to the end of the continent, and then politics took me back again: Revolution, the Presidents, the cotton crops, slavery, the Underground Railroad, the expansions, the trumped up fight with Mexico, Lincoln and the Civil War. Reading always happened on a map, and Daddy had provided the first map.

In the world around me I couldn't see the resistance to oppression, but in the books I found heroes—Harriet Tubman following the North Star to lead her people to freedom, stopping for the last time, I imagined, in Mrs.

Dixon's fruit cellar in our basement, only three blocks away from a dark moonless night and a crossing of the mighty Detroit River.

Davy Crockett used a powder horn made from a steer's horn to store his gunpowder and keep it dry. One day I ducked behind the two rods of Mama's dresses hanging in the back closet to look up and see the shelves of stuff that Daddy left. Among the things, I found a powder horn. Smooth, faded, old, smelling of nothing, hanging on an ancient faintly leather-smelling shoulder strap. I brought it out, trembling with excitement. How did it get there? I knew it had belonged to Daddy.

I brought it out to Mama, who was trying to clean off the clutter on the dining room table.

"What's this?" I said.

"Let me see," she said. She took it in her hand and examined it a while. "Oh, that's Omer's powder horn. He had that when he was fixing up those old rifles."

"Where are the rifles?" I said. I'd already heard that Daddy used to buy old gun parts and put them together into new guns that worked, although I never remembered seeing him working on them.

"Oh, he sold the whole collection," she said. "I think that was during the War. He got a lot of money for it." She handed the powder horn back to me.

"This is just like Davy Crockett's," I said. She let me hang it on the mirror on my dresser, along with the ribbons, scapulars, and amber rosary. I took it down to feel the soft cool ivory of the horn. It reminded me of Davy, and it reminded me of Daddy. Mama thought it only reminded me of Davy.

I didn't respond to Davy Crockett like most of the other kids at the time. They adored him, too, but they seemed to be focused more on his adventures. I kept the Daddy reason for my deep devotion completely secret. I also kept my reading secret, as it fueled my longing to travel across my sadness to myself. I figured Daddy would like me reading. He'd gotten me interested in geography.

Once, like many of the kids, I made a coonskin cap out of a brown paper bag, stapling a paper tail onto the cap, and drawing a few brown waves on the tail to simulate a pelt. Bobby Gardner lent me one of his toy rifles, and we aimed at each other, took cover, and shot imaginary "ping, ping, pings" that ricocheted down the alley. We took turns, and I liked it better when I played the Indian. "Come out from that tree, you varmint," Bobby yelled, and I drew in further behind the telephone pole, aimed my rifle around and shot. "Ping." Of course he got me and I died. We didn't play Davy Crockett again, although I think Bobby did a few more times with the boys from McKinstry across the alley.

One time a college friend suggested that Mama's objection about how many books I brought home was evidence of wisdom. Mama knew I'd read every book if she told me I couldn't. My friend's interpretation was generous, and sensitive, based on what she could clearly see was my great affection for Mama. Still, I never believed Mama was up for that.

With Mama it was simpler. She worried about the possibility of the overdue fines—two cents per book per day, with the possibility that some of the books would be forgotten or lost in the mounds of junk. If she could moderate my book consumption, she could feel a little less anxious about the fines. It was just part of her irrational thrift that went beyond that of others who'd survived the Depression. In the end it didn't matter. The books were rarely overdue, never lost, and nothing would have stopped me from reading.

CHAPTER EIGHT
PATSY'S BURDEN

About a year after Mama bought the house, with Lois Farrell and her grown son Jack Ramsey installed in the downstairs flat, Jack surprised everybody when he suddenly got married. For the first time that flat offered me more than old, odd or dying people. Now there was Dean Ramsey and Patsy Walker, her seven-year-old daughter.

Jack's new wife, Willa Dean Walker Ramsey, spoke with a cute, thick twang that she carried from her home state of Alabama. "You can call me Dean, for short," she said. Nobody could have been more opposite to Jack as this blue-eyed, brown-haired Dean who stood 5' 2" and weighed ninety-seven pounds, while Jack weighed in around three hundred. Either she loved him or took him on as a project. "He's just going to have to change his ways," she said once with a determined little half smile.

What Willa Dean Ramsey lacked in height she made up for in energy. Starting from the day she moved in, everything downstairs started to glisten and gleam, everything that had been stagnant started to flow. The first week the furniture truck arrived at the front door with the new modern living room couch with stick legs and two winged chairs. Brand new gingham ruffled café curtains, new window shades, new lace doilies starched so that the ruffles stood on end on matching blonde end tables with matching lamps that looked like big coffee urns. A week later Dean introduced the new blonde bedroom suite with a bookcase at the head of the bed and a black-panther ashtray on the shiny blonde dresser. She bought the stuff on time at Crown Furniture up on Fort Street. After it was all in place, she rang our doorbell and called up into the stairway, "You all come down and see it." With that simple down-home invitation she opened up the downstairs flat, which I'd never really seen, to my eager eyes.

Dean waxed the oak floors so that when you looked in at the front door you could see down the entire length of running glittering planks all the way back to the kitchen. And you knew that if you pitched a bowling ball down the hallway, it would probably slide all over the place before it ever got to the kitchen. The floor of the flat was slipperier than a bowling alley. Dean "dressed" the toilet in a fuzzy yellow halter with a matching wrap-around rug and a cover for the seat. I'd never seen or contemplated anything like it. An extra roll of toilet paper was disguised in a white and yellow crocheted bonnet on top of the cuddly toilet. She emptied Jack's ashtrays as fast as a cocktail waitress on duty just waiting around to do something for somebody. And that was no coincidence. She also worked as a waitress all afternoon at one of the Southern down-home-cooking joints on Fort Street.

While Jack and his mother Lois were at work in the mornings, Mama and I, sitting at our own cluttered dining room table, heard the sounds of Dean happily performing her housewife duties. When it sounded as though Dean was moving furniture around, Mama shook her head in bemusement, "Now how is she doing that without anybody to help her?" And then, more bemusement, "Didn't she move that furniture last week?"

We heard many happy picture hooks being driven into the walls so Dean could hang all the pictures of her large Alabama family. We heard the sound of extra-happy hooks insuring that in Dean's kitchen pots and pans and spatulas and spoons stood ready to jump from the wall to do Dean's bidding at the stove. When we descended the back stairs to go outside or to the basement, we heard the vacuum running over the cheerful chirp of Dean's parakeet that perched in a cage hung in front of the wafting new back-window kitchen curtains.

Watching Mama nurse her morning coffee, as she vaguely gazed above and beyond the mound of newspapers, coat hangers, crocheted throw rugs, fountain pens, pins, needles, darning hams and flower pots that stood opposite her on the table, and listening in our silence to Dean's industry below, brought to my mind an extremely useful concept: *contrast*. How different people were, and in the same house! I didn't know it at the time, but that airy well-designed flat below, with its parade of tenants, was going to provide me with a steady check on how we were and how I wanted us to be. Even, sometimes, on how I wanted the people below to be. Perhaps it wasn't such a bad decision I'd made, after all, to buy the house.

The smell Dean introduced into the house was a medley of Pinesol, Ajax, Murphy's Oil Soap and Bruce floor wax alternating with the three rounds a day of Southern cooking. Dean didn't stint. Breakfast was a symphony of biscuits, eggs, sausage, ham, bacon, grits, gravy, coffee and orange juice. Lunch was as big as dinner, and dinner was a smoky kitchen full of whatever she could bread and fry—chicken, fish, pork chops or hot dogs. She even breaded and fried sweet potatoes and onions.

When Dean wasn't doing serious cleaning, she buzzed around with her feather duster, and Lois Farrell claimed to be so happy for the newlyweds she decided to move out and give her son and new daughter-in-law the entire flat. Lois was one of the first in the neighborhood to leave Detroit to move to the far-away little suburb we'd never heard of—South Lyon. Mama always wondered what it was south of, and why anybody would want to live in the sticks. A couple years later though, others from the neighborhood would join her after Ford Motor Company opened the assembly plant in Wixom.

Dean never did get Jack to change his lazy ways, at least not that I could see. Whenever he wasn't at work he sat as though he'd been poured into the front porch rocker, or draped himself over a red-and-white plastic cushioned chair at the matching Formica kitchen table, or lounged on the sagging white couch with the pin-point legs in front of the 14" console TV set. While Dean cooked and cleaned, Jack drank beer and devoured Dean's perfect Southern fried chicken cooked in an electric skillet, or he gobbled down scrambled eggs, ham, bacon, biscuits and gravy, or munched on a big brown bag of the potato chips crumbs we all bought from the potato chip factory up past the dime store on Vernor.

Dean was a great person to study, and so, motivated by longing, I learned from her through careful observation how to efficiently clean a house. The best thing though about the new situation downstairs was that Dean had been married before, and she brought along her daughter, Patsy. Patsy was seven going on eight, and I was nine going on ten. We quickly became friends.

Patsy was a wiry talkative little girl who hopped from one foot to the other when she stood and rubbed her nose with the back of her hand. Remarkably convenient, Patsy required no coat or hat to get to. She was just a back stairway away. I learned that sometimes I could even set in motion the chain of events that would summon her at will. When Saturday mornings rolled around, the Ramseys liked to sleep in. Since I couldn't wait for Patsy to wake up, I started making a racket. Sister Callistus said virtuous families should rise early, so I figured I was doing the Ramseys a favor. Soon I smelled the bacon and eggs and the biscuits cooking, and not long after that, Patsy tramped up the back stairs and knocked at the back door. "My mother says you're like an elephant thumping around up here," Patsy said the moment I opened the door. I didn't care. I wanted to play with her.

I appreciated Patsy for reasons beyond convenience. She lived in the house, and even though the downstairs flat clearly presented a cleaner, better organized, more modern and normal place to be, it still belonged to our odd house. The house drew you in with its ghosts and mysteries, the garage and the back yard, and especially the crevices and corners and ancient fruit cellar of its spooky dim cobwebbed basement. Another kid dwelled in the house now, a kind of witness. We were in it together.

Patsy, like me, also had troubles, and for that reason she fast became my best friend. My exposure to the kids in Sister Florita's class at Holy Redeemer, especially the girls who were so well cared for and confident, had led me to believe I was the only child with troubles. Yes, Patsy had her troubles, the biggest being the experience of living with her new stepfather.

When Patsy moved in she had a nervous tic in her throat, something like a cross between clearing her throat and a hiccup. She'd get excited talking and then she'd rock on her heels and do it, "Hic." Her head jerked a little as well. She did it every other sentence or so—"Hic."

The first time she came up the back stairs to play with me, Mama asked, "Can I get you something to eat, Patsy? I've got some grape juice. Or I could peel you an orange."

"No, thank you, hic, Mrs. Rhodes. Hic."

"Now where do you come from in Alabama?"

"Decatur, hic," Patsy said.

"Where's that near?"

"I don't, hic, know," Patsy said.

Mama ignored Patsy's clearing-throat hiccups and continued the conversation as if they didn't exist. Often I thought Mama asked too many questions, believing kids were ready for adult conversations when they weren't. But ignoring the "hics" was right, one of the rare times when Mama knew the best thing to do. Once Patsy got used to us, she stopped clearing her throat so much. When she was really having fun she hardly did it at all. And if she did continue to "hic" every once in awhile, it just became part of the way she spoke.

That didn't stop Jack from trying to break Patsy of the habit. The irony of Dean trying to improve him, and his going to great lengths to change Patsy wasn't lost on me. It was clear by his bulging eyes, swollen red cheeks and sudden expulsions of breath that Patsy's hiccup sounds got under his skin.

One time we were sitting on the floor in the huge closet off her living room that ran underneath our front stairway. We played with Jenny dolls and left the door open for heat. Patsy talked a mile a minute about her grandma making clothes for her doll. Jack, who sat in his new oversized La-Z-Boy watching a bowling match on TV, suddenly turned to us.

"Stop that!" he said.

We looked around while inserting doll arms into doll clothes, wondering "Stop what?" but said nothing.

"Stop that. You're driving me crazy." He paused. "Why do you keep doing that? You're driving me nuts. Nobody else keeps clearing their throat and jumping. Mary doesn't do that. Why do you?"

He turned to me, still yelling at Patsy. "You're not to do it anymore. Mary is going to correct you every time you do it." And to me, "I want you to correct her. Every time. I want you to do it." And back to Patsy, "She's not going to put up with it." His face read disgust.

I cowered. He adjusted his chair and got up, sniffed and padded off to the kitchen for something to eat. I turned to see Patsy's reddened face, tears welling up in her eyes. Afraid to say anything because Jack would be on his way back, I couldn't think of what to do. I felt for Patsy. I could relate. Jack treated Patsy like Sister Florita treated me.

Later, as Patsy shared her heart and her experience with me, she opened my eyes to the world beyond that of my strange family and the "normal" families of Holy Redeemer. When her grandmother came to visit, Patsy let me in on a secret. The two younger children her grandmother brought along, and who called her grandmother "Mommy," were really Patsy's younger sister and brother. Her mother, Dean, had been divorced from a man in Alabama who used to drink and beat Dean up, but when Dean came up to Detroit to find a job, she could bring only one of her kids, the eldest, Patsy.

"Will your grandmother be giving them back to your mother?" I said, thinking about my sister living with my Aunt Marie.

"No, they don't know about it. They think Grandma's their mother." I swore I wouldn't tell.

Patsy wasn't doing well in school either. She went to Maybury Elementary, right down the street and a lot closer than Holy Redeemer. She read everything out loud in a halting stuttering way. Whenever she read, she reverted to her "hic," and even though she'd been placed in second grade, she was still on *Dick and Jane*. It was hard to listen to her because she sounded like she was being tortured, or like a world of shame and sadness was coming out in her voice. My problem wasn't reading, even though I got Ds in reading for not paying attention. I could read. I just didn't want to in school.

Jack got Mama and me invited to go along to the Ternstedt's annual company picnic, held that year at Wampler's Lake. Several other people in the neighborhood were going, as several other fathers also worked at Ternstedt's. Mama's best friend Smitty and her husband Roy were going. Roy worked at Ternstedt's making chrome parts that were shipped to Fleetwood down the street where they were attached to car bodies shipped up our street to the Cadillac plant. Roy sometimes bragged that it was he who made the famous Cadillac crests.

Dean and Mama rode in Roy and Smitty's car out Michigan Avenue, and the kids—Linda and Norma Smith and Patsy and I—rode with Jack in his brand new 1954 Chevrolet. Patsy and I slid into the roomy front seat. For as many miles as we could, Jack took the new expressway and gave us a demonstration of just how fast that car could go. When we got to a sign that said "YPSILANTI," Jack quizzed Patsy about reading it. "What does that sign say, Patsy?"

Of course Patsy couldn't read it. She didn't have a clue. Her face reddened. Humiliated and embarrassed, she said, "Hic. I don't know, hic."

Then he turned to me. I cheated. I couldn't read it either. I wouldn't have been able to sound it out. But I already knew about the town called Ypsilanti. Mama and I had passed it before on our way to Ann Arbor, and Mama had told me a story about how Greeks settled in the area, named the town a Greek word, and that was why "Ypsilanti" was hard to say ("IPSA-lantee") and spelled so funny.

"Ypsilanti," I answered too quickly.

It was all Jack needed, and once again he hurt Patsy by using me. "Now, Mary can read. She's a good reader. Why can't you? What's wrong with you?"

I never figured out how to get him to stop berating my friend. I never said anything to Patsy about it either. I felt the unfairness, but I didn't have the words yet to express it or stand up to a grownup—other than Mama, of course.

Jack alternated working between days and afternoons. Dean worked at the restaurant until around five in the afternoon. Patsy kept a front door key on a string around her neck all day, just like a roller skate key. She frequently fingered it nervously when we played outside. Sometimes she chewed on the string.

One day after school she rang our doorbell. "I can't find my key. My mom's going to kill me. I lost the key."

"Don't worry," Mama said. "Your mom will have her key when she gets home. Maybe you and Mary can find your key in the meantime."

I got my coat on and went downstairs. Patsy and I looked all over the porch, all over the front walk, and retraced Patsy's steps all the way back to Maybury School. Too shy, we stopped short of entering the big double doors, even though we saw the lights still on. We retraced our steps back home, satisfied at least that we'd looked thoroughly on the sidewalk and surrounding grass. Patsy was getting more and more anxious. "My mom's going to kill me."

I couldn't think of a solution. But when we opened the door at the top of the stairs, I knew what to do in the meantime. Mama had stoked up the furnace pretty good. It was warm upstairs, and I heard *Howdy Doody* just starting on the TV.

When Dean got home she rang our front door buzzer and spoke into the stairway as Patsy and I leaned down. "Is Patsy up there? How come you didn't open the door? Hand down your key."

"I don't have it, Mommy," Patsy said.

"What do you mean you don't have it?" Dean said. Her voice rose in volume.

Patsy looked at her shoes. "I lost it, Mommy."

"What did you say?" Dean's voice rose even higher.

"I lost it."

"How are we going to get in? I left *my* key on the kitchen table!"

At this point Mama came to the stairway. "Come on up, Dean. Maybe I can find a key for your door in my drawer."

Dean trudged upstairs with a heavy foot. She was seven months pregnant and already parading an enormous belly. She stole a menacing glance at Patsy as she exchanged pleasantries with Mama.

"Make yourself comfortable, Dean," Mama said, and Dean sank down into the nearest easy chair. Mama ambled to the dining room to look in the top drawer of the buffet. "I'll look in here," she said. I knew already that even with her bright talk she probably wasn't going to find the right key among the hundred or so unlabeled unsorted keys she housed among the other miscellaneous objects such as shoe strings, Immaculate Conception medals and plastic accordion rain hats that crowded all four of the velvet silverware dividers.

In the meantime, Dean grilled Patsy. "Jack won't be home until midnight. Just what do you think we're supposed to do? I told you not to lose that key."

Mama scooped up two hands' full of keys from the buffet drawer and immediately let them slide back, apparently losing hope in her quest. She returned to Dean in the living room. "You're welcome to stay, Dean. There's plenty of supper for you and Patsy."

Dean maintained her politeness, but it was easy to see Mama's solution wasn't what she wanted to hear. Dean was a woman of motion, and no doubt hankered to be moving in her own kitchen, getting a household job and a load of laundry done before kicking back on her own modern couch, raising her swollen feet, and watching her own TV. Mama always suggested the slowest solution to any problem, and she didn't seem too concerned that she didn't have the most obvious one. I felt certain that if Dean had been the landlady she'd have kept a neatly labeled extra key.

When Dean didn't respond to the dinner invitation, Mama offered other suggestions.

"What about the door to the basement?" Mama said. "Do you keep it locked?"

Dean nodded.

"The backyard door?" Mama said.

Dean nodded her head again, clutching her coat that she'd unbuttoned but neglected to take off. Her eyes cut to Patsy. "You're going to get the worst spanking of your life."

"Maybe a window is unlocked," Mama said, still maintaining her polite cheerfulness.

"That's an idea," Dean said, already adjusting her weight sideways to extract herself from the chair. "Have you got a step ladder?"

"I'll get it," Mama said and took off to get it from behind the kitchen door.

Outside, Dean moved the step ladder from one window to the next, yanking hard on each as Patsy and I watched and prayed. The sun had already set. The ground was hard. The limpid leaves swirled on the ground. Her face red, Dean railed at Patsy with each yank. "Just wait until we get in. I told you not to fiddle with that key."

I watched, scared for Patsy and scared Dean might topple over from the uneven distribution of her weight. In the fading light I saw her silhouette, surprised at just how large her belly had grown.

Every window was checked and found locked. As the three of us mounted the stairs again, Mama called down and offered the same invitation. "You're welcome to stay, Dean. I've got hamburgers, and there's plenty for you and Patsy."

Dean propped the folded step ladder against the wall near the piano. She looked defeated, seeming to be deciding to finally take off her coat.

But then she hit on a solution. She called her mother-in-law, Lois Farrell, remembering that Lois still had a key to the flat. While waiting for Lois to come, Mama tried to entertain Dean, talking about everything under the sun. Dean sat with her coat on, nodding at Mama, thinly concealing her fury, glancing at Patsy every once in a while. Patsy sat twitching on the edge of a chair, as scared and nervous as I'd ever seen her, hiccing like crazy. She looked like she might pee in her pants. She knew she was going to get a spanking.

When Lois arrived, about an hour later, it seemed Mama had forgotten a crisis was going on. "How do you like South Lyon, Lois? Are you settled in yet? Gee, you look good. It must be agreeing with you."

Lois, who didn't have any makeup on, didn't say much. I guessed she'd been in the middle of something and wasn't happy about driving to Detroit to give Dean the key. She directed a few of her own scornful looks toward Patsy.

Dean took the key, Lois extracted herself from Mama, saying she had to run, and Dean and Patsy followed her down the front stairs.

I never got spankings, and I was curious. I snuck down the back stairs to listen. Patsy had told me how her spankings went, with her mother sitting on the toilet, Patsy draped over her lap with her pants down, her mother whacking her with the back of a hairbrush. She got the kind of spankings most kids got. Deliberate. Planned. With stated parental clear intentions.

I stood in the downstairs landing, leaning against their kitchen wall. I heard everything. The "whack, whack, whack" of the hairbrush, Patsy's crying, Dean's shouting. At first I enjoyed it. All my attention to the brutal suffering of the saints and martyrs had turned me into a little sado-masochist, and, from all I'd heard, I knew that in normal families the children were shown love, concern and guidance through the spankings I never got.

But then the sound of Patsy's pitiful wailing, the sound of the fear and misery in her voice, the loud whacks, transformed me. My body trembled, my stomach roiled and my skin broke out in a cold sweat. I started to become alarmed. Patsy was wailing, and it went on so long.

Even after the spanking was over, Dean continued to extract promises and hurl threats. "Tell me you'll never lose that key again. Tell me."

"I won't lose it again, Mommy," Patsy whimpered.

"If you lose that key again it'll be worse. Do you hear me? Do you understand me?"

"I understand."

I continued shaking, unable to hear Patsy after that, her whimpering fading as they no doubt moved into one of their front rooms. Finally I climbed the stairs, as quietly as I could, feeling the chill in the unheated stairway more keenly than usual. Something very bad had happened that was different from my own profound loneliness and feelings of abandonment.

*   *   *

I returned to the dining room where Mama sat, listlessly sorting keys by their shapes. Behind her, the windows had steamed up from the potatoes boiling on the stove.

"Mama, Patsy didn't deserve a spanking. She's only seven, and that's the losing age."

Mama looked thoughtful. "What do you mean, losing age?"

"Seven is the age when you lose things," I said. "Patsy shouldn't have gotten a spanking for losing the key. She couldn't help it. Seven is the losing age."

Mama looked at me, one of her long looks with her hands rising to prop up her chin. "You may be right," she said. "Poor Patsy."

I knew I was right. I'd already heard that two-year-olds said "No" all the time, and nobody blames them for it. Based on my own theory—all seven-year-olds should be forgiven for losing keys and lunchboxes and barrettes and doll socks and pretty flowers and shouldn't be spanked for it—all other children should be forgiven for whatever faults they're supposed to have at a given age. What was the fault of ten-year-olds? I wondered. I'd have to figure that out.

The next day Patsy had bruises on the backs of her legs. She didn't say anything mean about her mother, and she didn't say anything about the spanking. She was as cheerful as usual when we played Jenny dolls after school. It seemed as though she'd forgotten what happened. I, though, would never forget.

One day in early January, the moment I opened the front door downstairs when I came home from school, I saw Mama leaning into the stairway. "Jack took Dean to the hospital. The baby's coming. Keep an eye out for Patsy." We'd already arranged it. Patsy was going to stay with us while her mother was in the hospital.

When Patsy came home from Maybury we arranged my bedroom for her stay. She brought up all the things she needed from downstairs—teddy bears, blankets, a musical jewel box she'd received from her grandmother. We knew a bit about where babies came from. At least we knew they grew in a mother's tummy. Mama had told me they came out from a "body opening," so I believed the mother's tummy opened on a hinge. I imagined it as something like I'd seen when a lady in a costume emerged from a pea pod as the Empress of Detroit at the city's 250th birthday party a few years before.

While Patsy and I waited, Mama fielded calls from the neighbors. "Yes, Jack took her over to Delray Hospital around two. Haven't heard anything. I'll let you know."

To someone else, probably Smitty, "Yeah, Jack was real cute. Maybe he's going to grow up now. We'll see. I hope it's a boy."

Jack was hoping for a boy. He'd made it known all along. The way he talked you had to worry that if it turned out to be a girl, he might not treat her any better than he treated Patsy.

Around seven o'clock, after we'd eaten the usual—mashed potatoes, overcooked round steak, and fresh green beans too snappy for my taste, all washed down with milk—Mama received *the* telephone call. Jack was deliriously happy. At least it seemed that way from the long pauses on our end.

"A boy!" Mama said. "Oh, you must be so happy."

Patsy and I started jumping up and down, and Mama waved her hand to shush us. I guess Jack was rattling on. Or at least Mama's end of the conversation was "Uh-huh," and "Yes," and "Really?" As the conversation was about to end, Mama said, "Don't you worry about Patsy. We're taking care of her." I don't think he'd asked about Patsy, but maybe Mama wanted him to remember her.

After Mama hung up, she gave us the vital statistics and started cooing at Patsy about her having a new little brother. "Your father says he's going to name him Newell. That's such a nice name." I don't really think she thought it was a nice name.

On Saturday Jack rang our bell. Patsy had gone with Lois Farrell, who wanted to take her downtown to have lunch at Greenfield's. "Come see what I bought for Newell," he said to us.

Mama found her shoes and we went down. There, in the middle of the living room he'd assembled a pile of toys—a big teddy bear, a big giraffe, all sorts of other smaller stuffed animals and baby toys—bells and soft balls and rattles, a mound of blue clothing, a football, a baseball glove and bat, a train set, and even a shiny red boy's two-wheeler with training wheels. Mama's eyes got big as saucers while I got a little sick to my stomach. Jack explained. "If it had been a girl, she would have gotten what she needed. I would have been happy. But since it's a boy, there's no telling what he's going to get." Jack, all three-hundred pounds of him, started dancing a jig around the heap of presents.

The story made a great one for Mama to tell, and for me to overhear, as she and Smitty, or sometimes she and the other neighbors, discussed it.

"The kid isn't going to need that stuff for a long time."

"What are they going to do with it in the meantime?"

"You know, Jack never really grew up."

"And what's Dean going to do when she finds out he spent all that money?"

"You know Dean has a hard row to hoe with that one."

"Well, at least he got excited," Mama said. She had a way of ending conversations such as these on a positive note—I think to honor the person who had made such amusing conversation. She never gossiped maliciously, as her sisters did, and Mama was a good storyteller. Besides, Jack and Dean Ramsey were great entertainment. Just thinking about how they looked together, her body less than a third of his mass, yet twice as smart and strong, made me smile. Having a baby in the house would make me smile even more.

Chapter Nine
Davy Crockett Rhodes

In 1955 almost everybody in the neighborhood owned a parakeet. Parakeets chirped from cages in living rooms or in kitchens large enough to accommodate a cage hung from a window or door frame. The Southern neighbors owned them. The Polish neighbors owned them. Even the German and Irish Old Guard owned them. Parakeets provided the musical accompaniment to being invited inside.

Mama's friend Smitty owned what I thought was a remarkably talented parakeet. Of course, Smitty, a Tennessean, was pretty good at boasting about her bird, and pretty good at demonstrating that Southern flair for exaggeration. Smitty herself was remarkably talented—confident, daring and energetic, and good with children, adults, and animals. She often led others into adventures they'd never have on their own. Smitty was the first mother to introduce pizza pie to the neighborhood, experimenting with six Apian Way mixes for her daughter Linda's birthday party. She even fixed Mama up with a nice widower one time, and though it didn't work out, it wasn't for Smitty's lack of trying. Smitty also kept a watchful eye out for me.

Try as I might, I cannot remember the name of Smitty's amazing parakeet, and so I'll call him Gabby. Green Gabby did all a parakeet was supposed to do—talked, parroted, sat on shoulders to eat Nabisco crackers, flew back into his cage when ordered, and otherwise continued an incessant cheerful chirp.

But Gabby seemed to go beyond his duties as parakeet and, according to Smitty, could carry on a conversation. If she asked him, "How you doing today, Gabby?" unlike other parakeets who parroted, Gabby would answer, "Mighty fine!"

Smitty claimed that she also trained Gabby to take over a few of her duties as mother. For instance, when Smitty's older daughter Norma came in the kitchen door, Gabby cautioned, "Shut the door!"

When it was Linda, Smitty's younger daughter, Gabby was on top of that too. "Take off those wet boots!"

"Shut the door!" "Take off those wet boots!" "You're letting in the flies!"

Smitty's husband, Roy, a red-faced Southerner with a drawl, who worked two shifts, came home dog tired all the time. It didn't matter what time Roy stumbled in, even after midnight, even long after the cage had been covered with a dish towel for the bird's bedtime. "Hello Roy." Gabby the Parakeet greeted Roy with cheerful good manners. "Hello Roy, Hello Roy, Hello Roy." What was astonishing was that Gabby never called anyone else by Roy's name. How the bird knew it was Roy who'd come in was a mystery. Roy never played with the bird and rarely talked to it. Of course I never witnessed the midnight greetings, but one rare Saturday afternoon, when Roy wasn't working and joined the conversation at the kitchen table, he confirmed it. The truth of it amused and bedeviled him. He scratched his head, saying, "Now how does that darned critter know it's me?"

I never witnessed most of Gabby's exploits that Smitty talked about, but I did learn that if you thought you could dismiss Smitty's stories as tall tales, you'd be called up short when the bird went on to flaunt its learning of new things. The day Mama was called for the first time to substitute as an attendant on the bus for handicapped kids, we sat in Smitty's kitchen. Mama was anticipating the challenge, wondering how early she'd have to get up. She told Smitty she was supposed to report the next day to the bus terminal on Schaefer and Schoolcraft. "What do you think is the best way to get there?"

"Hmm, Schaefer and Schoolcraft," Smitty said.

That was all the bird needed. "Schaefer and Schoolcraft," said the precocious parakeet. "Schaefer and Schoolcraft" ad nauseam, and would have gone on all afternoon had Smitty not said, "Would you please cut that out?"

In the flat downstairs, my friend Patsy's family owned a parakeet, a green one a little paler than Smitty's. Whenever they went back to Alabama for vacation, they set the cage in the back stairway, and Mama fed the bird. She always stopped short of bringing the cage upstairs. I guess she didn't want to encourage me too much.

I wanted a parakeet. A parakeet would be a friend, someone to talk to, someone to train, someone to make us more like everybody else. You could buy a parakeet from Kresge's on Vernor for around $6. And you could buy the cages for a little more. I started stopping at Kresge's on my way home from school to watch the dime store ladies playing with the parakeets. Some of the young parakeets, already tamed, ate carrot sticks from the ladies' lunches. The dime store lady with the penciled eyebrows showed me one that talked and gave kisses. I think she talked to the birds so she wouldn't get bored, and she and one little blue parakeet I liked a lot had a nice routine.

I figured up the cost. Parakeet goods were needed: bird seed and that sharp stick-like gizmo so the bird could sharpen its beak. You put the water in one of the two glass bowls that stuck out of the side of the cage. You put the feed in the other one. The bowls came with the cage, so no extra cost there. You hung a mirror for the bird to see itself and, being bird-brained, think it was another bird and not be lonely. You bought some medicinal powder to use in case the bird got fleas. You lined the cage with a special material that looked like medium grade sand paper. You could invest in a plastic fitted cover for the cage, a choice of one in beige, or blue, or cherry red. I wanted a parakeet and I tallied the cost of one, the initial investment and then the continued cost of feed. I wrote it all down on school lined paper and did the math—a $20 dollar initial investment.

I had enough sense not to tell Mama right off. If I wanted a parakeet I'd have to start a campaign of persuasion. First, I reminded Mama it was not a dog or a cat, which she'd already declined. "You shouldn't have a dog if you live upstairs," she had said a few months earlier. Now I opened up a new discussion.

"A parakeet can live in a cage upstairs."

"But who'll clean the cage?"

"I will."

"What if it gets out?"

"We'll train it to come back. Mrs. Smith's parakeet comes back when you call it."

After hours and days of argument I knew she was considering. "Well," she asked, "how much are they up at the dime store?"

"Six dollars."

"That's too high." Mama went on to mention the other expenses. "It costs more for the supplies than it does for the bird."

I knew she'd say that, and I had no counter. It had struck me too as strange when the bored Kresge lady had given me higher price quotes for the inanimate objects than for the pulsing-hearted bird. I'd been taught to think that that which lived was more precious, more dear, than that which was metallic.

The argument hit a stalemate when Mama ended the discussion, "I'll think about it."

At ten years old I already knew the art of letting her be, knowing that the biggest obstacle rested on her extreme reluctance to part with money. It was best to let it settle in her mind, perhaps do some subtle mentioning of prices for other things she'd buy without question in the next few weeks. It would take patience.

And then Smitty saved me. Smitty, my guardian angel. It just seemed to happen that when I wanted something in particular to happen it was Smitty who intervened to make it happen. It was Smitty who'd insisted that Mama buy me a Jenny doll for Christmas.

Back at that oil cloth table in the row house kitchen where Mama and Smitty sat and drank their coffee, and I sat listening to the stories, a new conversation opened.

"I just learned from Roy there's a Polish guy over on Greusel who raises parakeets in his basement. He's got lots of them, and he sells them cheap."

"How much?" Mama said.

"Two dollars," Smitty said.

"Two dollars," said Gabby. "Two dollars, two dollars, two dollars." When Smitty rose from her chair and pitched a stern close-up look through the bars of his cage, Gabby shut up.

Mama took down the phone number. She broke down and bought the cage up at Kresge's, along with the sand paper, the mirror with a bell hanging from it, the flea powder, the vitamins, and the beak-sharpener. She even bought a blue cage cover for night time. Arrangements were made for us to go over to the house on Greusel to pick out a parakeet.

I knew I'd pick a boy parakeet because I already had a name for him. His namesake would be Davy Crockett, and with our name he'd be Davy Crockett Rhodes. He'd be named for Davy Crockett, proud citizen born on a mountain top in that mythical, to me, state of Tennessee, named for my deceased father born in the foothills of that mystical, to me, state of Tennessee. The bird represented the flight toward getting there—pretty hefty expectations for a little bird.

To pick out our parakeet, we needed to drive to the Polish neighborhood around Michigan and Junction Avenues, about a mile away. In those days, unlike our own immediate business strip on Vernor Highway that served a diverse or diluted population, the strip on Michigan Avenue, from east of Junction at least on down to west of Martin, was homogeneous, impressively and imposingly Polish. On broad Michigan Avenue, the same Michigan Avenue that Mama said you could take to Chicago, most of the storefront signs were in Polish. And the ones written in English, like Witkowski Clothing and Jarzembowski Funeral Home, along with the White Eagle Restaurant named for the Polish bird of freedom, told you the proprietors were Polish anyway. Most business was conducted in Polish. If you wanted to shop there, which we occasionally did, you had to point at things in the display cases, like the *pierogis* or the lambs made out of butter. You had to know what you wanted. And you had to be prepared for a glance from the clerk that told you that you were an outsider.

The big businesses, of course—the banks, the Cunningham's and Kinsel's drug stores, the Kresge's and Woolworth's dime stores, the Kramer Theater—all displayed signs in English, but the fact that there were so many of these businesses on Michigan Avenue, including a Federal's Department Store, told you right away—the Polish neighborhood was more prosperous and stable than our area on Vernor.

It didn't seem fair. On our part of Vernor Highway near Clark Park we had the Southern honky-tonks, and we also had a few anomalies among the clean-windowed dress shops, dry cleaners, meat markets, and jewelry stores that heralded the start of more troublesome changes—a plumbing supply store, an auto parts dealer, a couple of second-hand furniture stores, and a Jesus-the-Mighty storefront church.

Later on, when a little older, I'd respond to the sheer excitement of the fast-changing storefronts, the many migrations of new people, and the Friday-night foolishness. But at the time, I was still of the opinion I'd held from when I was much younger and had paid attention to Mama pointing things out. I loved traveling through the ethnic neighborhoods—colorful, mysterious and exotic. It would be better to be all of one thing—all Polish, all Hungarian, all Lithuanian, or all Irish—it didn't matter which, as long as you could easily define yourself, know exactly who you were. And count on a system of unchanging neighborly support.

All the residential streets off Michigan Avenue in the Polish neighborhood seemed to offer bastions of such support. Blocks and blocks of extended Polish families—grandparents, aunts, uncles, brothers—in two-family white clapboard or brick substantial houses, set no more than ten feet from the sidewalk, and no more than six feet from each other, all with full wide pillared porches up and down, all with a hawk-like set of attic windows in the front, extending and looking out over the upper porches.

We easily found the right house on Greusel Street, checking the address Mama had written down. I'd never been in one of these houses in the Polish neighborhood, although it seemed I'd seen them all. Standing on the porch, I waited in happy expectation, especially with the prospect of a pet of my very own. If I'd never been in one of these houses, at least, like all of us in our border neighborhood, I knew what to expect on the inside. Any time I entered an ethnic house, I could easily tell the difference between a Polish and a Lithuanian, a Hungarian and an Irish, a Maltese and a Kentuckian, and of course the one-of-a-kind messy mixed up house of our own.

When the man opened the door, I quickly saw that this house was no exception. The statue of the Infant of Prague, the many wedding photographs of brides posed with the long trains of their dresses spread in front to show the details, the embroidered doilies, the sick-call crucifix, the pungent low smell of slow-cooking chicken soup: yes, recognizable. Just like the Markowicz's house on our block, just like the houses of Mama's Avon customers, Mrs. Kowalczyk and Mrs. Czarnecki, and just as clean as all of them. This house was definitely Polish.

The man who answered the door presented himself as a typical working man—no unnecessary smiles, no unnecessary expressions. He was tall and thin, with one of those long Polish abdomens that appeared strong. He wore the typical working man's costume, blue twill shirt and blue cotton work pants, with a substantial belt, and his clothes were starched and ironed impeccably, the creases in his pants as good as what a man in our neighborhood wore on Sunday. He conducted himself with a certain formality, as though he was inviting us into a store. After all, he was an entrepreneur. Or an opportunist. He knew a good thing as he invited us in. Everybody wanted a parakeet.

He led us down the basement stairs, so clean it seemed that a toothbrush had been taken to the corners, and in being so clean, so unlike our own. The basement, completely finished in knotty pine, included a rec room with a carpet, a television, a black-and-white plaid Sears' high-back sofa, a matching chair, and a clock like a sunburst hanging on the wall. Beyond that was a tool room with peg boards from which hung many tools, each offered an equidistant comfortable space around it so the overall effect was that hammers, saws, screw drivers, drill bits, boxes of screws and nails, and power tools of every sort had learned to live in perfect harmony. It was no wonder the man needed another hobby. He wouldn't have to clean his basement for years. He led us to a doorway off the tool room that was most likely a converted coal bin, with a shed-like door. There was a small window in the door, and to see in I had to stand on a stool.

Inside were hundreds of unfettered parakeets. Hundreds of blue and green streaks darting back and forth in the kind of frenzy I imagined as bedlam, in a frenzy I had never seen and wouldn't be able to visualize again until Alfred Hitchcock's *The Birds*. The steady cacophonous chirping was only partially muted by the door, the chaos, the randomness. The second I peered in I wanted to bolt. I wanted to run up those immaculate basement stairs. I wanted to tell Mama we should go home. This was too much. None of these birds would achieve the peaceful playfulness of Smitty's parakeet Gabby. They were birds totally out of step with my own loner personality. After all, each of them contended with at least a hundred murderous siblings. As they darted back and forth in a furious battle of convoluted zooming, and savage pecking chase, I noticed the floor full of droppings, the troughs of bird seed on the left, the shallow boxes of about eight inches square on the right, in which two or three dull hens squatted, apparently warming eggs. I had to marvel at the efficiency of it all. What if two birds, a mama and a papa, were simply given a room this size? From what I later learned about the breeding habits of parakeets, they could start when they were six months old, hatch five eggs in two and a half weeks, and in no time they could produce this inbred hell.

I thought the process of picking my bird would involve judicious consideration, that I'd be picking from two or three, possibly more, possibly less, than the nine or so of them they had at Kresge's. I hadn't quite decided. Would it be green or blue? I knew I'd need help determining the sex. I couldn't call a female Davy, and I had no idea what to look for beneath the abdominal feathers of parakeets. How I longed for that cute little blue six-dollar bird I liked at Kresge's.

I felt the Polish man's urgency to get the transaction over with. Perhaps his wife's soup, or Milton Berle, or something better on TV was waiting. Sensing that, seeing that I couldn't talk to Mama alone, and sensing the hopelessness of consideration, I made a quick decision. "A blue one. A boy."

He told us to stand back from the door. In a practiced move, he unhooked the door, swooped away, and, as though he'd disappeared into thin air, joined the crowd in bird land. We heard him hook the door inside.

It was lucky I wasn't tall enough to reach the window. I couldn't have watched, but Mama was fascinated. "He's catching one!" she called out. Within another second or two the door swooshed open, and the Polish man swooped out again. In his hand trembled a terrified, rather dumbfounded-looking blue bird with peck marks and rheumy eyes. "Is it a boy?" I said. "It's a boy," he said.

The Polish man released Davy Crockett Rhodes into the cage we'd brought. I noticed even then, as Mama was paying for him and conducting the final pleasantries, that Davy seemed not to make a fast recovery from being rescued from his crazy life. He sat on the floor of the cage and not on a perch. I felt sorry for him, and I already felt ashamed of him. I suspected he was a loser. Odd, like us.

Almost immediately, like most kids I suppose, I became disinclined to take care of the bird. And in Davy's case, his habit of sitting on the floor promptly intensified my embarrassment. The responsibility for his care fell to Mama. And then the nagging began. "Talk to him," she said, ambling over to his cage, which hung on the side of the archway between the living room and dining room. "Davy. Davy," she said. "Davy."

And turning to me, "Talk to him. He's your bird."

Davy never said a word, although he did get so he cocked his head in a kind of exaggerated version of a wink when we uttered his name. "Davy, Davy. Day-vee!"

Occasionally he stopped sulking on the floor of his cage, ascending to his perch. When he did that we rejoiced in seeing he was having a good day. "Davy. Davy. Are you sitting on your perch?"

Mama got attached to him, demonstrating the acceptance she'd later exhibit when she became a regular working with handicapped children. She didn't seem too disappointed in Davy. Every month or so she decided he needed to be bathed. Since he was incapable of taking his own bath like Smitty's Gabby, who knew to demurely splash around in the shallow bowl offered through the door of his cage, Mama had to figure out an alternate strategy. She placed the cage on newspapers set on the clean spot of the dining room table. She grasped the same bottle with the shaker she used to dampen her clothes to be ironed and shook a thunderstorm's worth of water through the top of the cage. Davy flailed around, squawking in outrage. It was for his own good, she said. "You don't want to be a dirty bird, now do you?" I learned that Davy's bath time was also the time for me to be anywhere but around.

I can't say I grieved much over Davy's failure to meet my expectations. He was consistent. He failed in the first moment I saw him, and he never stopped failing. I sublimated my longing for a pet companion by reading, reading all the Lassie books, reading Old Yeller. I almost flew across the borderlands of England or leapt through the prairie grasses of Texas with some mighty intelligent pets. I did stop at the cage, though, when I passed by. "Davy, Davy. Day-vee!"

A year or so later my friend Patsy and I found a green parakeet on the ground in the park. We brought the bird back to dwell in the cage with Davy. Davy didn't seem to notice, didn't seem to mind. Mama accepted it, although she complained a little about another mouth to feed. The new bird must have been sick, because within a month or so, we woke up one morning to discover that both it and Davy Crockett Rhodes had died.

I didn't grieve too much about it, although Patsy and I made an elaborate ceremony of laying the birds out in a satin-lined box and burying them as true lovers, on the side of the house, forever side by side. Mama cleaned Davy's cage and propped it up on the pile of junk on the dining room table where it sat for several months. It eventually ended up in the way-back room.

CHAPTER TEN
THE DREAM OF THE SUBURBS

In spring 1956, when baby Newell was just a little over a year old, Jack and Dean told Mama they were moving out of our downstairs flat. Dean was pregnant again, and the flat was getting small, they said. They had bought a house in Inkster, a working-class suburb out Michigan Avenue about fifteen miles away. The idea for the move to Inkster came from a common deal being hawked on television and radio at the time. We couldn't help but memorize the mantra: *A three-bedroom ranch house in Inkster, all for ninety-nine hundred dollars, and ninety-nine dollars moves you in!* The guaranteed loan for veterans sweetened the deal, and Jack was a veteran, having had the luck to serve smack-dab between World War II and Korea.

In May, Jack, Dean, Patsy and Newell moved. Patsy and I both cried, and I felt like I was going to die as I strolled from room to room in the airy, empty, sparkling clean, echoing oak-pillared, oak-woodworked downstairs flat with the roomy kitchen.

Mama and I visited the Ramseys in the summer. Their house in Inkster was nice, with wall-to-wall carpets in each of the three bedrooms. In fact, the whole house was carpeted, and I figured you could run the vacuum everywhere without stopping except for the kitchen and bathroom. Dean had the whole place, even the basement, looking really cute. I thought I'd like to live there.

It was no surprise that Jack and Dean decided to move away. The middle 1950s saw the biggest exodus of neighbors to the Detroit suburbs, a kind of frenzy of leaving. We who remained in the neighborhood were keenly aware of being left behind. We functioned under a steady barrage of pressure to leave, as the real estate developers who sold the suburbs worked to create a malaise of discontent. The newspaper and magazine ads, the television and radio ads, the attitudes of the larger culture coming from beyond anything local that we could see, all told us we'd be happier somewhere else. We had being taught to hate our surroundings so that we would to want to leave them.

The filters placed on our eyes led us to see the neighborhood as ugly. *The air was dirty. The traffic was loud. The sidewalks interfered with the lawns. The houses sat too close together. Most of the houses were two-story, which meant climbing stairs. The houses weren't modern, and hardly any of them featured a picture window. The houses needed paint;*

they needed upgrades, and they were all different—aging, becoming eccentric. Wouldn't it be best to live in a neighborhood where all the houses looked the same?

Life would be better in a ranch house with a sparkling white kitchen with a double sink and plenty of counter-space to display and use the new appliances—electric mixers, blenders, can openers, skillets and knives. You needed a new non-spooky basement for your new electric washer and dryer and fancy ironing table. You needed a driveway in the front where you could watch your car all day, not leave it languishing in the garage in the alley. A driveway in front meant you could zoom in and out whenever you wanted to, steps away from your own front door. Some houses in the suburbs even featured garages attached—a brilliant idea, the epitome of convenience. Owning a ranch house equaled the dream of a deserving Cinderella who brought that matching slipper to the prince and lived happily ever after. Happily ever after in a ranch house, a low-slung castle of luxury and freedom. None of us, except for Mama, were exempt from thinking so.

When neighbors made the decision to move to the suburbs, they didn't see money or lack of it as the most significant factor. It wasn't necessarily the well-off ones who left and the poor who stayed behind. Leaving the neighborhood required no more financial resources than staying, even if people perceived living in the suburbs as a moving up. After all, the houses in the suburbs that most of our neighbors fled to—Melvindale, Allen Park, Lincoln Park, Inkster, Garden City, Wayne, and Romulus—were quite affordable. All you needed was a job and a willingness to buy on credit.

The suburbs lured us, while the forces of neighborhood cohesion mounted a fierce resistance. Holy Redeemer Parish, particularly, fought the trend by holding many parish seminars on neighborhood conservation and by starting a credit union for parishioners with competitive credit deals, not for home purchase, but for home improvement. Home improvement, even in some cases cutting out new picture windows in the clapboard siding, offered the best alternative to leaving the neighborhood and buying a new home.

Father Forbes, the pastor, addressed the issue in his inimical way several times throughout those years in his "Views from the Rectory" column in the *Holy Redeemer Weekly.* Mama always sat and read his weekly "Views" columns after lunch on Sunday. She was often moved to laughter, and started making calls to her sisters in River Rouge, lacing her stories with generous quotations. Some people disliked Father Forbes because they didn't understand his sense of humor. If you believed that, behind his sarcasm and scolding, a gentler, more fatherly, spirit lurked and, more importantly, if you agreed with him on the issue in the first place, then yes, he was a stitch. He went out of his way to write an entertaining column, choosing a bevy of the exact right words.

In one of his typical columns on the issue of leaving the parish in February 1955, he writes under the caption, "Thinking of Moving?" addressing it to the women of the parish, either correctly or incorrectly assessing that it was the women who were the bigger suburb dreamers:

[Thinking of moving?] *Why? Maybe you want to get farther away so your husband will have farther to travel getting to work. And this will make the old bear get up earlier and stay away longer. Let's say it takes him fifteen minutes to get to work now. Let's move out farther so that he has to add another fifteen minutes to the time it takes him to get to work. That will give him an hour away from home each day, five hours a week, just shuttling back and forth to the mines. At the end of the month, he has spent almost a twenty four hour day away from home. We won't count the extra gas and oil and use of the car. The broadening influence of travel, you know, was well worth the sacrifice—his sacrifice.*

Perhaps you would just love to help build a new parish. You get very tired just supporting an old one, where the church and school and parish house and convent are all paid for. You want opportunities for bigger sacrifices, more noble generosity. You'll get it. Especially when you find that they haven't got room for eleven hundred children and have to build a new school, five years after they put up their first one.

You want better surroundings for your children. It is well known that pagan neighbors, immoral companions and juvenile delinquency are not allowed in the suburbs. (Note to typesetter: Carry on, boy, no matter what YOU think, the previous sentence was not meant for the joke column.)

The most succinct representation of the suburb hysteria and Redeemer's position on it appeared in an ad for the new Holy Redeemer Credit Union on May 15, 1955. The ad features a smiling man sprawled on the ground, roped to the rear axle of a moving van he has just dislodged from under the truck with his resistance. *Sorry, but I'm staying!* he shouts in a balloon. The moving van driver stands next to his damaged truck hurling stars and exclamations while the spire of Holy Redeemer rises in the background. The ad lists the man's reasons for staying in bullets: cathedral-like church, grade school, high school, gymnasium, rectory, adequate teachers, fire and police departments, transportation, large homes and paved streets, and shopping district. *And, the credit union allows you to stay in the parish*, the ad boasts. *If you need improvements,... just borrow from your parish credit union at very low interest.* It was all true. Redeemer Parish offered all those resources, and if you included the resources of Detroit city, we had many times more. Nobody needed to leave. But they did. And when they did, we missed them.

In those days, the issue of race did not present a significant reason for people's moving out, as it would later in the history of the city. After all, the rigid segregation in Detroit neighborhoods at the time ensured that blacks would not be moving in. Hence whites who feared blacks felt no cause for alarm. For the most part, in those days, the people who moved to the suburbs were not fleeing others. They became convinced, and probably continued to convince themselves, that life in the suburbs was better.

Questions of race and ethnicity in the neighborhood were complicated. An incident that happened the summer before Jack and Dean Allen moved out showed it pretty well. An upstairs rental flat on McKinstry just behind the Y became vacant, and a week or so later one of the neighbors saw a black woman with a head scarf shaking out a mop at the back door.

Some of the Southern men on McKinstry felt called upon to appear on the downstairs front porch to point it out to Jack. Patsy and I sat on the steps cutting out paper doll clothes while Jack and baby Newell wore out the wicker rocker. Jack was learning to be gentle for the baby's sake. And Dean had recently persuaded him to go on a diet, although he complained bitterly and often about how hungry he was.

The three men who moved around us on the steps were canvassing the neighborhood, looking for support. "Did you know there's Negroes moving in on McKinstry?" They waited a few beats to let the news sink in.

One of them I recognized as the man who broke bottles in the alley whenever he was drunk. "We're going around the neighborhood talking to people because you know we're going to have to put a stop to it. Nip it in the bud."

With their ruby red scowling faces, loud talk and taut muscles, all three of them seemed fired up by the righteousness of their cause. "We're going to have to go over there! Tell 'em they're not welcome here, and we need some fellows to come with us." They got nastier, tag teaming each other with overlapping comments about Negroes, and how they knew what to do and weren't afraid to do it.

Jack had just rocked the baby to sleep and didn't seem particularly interested in being roused to fury. "Mrs. Rhodes owns the house," he said. "Why don't you ring her bell?"

Answering the bell, Mama saw from the top of the stairs that the bottle-breaker and another man wanted a word with her. She must've decided it was safer to come down and talk to them on the downstairs porch. When she heard their allegation, she said, "Well, are you sure? Maybe it's a cleaning lady."

Nobody in the neighborhood used a cleaning lady. Most of the women would have considered such a luxury a sign of incompetence. Any woman worth her salt did her own housework and did it well. Mama probably wouldn't have thought of a cleaning lady if she hadn't just counseled my Aunt Kay, who was hurting for money, to advertise for such a job. The men didn't want to believe it. They were enjoying themselves more thinking they'd have a good old Southern battle on their hands. Maybe the bottle-breaker wanted to break more than bottles.

"It's no cleaning lady," he said. "We seen her. She's been there all week."

"Did they move in any of their furniture?" Mama said.

"Not yet. And we reckon that's why we ought to do something now."

Mama took part in conversations over a few fences as the vigilante group continued to make their case with other neighbors. Apparently they'd gotten angrier and angrier and a little crazier as they moved on down the block. By the time they got to Lafayette, I guess, they were screaming at the top of their lungs, probably drunk.

The following week, when a milky white Kentucky family with honey-blonde hair and two small kids in diapers moved in to replace the pink-faced Georgia family, the vigilante group could only sulk. "You see," Mama said, "they were so worried. And it was the white hillbillies who left that house so dirty they needed a cleaning lady. Some of those people just up from the South don't know how to live in the city."

Mama had more to say about the bad renters as the talk about the vigilante effort in the neighborhood spun out. "It's one thing keeping a dirty house, but it's another leaving it dirty for somebody else. If they had to have that cleaning lady there all week, it must have been filthy." In the end, though, Mama always came to the same point, which she believed and usually upheld, "It just goes to show you, there's good and bad in all the different groups."

That was the first time I'd seen a mob of men, albeit a small mob, and in light of Jack's and Mama's reactions to them, they didn't scare me. They seemed more scared themselves than persuasive, and in the neighborhood hierarchy, they didn't rank high.

Ironically, the neighborhood hierarchy was complicated by the fact that these red-faced white Southern vigilantes, and not blacks, represented the group that the Old Guard most feared might take over the neighborhood. Father Forbes was trying to hold the Catholic line, and these Southern "pagan neighbors" were Protestant. Holy Redeemer Parish was the largest, densest group of Catholics in the city, some said the largest, densest group of Catholics in the entire U.S.A.—it didn't matter if they were German, French, Lithuanian, Hungarian, Polish, Italian, Maltese, Mexican or, as they still mostly were, Irish—as long as they were Catholic.

Father Forbes, and most of us in the parish, held an attitude of Catholic chauvinism—after all, we were "the one, the *only*, holy" church. Like many in the Irish-American parish, Father Forbes also viewed Protestants through the prism of Irish politics and history.

To be fair to Father Forbes, though, and to acknowledge his shepherdly spirit and considerable intelligence, he chiefly didn't want to lose his flock to what he saw as rampant consumerism in the building of the suburbs. Many of his "Views" columns turned out to be prophetic. In one, for instance, he scolded women who took jobs outside the home to provide the family with "modern conveniences." He seemed to know, like no one else at the time, that the "conveniences" would lead to restlessness, that restlessness would lead to flight, and that so much flight might eventually make a shambles of the neighborhood and city.

It was a period of remarkable change, and the changes in our immediate neighborhood on the east side of the parish, came early as it became *the* mecca for white Southerners. Our area around the park had always supported a more diverse population than the solid blocks and blocks of Irish Catholics who resided closer to the church. I played with several Protestant kids on Clark Street; although, of course, I reserved the ritual games such as "Christian Martyr" for the Catholic Faithful. The housing stock supported a considerable population of renters, with two-family and four-family homes and an apartment building on Clark Street, and on Lafayette, Fort Street and Vernor, huge apartment buildings sharing the strip with businesses and stores. While the renters of prior decades, like Mama and Daddy, planned to keep renting, enjoying the convenience and culture of the city, the renters in the 1950s were smitten by the dream of ownership. They were renting to save enough to buy a home. Thus, our part of the parish saw the most transience.

As these changes that started in the early 1950s progressed, and as businesses on Vernor Highway changed hands, we too started to change our attitude. If we missed the people who moved away, we couldn't help but embrace the optimism of the people moving in. Coming up to *Dee*-troit in droves. Heading straight to our neighborhood to enrich it.

It was a high time in the neighborhood. The folks from Tennessee, Kentucky, Georgia and Alabama saw *Dee*-troit and the neighborhood as a new beginning, and they rarely hid their exuberance. We couldn't help but look at the city from their point of view. They took the train or drove their old jalopies up to *Dee*-troit, and in a day or two they secured the best job with best pay that they had ever earned. Just like that, it seemed they traded rural poverty and the slow pace of the Appalachian South for the big city. Many often got rip-roaring drunk on Friday nights, slept it off on Saturday mornings, and were back at it—the shift work and the Vernor Highway honky-tonks— in no time. Typically they stayed at the Y until they'd saved enough from their paychecks, and in a few months sent back down south for their wives. They met them at the Depot and took them home to an apartment or a rented flat to make the biscuits and gravy. *Dee*-troit was hopping. The neighborhood was hopping. It's no wonder the pedestrians sauntered and jaunted and swaggered and bounced up and down Vernor Highway.

Even Mama, more accustomed to her languorous slow-footed gait, put a little spring in her step while walking down Vernor Highway. As for me, I fairly flew, letting my eyes capture in peripheral vision the string of silly fly-by-night businesses, down-home diners, and the honky-tonks that blared their juke boxes out of open doors. On the street side, I witnessed the parade of hissing busses, big fin-tailed cars, old trucks with out-of-state license plates, jalopies with shot mufflers, new Cadillacs, and an odd assortment of eccentric vehicles that idled or rolled past at a crawl. Drivers dangled cigarettes out of open car windows and started friendly conversations with anybody on the sidewalk, getting directions, sharing the news, exchanging information about where they came from. It was something to do while waiting for the light. When the light changed and the line of cars started to inch onward, they tooted and called out, "So long." It was like a party and it rubbed off on everybody.

Exposed to the many Southern accents, I started to feel something stirring in me. Everybody told me I looked like my father. Although I couldn't remember what he looked like, I could see that many of the new people who thronged to the neighborhood bore a resemblance to me. And then people started mistaking me for a Southern gal. "Where you from, honey?" they asked.

It was a shock to me and a call. My conscious mind had excluded it. Only fleetingly, and in deep secret, had I dared to wish it—to walk with Davy Crockett through Cumberland Gap, to ponder Daddy's things, to hold a secret homesickness for the green of Tennessee. And now people were calling out to me—innocently, as though it was no big secret.

"I'm from right here," I said, " but my father came from Westmoreland, Tennessee." I longed to say, but couldn't breathe the lie: "My father *comes* from Tennessee." Still, they were noticing what had been denied—the Southern half of me. In those remarkable years of transformation in the neighborhood, the South came north to claim me.

CHAPTER ELEVEN
FILLING THE CRACKS

During the spring and early summer of 1956, I consolidated my status as a competent and persistent child. I finally learned to ride the bicycle I'd inherited from my sister and soon was riding to neighborhoods near and far. In May I started taking piano lessons from Miss Craig, a frail elderly Scots lady who draped her coat over Mama's chair by the window and backtracked to work with me at the piano near the door, and hence she never ventured far enough into the flat to see the dining room clutter, much less the way-back room. That summer I followed the Detroit Tigers and ended the season with a perfect attendance record: I either attended in person, watched on TV, or listened on the radio to every single Tigers game. I calculated batting averages, refiguring them daily for my beloved outfielders Al Kaline, Bill Tuttle and Charlie Maxwell. I often spent time on my favorite bench in the park reading thick books and gazing at innumerable comic book issues of *Little Lu Lu* and *Nancy and Slugo*. Both Lu Lu and Nancy were resourceful girls, and I liked their wisecracks.

Right after school got out after sixth grade, Mama hired a painter recommended by our neighbor Bill up the street. The painter, a likeable Irishman named Mr. Gowan, was trying to get off the bottle and needed work to keep him straight. He was supposed to paint the dining room and then the dark hallway, and when he showed up one morning to negotiate the job, he said with confidence, "I'm a good painter. It shouldn't take me any longer than two or three days." He was a charmer, earnestly complimenting me on my freckles and beautiful red hair. I liked him, but I soon became ambivalent about having him in the house.

First it was Mama and her ways. When he showed up bright and early the next morning, Mama asked him the same round of questions she put to every person who entered the house. "Are you hungry? Can I fix you something to eat?" He hadn't even stirred the paint or gone down to the basement for the ladder.

First he politely declined. It looked as though he was set on doing what he said he'd do, which was to work. To work, though, he'd have to use an accelerated bit of energy to get started. He was clean, his damp hair slicked back, and it looked like he'd just shaved. But Mama did her usual. She nagged. "Are you sure you don't want something to eat? I can squeeze you some orange juice. Or I can make you some eggs." I found it embarrassing, hearing her list all the foods she had in the house. She assumed, I guess, that food for him was like food for her—the highest order of concern. And then she turned toward me. "Mary can make you some eggs."

Trapped, Mr. Gowan possessed enough sensibility to see he couldn't get out of it, especially since the young woman-in-training had been drawn into the offer. "OK," he said. "Do you think you could make me a couple of soft boiled eggs?" Mama didn't budge from the chair she'd plopped down into. He sat on the edge of the couch in his clean work clothes. She was parading me. I boiled the eggs, somehow remembering that soft boiled took three minutes. I peeled them and served them at the dining room table that hadn't yet been moved aside, and he commented, "These are exactly the way I like them." He went on a little after that.

Although pleased I'd boiled them correctly, and pleased by his attention, I kept wondering when he was going to get started. Mama offered so many excuses and postponements. She talked to him about the neighborhood and listed possible friends they might both know from the Parish. Of course she was by now cheerfully desperate: her fear of change became most acute when change loomed as inevitable, when the agent of change—in this case Mr. Gowan and his painting—was absentmindedly carding the bristles of the dry paint brush he held in his hand.

Around eleven in the morning he finally got going. He moved the furniture out from the walls, brought up the ladder from the basement, spread a few newspapers around, covered up the table, buffet and china cabinet and stirred the paint.

When lunch time came, Mama started the whole ritual over again. I didn't want to get commandeered into showing my cooking skills again, so I made my exit. "I'm going over to Jodie's," I said. "And then I've got to go babysit." It was true. I had a regular babysitting job that summer entertaining three blond Polish girls on Plumer Street who looked like matryoshka dolls. Their grandmother turned them over to me at two o'clock to get a respite from their constant talking. I said so long and took off on my bike.

When I got back a little after five-thirty, Mr. Gowan was wrapping up for the day. He'd gotten three quarters of the ceiling done and was washing out his brush and roller in the kitchen sink. Beads of sweat and fine white flecks among his freckles dotted his face. After drying his brush with a dishrag, he set it on the paint can on the dining room table. "I'll be back tomorrow bright and early," he said. I could see a hint of blond whiskers on his chin. He was a handsome man.

"I should pay you for the work you did today," Mama said.

"You can pay me tomorrow, Mrs. Rhodes. Or when I'm finished."

"No, I want to pay you today. How much do I owe you?"

He didn't come back the next day until around noon. And when he stood on the ladder to finish the ceiling, he started to reel.

I was terribly afraid of drunkenness in those days. I didn't understand the rhythm of it, and I couldn't judge the symptoms, especially since the people in the neighborhood who drank showed different symptoms—like getting funny, or louder, or sullen, or staggering and slurring, or showing no outward signs, but simply getting mean. Some got violent, like the man on McKinstry who broke the beer bottles in the alley. Others, I learned through overheard conversations among the women, showed bad judgment, bought things they couldn't afford and gave away money needed for the light bill.

The reeling man with the roller full of white paint in his hand leaned out in front, listed to the right side, almost toppled the ladder, and spun around to splash the paint for the ceiling over his left shoulder. Mama stood below pretending all was well, revealing her nervousness only in her exaggerated flirting. It was too much to bear. A wave of terror washed over me. And then despair.

Why was it that the only men who came into our house, the only men who came into our lives, it seemed, were neither trustworthy nor helpful? Like Mr. Yost, who over the years rendered practically every single line of plumbing in the house, both upstairs and downstairs, into nubs of eccentric turns and braces, and installed mismatched ancient fixtures on the sinks that demanded that you know that hot was really cold and cold was really hot. For awhile, even the traditional placement of the pipes, hot water on the left and cold water on the right, didn't pan out in our bathroom sink. Most of our visitors were baffled, and they often came out of the bathroom asking questions until they gave up. Mama liked Mr. Yost because he was cheap, doing everything for next to nothing, figuring, I guess, that helping out a widow would earn him grace in heaven. Besides, as old classmates, they gossiped while he worked about what had happened to whom from Saint Pat's.

He also might have shared her values. I distinctly remember him, with one of his smiling winks, proudly holding up for her inspection one of his greatest finds, a crusted old faucet with a broken porcelain handle he was about to install in the tub. "It didn't cost me nothing," he said. I knew Mama had the money to buy a shiny new faucet, but she wasn't letting on. She preferred to play Poor Widow, while once again I witnessed the cheap, ugly, shoddy, and pathetic assigned to our home and lives.

I knew some men who were helpful and knew what they were doing: all the men on TV, my Uncle Pete and my uncles in Tennessee. But these were not the kinds of men who came to help us. Instead, we had men like the one named Ray, who she'd hired the year before to paint the exterior of the house. He laughed at me but never explained when he saw me trying repeatedly to push our lawnmower to cut the grass with its seriously rusted blades. He left permanent gray paint drippings all over our dark front porch and painted most of the windows in the house hopelessly shut. Mama never hired anyone to open them.

I'd been practicing on Mr. Gowan to overcome my shyness of men because I liked him. He'd been attentive to me. I suspected that the only way

I was going to get used to male voices, overcome my fear, and understand men's mysterious ways was through these brief visits. I feared men, yet I wanted their attention. I used to track how many times I'd hear an adult male voice in our house, not counting the voices on the radio and TV. Sometimes we'd go for months without a single word.

Once again Mama paid Mr. Gowan at the end of the day. "I'll be back tomorrow," he said.

After a few days she called Bill, and from what I heard of her side of the conversation, and from her sad face and weak protests, I understood she'd been unwise to pay Mr. Gowan before he finished the job. She was giving him enough money each day to get good and drunk.

In the meantime, the dining room stayed in its disheveled condition. Mama cleared a corner of the table so we could eat, but the ladder, and newspapers covering the mounds of clutter on the buffet and china cabinet, and the chairs cast out into the living room, remained where they were. We lived around the mess. When the phone rang she grappled for it under the newspaper. "Maybe it's Mr. Gowan," she said. I couldn't stand it.

Every day, as she pulled the morning shades down in the living room to keep the sun from making the rooms hotter, she pondered aloud: "Maybe Mr. Gowan will come today." A few dusty sunbeams made it in through the slits between the window edges and the shades. The scene in the dining room was even gloomier without much light getting in.

After three weeks I decided I needed to learn how to paint. Mr. Gowan had finished the ceiling and started on one wall—a goldish color that clashed with the wallpaper in the living room, but Mama liked it.

I learned to use the roller pretty well, although Mama had a fit every time I took it into my hand. "Don't use too much, it's going to drip." "See that streak?" "Don't strain yourself." The "don't-strain-yourself" comment always seemed to come precisely when I'd gotten my body into a rhythm and was using it with grace and confidence. It wasn't hard to interpret it as "Don't be any good."

The thing I couldn't do, or at least couldn't do competently, was patch the long crack that ran on a slight diagonal the entire length of the wall behind the buffet. Mama provided leftover spackling compound from three years earlier when she'd hired the Kentucky brothers to paint the way-back room for my sister, and she supplied an old putty knife that had belonged to Mr. Dixon.

Although I tried and tried, every time I pressed a knife full of the dried-out stuff into the crack, it fell out, landing with a dry thud on the newspaper below. I discovered wetter paste under the surface crust deeper in the jar, but when I worked with that, I used too much. My patchwork and knife marks visibly stuck out beyond the wall. It didn't look good.

"Let's wait for Mr. Yost to help us," Mama said, but I wasn't going to stop and wait when I'd almost finished and could see the end of the chaos that I would set into order. I patched and patched and patched the crack all the way up to the ceiling, leaving a fresco of impatient horizontal strokes of the knife. Then I painted over them.

After I finally finished painting, disposed of the newspapers, got Mama to help me take the ladder back to the basement, vacuumed the floor, dusted the furniture and put it back where it belonged, I carted the paint cans, brush and roller, and Avon boxes stuffed with clutter to the way-back room.

It wasn't exactly pride in my accomplishment that I felt. Rather I felt sorry for myself. Painting had been an action borne out of expediency. I hadn't planned to do it. If pride would soon follow—"Yes, I can do it!"—so would the resolve: "If anything is going to get done around this house, it'll have to be me to do it." The dabs and slides of that angry putty knife marked the wall for forty more years.

Mama, Mary and Betty, 1945.

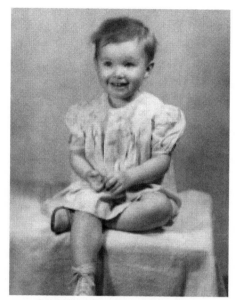

Mary at Eighteen Months.

Betty, Mama, and Mary, 1948.

Daddy and Mary, circa 1948.

Family, circa 1950.

Saint Mary of Detroit Among Her Mentors.

Present Community of Sisters
Servants of the Immaculate Heart of Mary

May God's Providence continue to bless Holy Redeemer through His Servants of the Immaculate Heart of Mary.

Holy Redeemer Faculy, 1955.

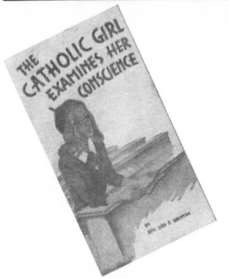

Holy Redeemer Grade School, circa 1950.   Mary, around age 10.

Holy Redeemer Auditorium, circa 1950.

The Holy Redeemer Weekly, May 15, 1955.

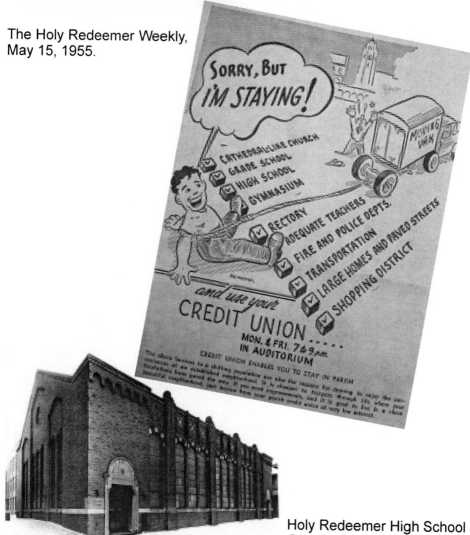

Holy Redeemer High School Gynmasium, circa 1950.

Holy Redeemer Church Interior, circa 1950.

Holy Redeemer Church, 1959.

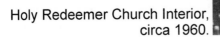

Holy Redeemer Church Interior, circa 1960.

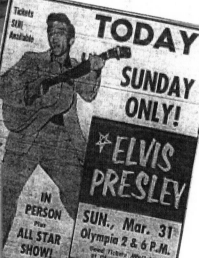

Mary at Elizabeth Park,
August 1956.

Debbie, Suzie and Mary, June 1956.

Mama and Mary, Lake Huron,
June 1963.

Easter, Clark Park.

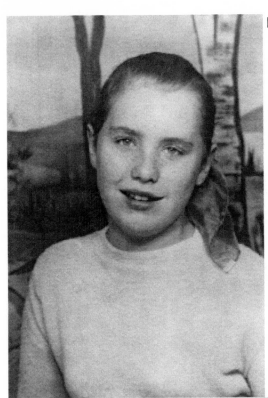

Mary, 1957.

Mary, Graduation 1962.

CHAPTER TWELVE
THE WAY-BACK ROOM

The thick ring loaded with keys of the late Mr. Dixon hid behind the decorative molding on top of the bookcase in the hall. No one but Mama and I knew where to reach for it. No one but Mama and I knew which key would work to open the way-back room from among the others that belonged to doors that no longer existed. No one but Mama and I knew what hid behind the locked door of the way-back room. It was our big dirty secret.

Since the bulb of the doorknob had fallen off years before, unlocking and opening the door required skill. After sifting through the keys on the ring, I inserted the correct one into the lock. While turning the deadbolt to the right I simultaneously grabbed the shaft of the doorknob to the left.

I pushed it open. The huge unheated, uncooled, unventilated room with its filthy green walls and filthy Venetian blinds hanging in front of the picture window sucked in the air surrounding me. I had to stand in the doorway a moment to take in the room's silence, and to adjust to its gloom. Then I smelled it, the dust, and saw it dancing in front of the tiny cracks of light at the edges of the blinds.

Beyond the window, I heard the backyard birds chirping as though they were in a far-off land. I then contemplated the lonely objects that waited here, enduring the changes of the seasons—the hot, the cold, the dry, the moist—either to be redeemed by someone in some unknown future or to return to dust. In the doorway, I could hardly hear the sounds from the rest of the house. If I ventured farther into the room, I heard nothing. Nothing but those strange, distant, unreachable and unseen backyard birds beyond the window. They performed their earthly prattle, oblivious to the far, far longer death awaiting them.

The way-back room, heaped with mounds of junk, measured twenty-four by fourteen feet. There were three narrow paths: one to the boxes of Avon products Mama sold, one to the paint cans where muriatic acid had spilled, making a gouge in the floor with charred wood around it, and one that stretched the length of the room, overgrown with stray papers, clothes hangers, crayons, pens and odds and ends. Though the floor underneath was still attractive, the stuff that seemed to be decomposing created a thick layer of earthly grit.

The jumbles of junk, much of it in Avon boxes, included practically everything in haphazard arrangement. Gallon vinegar bottles—Mama went through scores of them administering her weekly vinegar douches. Brushes and gadgets which the high-pressure Fuller Brush salesman had sold to her before the neighbors developed a call chain so no one, from Mr. Geis up at the corner near Vernor to Mrs. Sunlight down at Christiancy, answered the door when he came around. "He just doesn't take 'No' for an answer," Mama said.

There were Hudson's dress boxes full of eyeglasses, including her mother's and my father's. Her mother's hats and canes, her own unread stock market reports from various companies, magazines and newspapers, unread mail, and flyers (from coupons for front-end wheel alignments and mufflers to specials on hamburger at Banner Market.) Mama was unable to let anything in print go until at least one set of eyes had slowly and thoroughly devoured it. Broken furniture, end tables and chairs—some of it from the alley—floated on the waves of other objects and boxes, legs up, undersides exposed, some showing proprietary marks of ancient furniture factories.

In addition to Mama's own accumulations, she picked up what other people didn't want. A hideous green reclining chair, which resembled an inverted turtle, sat supine in a corner. She'd acquired it from Wilda Korn, the woman she worked for as a companion in Dearborn Township. An assortment of the same lady's extra dishes, pillowcases, slip covers and blankets was strewn around—all stuff Mrs. Korn threw out one day. Mama picked it up from the trash on her way home. When Wilda started cleaning house in preparation for her move to Florida, Mama brought home a second installment of Wilda's things. This time it included Wilda's paid electric bills and all the Christmas cards she had received. Mama tried to persuade Wilda to keep the stuff, but when she didn't, Mama again raided the trash cans on her way home.

In the middle of the room, along the path to the closet at the other end, were the few mementos to the short-lived inhabitation of my sister Betty three years before. Her school notebook with lined paper sat atop a precarious stack of boxes. Inside the notebook, on the only used page, was a vertical row of cursive signatures, "Elizabeth Rhodes," "Elizabeth Rhodes," "Elizabeth A. Rhodes," "Elizabeth Rhodes." Betty had been practicing her signature with neat feminine twirls. Other feminine reminders—a knobby milk-glass bottle of sweet-smelling apple blossom toilet water, a few sour-smelling tubes of spoiled lipstick.

At the farthest end of the room, the sanctum sanctorum that was the walk-in closet, were the artifacts of old man Dixon. In the totally packed space of that closet were all the treasures it seemed he'd need for the Afterlife. The closet was holy, mysterious, alien, smelling faintly of a man. Was it pipe ashes, or metal, or was it the leather bindings of the books and the mounds of stale paper?

As I struggled to find a flat surface to store the paint cans, brushes, roller and roller pan after I'd finished painting the dining room, I pondered one of my usual questions. Why was an old paint brush stuck upright in an old coffee can of evaporated turpentine on the floor? Finding even a foot of space in the way-back room was difficult. In the aftermath of my accomplishment painting the dining room, a solution floated into my head. How easy it would be to fetch the wastebasket and throw that out. Other questions followed. Why were the shards of glass from the broken window of two winters ago still sitting there pointing up? Why had that can of muriatic acid been allowed to spill and eat up the floor?

Why did we live the way we did?

No one else I knew slid their rubble into an unused room at the back of the house and locked the door. They threw it out or used their basements. They organized it. They knew what to throw out and what to keep, and they put what they were keeping in a place with like articles so they would have it handy when they needed it. Nobody lived like us. No wonder I felt ashamed. As I peered into the length of the way-back room, smelled the dust, saw the lampshades and pillows surfing on the Avon boxes, and heard those distant backyard birds, I made a resolution: we were going to clean up the way-back room. We were going to recast our messy abnormal lot.

I tried to involve Mama in my resolution. After all, it was her stuff, and it wasn't natural for me to be the authority at age eleven. Besides, I didn't know for certain what was worthless and what was valuable. I started by suggesting we take a couple of chairs to the way-back room. "Mama, we can sit in one of the paths and make a clearing. We can sort out some of the Avon boxes. We can fill up some bags with stuff to throw out."

Reluctantly, Mama obliged. She sat down sadly in the dining room chair I'd carried back and placed into one of the paths. Almost immediately her eyes started darting around. "Shouldn't the mail be here by now?" she said, changing the subject. Her breathing grew shallow, as if she'd seen something ghostly. After a moment, she turned, her face gray as death. At this angle, the boxes, stacked in lopsided increments with spongy, metallic, oblong, or papery objects mounding up or sticking out above them were higher than the shoulders of the flowered housedress she wore, in fact, higher than her graying hair.

"Are you getting hungry? I'm getting hungry," she said.

"No. We just ate breakfast."

"I've got to call Kay before she leaves."

I tried to keep control, to remember to honor my mother. I suggested a host of things to get the room cleaned up, all the while struggling to stay polite and calm. "Come on, Ma. We can make a pile of stuff to throw out, and piles of stuff to take to all the other rooms."

Finally, she reached over and started looking in one of the boxes. To my surprise, just when I thought we were making progress, she abruptly got up and left. When I followed her to our other back room, I saw she was carrying a single straight pin, *a single pin*. She opened the drawer of the sewing machine and stuck it into its rightful place in the pincushion. She turned around from the sewing machine, leaned back, and smiled at me with pride.

"Mama, what's wrong with you?" I said. "What is *wrong* with you? Why didn't you just throw that God-damned pin out? We've got a whole God-damned room to clean!"

I heard birds chirping, and thought of my bicycle, the summer, and my friend playing hopscotch. At this rate we'd never get done.

"Watch your language," she finally said. "What will the neighbors think?"

It took me awhile to calm down. I felt guilty for yelling at her.

"OK, Ma. Why don't I sort the stuff and you stay here and tell me what we need to keep?"

We tried that for awhile, but she kept up a steady stream of anxious objections to every decision I made. The ruined paintbrush in the ruined coffee can could be re-soaked, and the ruined can might come in handy. The vinegar bottles could be reused. An annual report of Detroit Edison stock, dusty, yellowing, dated 1949? "You can't throw that out. I haven't read it yet."

"Don't you have the ones from the last few years?" She ignored me.

I didn't feel much empathy for her agonized justifications for keeping eight-inch shards of broken window glass from the winter before last. Especially since the broken glass reminded me of the grim snowball event I prayed to forget.

"I can get Mr. Yost to cut that, and I can use it to frame a picture," she said.

"Which picture?"

"I don't know."

I persisted. "Can't we put the glass in the basement?"

"Who'll carry it down?"

"I will."

I should have known that was the wrong answer, as she started to pant, darted her eyes all over the room, and went on to describe several scenarios of me carrying the jagged glass down the basement stairs, falling and impaling myself.

"How much does glass cost?" I said.

"I don't know, but I'm sure it's expensive."

"How are you going to store it? It's pointy and dangerous."

"Well, just leave it where it is."

"But Ma, we're cleaning up this room."

She looked dazed and surprised, as though I were crazed.

She was going to balk at every suggestion I made, and I'd have to clean the room when she was either gone or busy somewhere else in the house. In fact, the more she resisted, the more determined I became to do it. After all, normalcy was at stake, and I wanted normalcy, if only a sliver of it.

The next day, alone in the room, I had to decide which things were valuable and which were not. What gems resided among the obvious candidates for the monthly bulk trash pickup in the alley? What valuable treasures might my eleven-year-old brain fail to appreciate and value? A dulling white dress box of some unknown person's cancelled stamp collection presented me with one in a series of quandaries that would continue to plague me. If I stayed at my current level of expertise, I could easily throw it out. To me it was worthless. But if I took the time to learn about stamp collecting, which I had no interest in whatsoever, then who knew? Maybe some of these stamps could be sold for hundreds of dollars. But where would I put the box in the meantime?

I started by separating the clearly worthless from the possibly valuable items. Old stock reports, old copies of the *Holy Redeemer Weekly*, old mail, old flyers, old announcements for meetings long past, safety pins, rubber bands, spools of thread, stray curlers and hairpins—if the value was negligible and the stuff looked old in the first place, it could be sacrificed in the interest of getting the job done.

Wilda Korn's old paid electric bills and chatty postcards from strangers—those could be tossed. Much of the other stuff represented what came into the house in any given month. I could have listed each day we had company because these were the cut-off dates for when newspapers and mail of different dates would have been thrown into a box together. If no one showed up for a week or two, or even longer, we filled and propped more Avon boxes in front of the way-back room door before one of us answered the door. The material in the boxes became miniature time-capsule clusters.

There was no telling what I'd find in a given Avon box since the things had never been sorted. Perhaps a rosary—all rosaries were valuable, perhaps a scapular, perhaps a button from the Gaelic League that said *"Erin Go Bragh."* Tiny treasures among the larger stuff, tiny treasures that tended to settle to the bottom of the boxes, along with the grit of just sitting there for months and years. Another tiny button that said, *"I like Ike."* A missing sock from last year that we'd looked all over for. A pair of warm slippers, filthy, but never used. A holy card from somebody's funeral. A broach with shiny rhinestones. A lethal hatpin that jabbed me when I dipped my hand into the box. A metal coffee can of Bingo chips. A telephone number written on a torn scrap of paper in Mama's fat assertive open handwriting. It might be important.

My hands got dry and chapped and dirty. The hair in my nose became a filter like we talked about in science. I blew innumerable strings of black snot into the new hankies I found in a see-through "Merry-Christmas" box. I tasted the dry energy of my fervor.

And then there was the larger stuff, all of it crying for attention. A twisted cotton dress with price tags snaking through sawdust and used sandpaper, a metal file, remains of the Kentucky brothers who had refinished the front stairway. Old squashed hats with torn veils.

Meanwhile, Mama, of course, was not going to leave me alone. She strayed back several times on the first day. As I tossed an old orange silk bathrobe tie into a box full of trash, she erupted in a piercing wail. "Don't! Don't throw that away!"

"Why not?" I said.

"It reminds me of my honeymoon."

Well, not her honeymoon, she explained, but the first year she and Daddy had rented the flat. "I told Omer he shouldn't have bought me that silk robe and pajamas," she said. "We couldn't afford it. It was the Depression."

How was I to know the twisted dirty tie I remembered fingering and using for dress-up as a little kid was something that reminded her of my father?

I tried to be generous. "Why don't you put it in the wash, and then you can put it in a drawer." Even the obvious solution seemed to deflate her. She just stood there, given over to grief, unable to bear anything being moved or put away.

Trembling with rage, I charged around her and dashed to the bathroom before she could stop me. I threw the tie into the hamper. I now understood why Daddy had yelled at her so much. Now the burden of not screaming at her and making her cry fell on me.

To get Mama to relax, I promised to fill boxes with objects that needed her judgment. I could clean during the day and then at night she could review.

I packed the unread stock reports as densely as possible into the trash boxes and covered them with torn newspapers. At least I knew they were worthless since more came every few months. I knew that allowing her to read through hundreds of dull quarterly and annual reports before I could dispose of them would defeat my project. Besides, she'd never read them, just keep them. I started to sneak boxes down the back stairs, across the backyard, to the garage, which had four partitioned stalls.

The stall I chose, to the left of the one for our car, had been old man Dixon's workshop. Though the door had a padlock, it was never locked. The stall was empty, except for a couple of Mrs. Dixon's beautiful antiques—a long mahogany buffet and an oak table. Several of old man Dixon's posters hung on the walls from when he did publicity for the Convention and Tourist Bureau. Three copies of one of them featured pictures of boats and waterfronts and skylines and buildings. *Beautiful and Dynamic Detroit,* it read. *An Ideal Convention City.* I thought fleetingly of Mr. Dixon, who I remembered from when I was very young. I'd come to believe in his importance by all the territory he claimed in and around the property—his workshop in the garage and his office in the way-back room, and the entire first floor of the house.

I didn't like the dishonesty I felt expediency had forced me to adopt. I trembled as I started making more and more secret trips out to the garage in preparation for the big trash collection day in the alley. I barely breathed through the whole trip, sick with worry that Mama would find me, start wailing and stop me. I had become as intent on getting rid of the trash as she was on saving it.

I felt my path to normalcy widen while hoping I could make it to the garage before the neighbors, downstairs or on either side, noticed just how much trash was being carted out of the soon-to-be-normal house to the alley.

Aside from the two antiques in the corner, the floor of the nine-by-sixteen-foot stall was bare and clean. I started stacking boxes at the back, in front of the big swinging doors that faced the alley. I set aside a separate area for large, awkwardly shaped objects that stuck out of the boxes. Upstairs, I kept a few boxes of the most obvious trash, sawdust and spent steel wool, envelopes from old mail, so Mama would be unaware of the more dubious boxes filling the garage.

What if Mama came down into the yard and looked at the window of the garage? To throw her off, I propped a huge box with worthless-looking trash sticking out of it—bent curtain rods, twisted coat hangers and ancient Palm Sunday palms—on the shelf behind the backyard window. I bent and twisted the objects more in order to advertise their worthlessness.

It didn't ease my anxiety any when she took me to task about the obvious trash I'd left upstairs. "Don't throw that sawdust out. We can use it on the sidewalk when it snows."

The worst thing that Mama didn't know was that I'd gotten into old man Dixon's things. Mama had always stressed, from the time she bought the house, that old man Dixon's things were valuable. By the time I got to tearing through his closet, though, I cleaned in a passionate white heat. On the shelves of his huge closet were pictures, many pictures, pictures of people I didn't know and would never know, sepia people in front of downtown buildings or on sailboats on the river, pictures that I knew, if I asked her, Mama would say to keep. There were dozens of little blue cloth notebooks, some used up in old man Dixon's jerky scrawl, some never touched, in mint condition. On each cover was written "Memoranda 1871." Passionless, I tossed most of them out. There were papers, plenty of them, dozens of cardboard magazine boxes full of papers, neatly labeled, one I remember titled "The Catholic Menace." When I looked into them they were full of newspaper clippings and little essays written in old man Dixon's fountain-pen hand. One I examined in detail. I learned that old man Dixon didn't much appreciate President Franklin Roosevelt, even though he'd collected the book about the Rough Riders and the autobiography of the first Roosevelt President, Teddy. Mr. Dixon thought Franklin Roosevelt's programs were ruining the country.

I didn't know much about it. The boxes were neat and organized, but there was nowhere to put them, and Mama had dumped them haphazardly into Avon boxes full of other junk. I became ruthless. I tossed them.

I did save a few of old man Dixon's pretty trinkets—a brass little girl holding up a brass little world, several other filigree statues done in the swirling style I later learned was Art Nouveau, a brass thermometer behind the U.S. Capitol Building, with the engraved inscription, "Capitol Washington D.C." They appealed to me, so I put them in the keep-and-reassign boxes. I also left all his books in place since they were neatly organized though extremely dusty.

*　　　　*　　　　*

In those days, the weekly trash procedures in Detroit still reflected the salvage efforts adopted during the War. Each household tightly packed the organic garbage—potato peels, orange rinds, coffee grounds and fish heads, and all the other food waste—into a paper bag, wrapped the paper bag again in another, and put it in the concrete receptacle at the fence line. The receptacle had a metal spring door that opened in the backyard and another spring door that opened in the alley. The doors sprung back firmly whenever they were let go, and, though we often saw maggots, we rarely saw rats.

We washed the tin cans and other metal containers and set them in a separate pile out at the alley. Anything paper we burned ourselves in a large metal drum with ridges that looked like a giant Campbell soup can without a label. Bottles, old clothing, anything made of fibers—from rags to rugs—as well as useful household items we didn't give to Saint Vincent's charity, we left in another pile for the Sheeny man who came down the alley with his horse-drawn wagon every week. We weren't aware at that time, not even Mama, that the term "Sheeny man" was a derogatory one for a Jew.

I thought about burning all the paper from the way-back room. There was a great amount of it, and I was already burning the household paper and cardboard waste in the alley almost every week. I enjoyed setting the contained fires, standing there after lighting with a kitchen match the paper bags of waxed-cardboard containers and newspapers and watching them burn each time in an original way. Staring into the fire was a good meditation at any time of year, especially in the winter around dusk, with the sun going down. While cleaning out the way-back room, though, I simply didn't have time. Burning would have broken into the rhythm of cleaning and carrying out the boxes.

Although large stacks of boxes, assigned for put-away in other rooms, remained in the way-back room, I was beginning to sweep big areas of the floor. To my delight, the room started to echo.

The Detroit Department of Public Works came once a week. The garbage men scooped the organic material out of the concrete receptacles into wheelbarrows and loaded it on the truck to become compost. They collected the tin cans to be recycled. If we weren't aware of the racial connotations of "Sheeny man," we certainly were aware that black city workers held the dirty garbage jobs. In fact, their presence in the alley was also the only exception to the complete segregation in the neighborhood, and in the weekly rhythm, the old white men who regularly spent a lot of time in the alley, at gossip and garage hobbies, cleared out on garbage day, an accommodation for the time it took to make the trash go away. The garbage men worked in teams. They were efficient, and it didn't take them long. They were fun to watch, and the kids who lived in the Markowicz four-family flat and I would go to the alley gates to listen to their conversations and see the zigzag process getting done.

The only other rubbish service was the monthly bulk-trash collection, and I was ready on the scheduled day. And nervous about Mama. There'd been too many things to sort, too many odd and unexpected things, such as jewelry, among the odd torn rubber overshoes and dead poinsettias. At least to a degree, I regretted not having Mama review more of it. I fretted about the stuff that had belonged to old man Dixon.

In the early morning, I snuck out of the house, quietly swung the big double doors of the third garage stall open from the alley, and started to stack the boxes across our entire property line for pickup. I made sure to keep the big box on the shelf in front of the window, hiding my activities. By the time I got the garage unloaded, the neat stacks of trash were at least three boxes deep and five feet high. With growing excitement I listened to the big garbage truck huffing in the alley of the next block, between Porter and Christiancy. My worry was lifting. The junk was about to be hauled away.

I was about to close the garage doors and duck back into the yard, embarrassed by the amount of trash, when Mama came flying around the gate.

"What are you doing?"

I'd never seen her so alarmed—her eyes darting, her mouth twitching, her forehead bunching into furrows. Even more unbelievable was the lightning speed with which she moved her body. I'd never seen her move so fast. She grabbed boxes and ran them back into the open garage, tears flying across her face. She didn't even take time to scream at me. She lifted boxes and ran, while I watched, humiliated, defeated, and mortified by what the neighbors might see. Particularly Mr. and Mrs. McCarthy, who lived in the yellow asbestos-sided alley house next door. All of the drama was taking place no more than five feet from their kitchen window. To ensure they wouldn't hear, I kept my mouth shut.

Standing there, dumbstruck, I watched the promise of a new uncluttered world—one I suspected existed in every other household, in every other castle in the city—as it crumbled and fell.

By the time the garbage truck got to our garage, Mama had rescued all but five boxes in less than five minutes. One of the garbage men gazed at us dumbfounded. After all, I'm sure he usually saw women in little flowered zipper-front housedresses like Mama's hurrying to get their rubbish out rather than in.

The garage was now a mess—a bounding main of tipping, turning, listing, leaning boxes, with all that had spilled in the fray piled on top, a briny deep of drifting, yawing, sinking and careening boxes, without any partings or paths. Mama closed the big alley doors, went around and closed the door from the backyard, and this time she worked in the padlock and locked it. She went up to Copp's Hardware later in the day and bought another padlock, and locked the alley doors as well. After a year or so she lost both keys among the more than hundred other keys housed in the top buffet drawer.

At a stalemate, she'd saved the junk, which no doubt consoled her, and I'd gotten it out of the way-back room. Yet we each carried our resentments. It all had been too hard for me.

I did follow through on my plan to make the way-back room a clean and livable space. I talked Mama into washing the imitation leather turtle chair. The bucket of Rosenthal cleaner and water turned black in the process, but the chair came out clean. Mama also washed the Venetian blinds, and I found some clean curtains in a drawer to hang in place of the ones caked with filth. I righted the other sticks of furniture and dusted them, brought the old broken 1949 Philco combination radio-record player and a magazine rack back from the living room, and tried to work them into a grouping with the turtle chair. The trouble was that nobody, including me, wanted to sit in the turtle chair and read or pretend the radio worked. When the way-back room still looked barren, I brought the three throw rugs from the living room and scattered them on the shiny waxed pine floor. Mama didn't like that and started a steady stream of nagging about how the bigger living room rug underneath would wear out without the throw rugs on top.

In the end I'm not sure I gained more than I lost through my effort to clean up the way-back room. At least it was clean. There was no reason to hide it. There was no reason to lock it. I was able to throw myself a little twelfth-birthday party, inviting a group of eight girls over to the house without feeling ashamed.

Still, the way-back room, so far beyond the dark hallway, the locked back door, the hallway to the stairway, with its own dark door, seemed too out-of-the-way to live in. As soon as the weather turned fierce, the room became way too cold. Mama persuaded me to bring the throw rugs back to the living room for the winter, and by spring, she was starting to fill up the way-back room again with "just a few" boxes.

Thirty-five years after cleaning out the way-back room, I turned on *Sixty Minutes* one Sunday evening. For the first time, I learned there were other people who behaved like Mama. *Sixty Minutes* was doing a segment on "hoarders," and the interviewees talked about why they had to keep what they were hoarding with the same matter-of-fact, though patently absurd, reasoning Mama used. Their houses, like ours, loomed up around them. Hoarding, the television program informed, was caused either by a compulsive disorder or deep depression. At the time we didn't have a name for it, much less an understanding of it.

It could have been worse. Mama didn't hoard bacteria-laden food or keep a host of messy multiplying animals. When it came to food and bacteria, Mama was scrupulous, never even leaving a spoon in the mayonnaise jar, never leaving dirty dishes to molder on the counter, always wiping the counters after she cut up poultry or fish. If her fridge was a little more crowded than most, and if the kitchen floor was scrubbed ten times less often than the neighbors, she cleaned the fridge and the floor very well when she got to them. She didn't have trouble throwing out moldy peaches she discovered in the recess of a bin.

Mama was also excellent at doing laundry, using her 1934 Maytag ringer washer until her death. She was good at ironing, and she sang love songs while she did it. Still, when it came to cleaning, dusting, vacuuming, making decisions about what to take in to the house and what to throw out, where to put things so that we could use them, she had a disorder as serious as any of the hoarders featured on *Sixty Minutes*.

Actually Mama suffered greatly because of her disorder. She bore horrendous criticism from her sisters and anger from my very organized, frustrated father. She lost her older daughter, in part because of her hoarding. She bore the bossy tough love of the likes of me, trying to deliver us from the repercussions of her compulsion. She hid most of the house from visitors. She knew she was different. "I can't seem to keep a clean house," she often said and hung her head in shame.

What did it do to me, knowing that to get anything done I'd have to lie to her or defy her? Those piercing wails of hers—almost in tone on the level of one shouting, "Fire!"—those predictable piercing admonitions, "Don't use too much!" "Turn out that light!" "Don't drop it!" "Don't spill it!" "Be careful!" the high-pitched accompaniment to so many of my actions that so damaged my self esteem. Those fears—of letting anything go, of even the smallest change, of even the smallest initiative of another—they were terrors she couldn't control, hiccups without logic. Even when she hid her fears under the mantle of virtue—thrift and "waste-not-want-not." It was nothing personal. It wouldn't have made it better to know her condition had a name because she couldn't have changed it. Mama felt her fears, but she hid the source of them from herself.

Even though Mama agonized most of her life, saying she wanted a clean house, she never really enjoyed it when it was clean. When I cleaned it, she could allow herself to admire the job I had done, but only for an instant. After that, her worry and anxiety returned. She would long again for the stock reports, the dated coupons, even the sawdust.

CHAPTER THIRTEEN
LOVE ME TENDER

When I lost my baby, I almost lost my mind... Pat Boone croons with a voice almost as smooth as Bing Crosby's. Again I've changed the living room and dining room furniture around. Mama is still downstairs washing. She'll review the rooms when she comes up, hungry for lunch, and she'll interrogate me about what I did with the smaller things—the magazine rack, the morning's mail, her purse, her coat, the hassock—anything she can't immediately see. I know exactly what she'll say. I know what she'll complain about in the new arrangement, and I know what I'll answer. I'll show her that although everything has changed, nothing is lost.

I've set the record player on repeat. *When I lost my baby, I almost lost my mind.* I stand here and there, checking out the new views in the rooms from each of their corners, adjust the setting of a chair or lamp or doily, see my work is good, see the cool blue autumn sky and golden leaves in the park through the front windows. The song plays again. I've earned the pleasure I take in the rooms, having worked to make them beautiful. My pleasure in the song that has accompanied me throughout my work is more than I have earned. It mystifies me, sensual and cathartic. At times like this, nothing is wrong with my life. Absolutely nothing.

Diane Porter and I used to walk the six blocks from her house on McKinstry near Lafayette up to the record store on Fort Street between Junction and Campbell. Diane was a tiny, dark-haired, skinny girl I'd met in Sister Frederick Marie's sixth grade, probably the shyest and least talkative girl I knew. She blushed and looked down and sideways whenever anybody looked too directly in her eyes. Still, she was adventurous in her quiet way. As implausible as it seemed for such a skinny girl, she'd already gotten her period. We didn't talk about it, of course, but she asked for Modess sanitary napkins at Cunningham's on one of our first trips up on Fort Street.

Fort Street thrived as a commercial strip, the whole ten blocks between Clark Street and Livernois, offering necessities and diversions to accommodate the wants of almost everyone: bowling alleys; movie theaters; bars and more bars; stage and show bars; large and small restaurants; furniture and appliance stores; beauty and barber shops; dress shops; men's shops; shoe shops; hat shops and jewelry stores; hardware, paint and wallpaper stores; pet shops; candy stores; large and small grocery stores. There were even two Chinese laundries. Fort Street surpassed Vernor Highway by a long shot, rivaling Michigan Avenue, but closer, more upscale and faster-paced.

We often headed for the two block strip past Junction to look at pretty things in store windows—ballerina skirts, angora sweaters, and high-heeled shoes. Our main destination though, besides the record store, was Cunningham Drugs, for inside were the magazine racks with the teen magazines. Two Cunninghams stood a block apart, one at Junction and one at Campbell, and we always stopped at both stores, spending hours at the magazine racks, browsing *Teen Magazine, Movie Stars, Modern Teen, Teen Idol, Hep Cats, Dig,* and *16 Magazine.* We could buy the magazines for fifteen to twenty-five cents an issue, but we didn't make fast decisions. After we wore out our welcome while standing reading at one store, we left and walked to the other store, discussing on the way if any issue was worth buying. We eventually chose an unread copy from the back of the stack, in pristine condition.

Pat Boone and Elvis seemed to be in a contest. That's the way the magazines presented it. But Diane and I already had it sorted out. Diane had a crush on Pat Boone and joined the Pat Boone Fan Club. That suited me fine because, from "I Want You, I Need You, I Love You" on, my heart, my mind, my body, every strange ungainly part of it, all of whatever it would become, was pledged to Elvis. Diane, the wispy delicate girl, made a perfect match for the gentle Boone. I thought I was nervier (though I wasn't) and so I made a better mate for the rougher, rawer, tougher Elvis. Diane and I, at least, wouldn't be in any contest. It's surprising how I thought we settled it—as though there weren't a million other girls in the running. I suppose I needed to believe it.

Diane needed to believe in Pat when Pat Boone and Elvis traded places for number one hits. In midsummer, Pat's "I Almost Lost My Mind" hit number one; then Elvis hit number one with "I Want You, I Need You, I Love You." In late summer, Elvis leaped ahead with "Don't Be Cruel" and "Hound Dog." Pat countered with "Friendly Persuasion" in early fall, and Elvis sprinted ahead again with "Love Me Tender" in November. We picked up the list of Billboard hits at the record store. We listened to them played on the radio in reverse order on Casey Kasem's and Mickey Shorr's nightly programs. If we liked them enough, we bought the records and listened to them again and again *ad delirium.*

I appreciated Pat Boone. He had a beautiful voice. He was handsome. He was a direct descendent of one of my old heroes, Daniel Boone. It helped that I could appreciate him because then I could analyze why I adored Elvis so much more. Pat Boone, it seemed to me, was dry, with his clean almost neutral airy good looks. Elvis, who lived on the bluesy, watery side of the state of Tennessee, was juicy. With his sweating energy, dark black, dripping oiled hair, full moist lips, crooked smile, turned down mouth and slurred phrasing, Elvis was a little dirty. Bad. Imperfect. A little self-conscious. Wild.

By early September, the first time I saw Elvis on *Ed Sullivan* and bought "Heartbreak Hotel," I was crazy about him. The sheer mention of his name made my heart faint. When I heard his voice, with his insinuating sprawling phrasing, and with his extra little rhythmic asides, the underside of me became so heavy that I had to sit down. I had no precise name for the feeling, but it was as clear as any I'd ever felt. In a bold, daring move of utter fantasy, I devoted myself to Elvis. Perhaps I could become the woman he wanted.

I knew what he wanted because someone on the staff of *16 Magazine* had interviewed Elvis, and he told them who he was looking for. His ideal woman would be 5'4", which at the time was my exact height. I would have to meet him soon because I was still growing. His ideal woman would have brown eyes. Perhaps I could get him to love green eyes. She'd be warm and tender, domestic, fun-loving and girly, and she'd have a good sense of humor. That was me exactly, or at least it could be, warm, tender, domestic, fun-loving, and eager to expand my sense of humor. I didn't know about being "girly." I had no patience with girls who laughed and rolled their eyes and asked a lot of stupid questions. I could probably explain that to Elvis.

I bought a lot of movie magazines where every week more stories and pictures of Elvis appeared. I started cutting out pictures. So many pictures. The ones I loved best showed him doing normal things: Elvis at the barber shop, Elvis on the telephone, Elvis alone in the picture puckering up his lips, Elvis at a carnival throwing softballs at a row of ducks, Elvis in a motel room lying in a bed with his shirt off, with the caption "Touring is the hardest." Elvis with his shirt off, lounging on top of or underneath the covers of many beds. Elvis with his shirt off, reaching for a bath towel his stout adoring mother is handing him from around a bathroom door that hides the rest of him. Elvis looking right at me, with his folded arms resting on a table … with his shirt off. The Elvis profiles—the noble brow, the shaded downward turning eyes, the straight perfect nose, and the sensuous beyond sensuous lips.

I was discerning. I didn't particularly enjoy some of the usual photographs—Elvis gyrating knock-kneed with his ankles splayed, Elvis signing autographs or playing to the crowd. I didn't like any of the still photographs of Elvis performing. They always seemed to catch him in an awkward position. For some strange reason, I worried about Elvis each time he performed on *Ed Sullivan*. Though he always laughed at himself a little, I could tell he was nervous. I wanted the song to be done, for Elvis to leave the stage, for Elvis to come to me waiting in the wings.

"How'd I do, Mary?"

"You were wonderful."

I judged each picture on its quality. I wanted Elvis to be shown in his best light. I loved the pouting pictures of Elvis best, Elvis with his full-hearted closed lips; pensive, simmering Elvis, looking off, looking aside; thinking, contemplating, longing Elvis, longing perhaps, although he didn't know it yet, for the girl of his dreams who might be me. It didn't matter if the fantasy was far-fetched. I invented all sorts of ways around the implausibility—most easily by ignoring who I was, what I looked like, how old I was, how awkward and inexperienced, how Catholic and protected, how far away. It could happen. Anything could happen.

When I look back at my fantasies about Elvis, I see they revealed more about me than Elvis. At first I fantasized being Elvis's sister—not because I was afraid of committing a sin by having thoughts of a sexual nature, but because it was safer. Besides, I imagined so many things we'd do together, and hardly any of them besides kissing were sexual. Being Elvis's sister was easy to imagine, and all I needed to do to fuel the fantasy was to keep reading about what he was doing and what he liked to do. I'd be his sister. With me around he'd be less lonely. After all, his twin had died at birth. He was an only child, pretty much like me. We'd laugh and play jokes on each other, and I'd be a steady source of support as fame catapulted my big brother even higher and higher into the sky of stardom. Elvis would grin and roughhouse with me. There'd be a lot of touching. There'd be the warmth of his body. And then the fantasy would turn to where my body started feeling good. I wasn't sure if I was still his sister. I'd halt the fantasy, say a quick prayer, "Please, dear God, don't let me think bad thoughts." Then I'd construct a fantasy of Elvis and me getting married.

It wasn't so difficult to fantasize, "El" and I getting married. Even if it was more difficult to supply a plausible fantasy of how we'd meet. The actual wedding scene was easiest of all. Elvis seemed thrilled to be marrying me at Holy Redeemer. He enjoyed visiting Detroit and the Southern bars on Vernor Highway, and, on his arm, I'd see the inside of the bars for the first time. In a completely unrehearsed and unplanned expression of joy, Elvis was moved to sing for free. I knew we'd have to get married in the sacristy, and not before the altar, because he wasn't and was never going to become Catholic. That was OK with me, although I was sure it would disappoint my classmates who would have loved to be invited to the big wedding. Though the wedding was small, I wore the most beautiful lace gown, yet the girl in that gown, who was clearly me, didn't look much like me. She was a beauty.

When I started sleeping, holding an extra pillow to my breast and thinking of it as warm Elvis, I was grateful we'd gotten married.

Only a year before my dresser looked like an altar, crowded with candles, and flowers and vials of Holy Water, the statue of Our Lady on her raised dais in the center, and statues of saints and angels, at least six of them by then turned to look her way. In early November, at the same time I was gazing at the bleached-out, sepia portrait of Elvis on the record jacket of "Love Me Tender" and listening over and over to the RCA reissue of the Sun recording, "Blue Moon," I decided that Our Lady should be somewhere where She could bless the entire household. So I took Her out of my bedroom, along with faithful Saint Theresa, and wrapped the rest of the saints in tissue paper to store in the front closet. Our Lady without her platform now stood centered on top of the high bookcase in the hall, with Saint Theresa in attendance in the corner. It offered a different perspective for the statues, and, to tell the truth, it was easier to ignore them when they were high above my line of vision. I wasn't exactly conscious of my shifting devotion, or perhaps I didn't want to be. After all, I would have found it an impossible confliction to make a choice between Elvis and Our Lady.

With Our Lady gone, I now had my room clear for Elvis. I joined the Elvis Fan Club, started sending away for Elvis buttons and 8"x10" glossy photographs, and continued clipping the action photos from the magazines. Up at Kresge's I bought three different 6" x 8" plastic-framed portraits signed, "Best wishes, Elvis Presley" in his own hand, an embossed mirror, an Elvis comb and brush set, and an Elvis charm bracelet. A little later I bought a thick ribbed plastic 3-D 8" x 10" portrait that showed two different Elvises, depending on which way you looked at it. I could stand with my feet apart, rock back and forth, and see Elvis pouting and then smiling. That portrait quickly lost its charm.

I didn't exactly make my dresser a shrine—at least not in the beginning. I had little "girly" things scattered on it as well—a pretty blue plastic box for safety pins and extra buttons, a milk-glass bottle of apple blossom toilet water I'd recovered from the way-back room, and the gold and black vanity mirror and hairbrush with the letter "R" that Daddy had given Mama some time before my sister and I were born. In a locked, carved, cedar souvenir box from Cumberland Gap, Tennessee, I housed my bicycle registration and a deliberate assortment of symbolic things from childhood: my First Communion prayer book, a rubber-banded stack of my best holy cards, an Indian arrowhead from Tennessee, and an embossed metal badge I'd bought off a cereal box that certified I owned a square inch of the Yukon Territory.

Still, the dresser attracted more and more Elvis relics—the several Elvis buttons pinned to a wide blue ribbon I tied on the mirror frame to accompany Daddy's powder horn. The framed Elvis portraits came with cardboard wings on the back that opened to prop them up on the dresser. My favorite was a soulful publicity shot from the film *Love Me Tender*. That's what it said, with Elvis in the portrait seeming to mouth the words, "Love me tender." At night, I sometimes kissed the portrait, a sign I would love him tender. One of the other portraits, Elvis sitting at the edge of a swimming pool in a red and white hound's-tooth wool jacket, included a wide white plastic frame with gold lettering, a treble clef and scattered eighth and quarter notes, guitars and hearts. I probably should have taken that one back to the dime store since its cardboard wing to keep it upright kept closing. When that happened, the portrait fell over, and then all the others fell over in domino effect. When I wasn't kissing them, I spent a lot of time repositioning them.

Gray patterned wallpaper draped my bedroom walls—one of those rose-bouquet designs roped by braided borders on each side that produced a vertical stripe. Against Mama's protestations—"You're going to ruin the wallpaper"—I Scotch-taped glossy pictures over the wallpaper on the walls. I then added the intimate extra pictures from the teen magazines. It wasn't long before at least three rows of Elvises at portrait level spanned the entire room. By Christmas, there were more. I counted them: seventy-eight beautiful, mostly glossy, pictures of Elvis.

In January 1957, Mama's friend Smitty told Mama that Elvis was coming to Detroit. Since Smitty knew I loved Elvis, she asked Mama if I would want to accompany her daughters, Norma and Linda, and their friends to Olympia Stadium on Sunday, March 31. Norma and Linda loved Elvis, too, but they were older than I by three and four years, and, though I didn't regularly socialize with them, Smitty always watched out for me. Of course I wanted to go.

She got tickets for the six-o'clock evening show. On the afternoon of the concert, I spent an hour deciding what to wear, changing into two or three different outfits. The weather was cold and gloomy, and as the afternoon progressed it started to drizzle. I knew it didn't matter in any personal way what I wore—it wasn't like the dreamed-of "date with Elvis" the magazines described. It was more about not knowing what to expect. I'd never been to a rock 'n' roll concert. I decided to go middle of the road. I wore my high-collared white blouse with the bow tie and my black and white checkered flared taffeta skirt. What to do with my feet was always a problem, but I had to pour them into some shoes, so I wore my white socks cuffed over three times with my brown penny loafers. It was cold, so I wore my shortie wool coat.

Mama drove all five of us girls to Olympia Stadium in our frowning, fish-mouthed, 1948 maroon Buick with the visor. As I remember, Mama was in a fine humor, laughing with all of the love-struck girls in her charge. As we got near to Olympia, we ran into so much traffic that she dropped us off three blocks away on the other side of Grand River. "Now, do you all have bus fare to get back home?" We did. "Have fun," she said.

After we'd piled out of the back seat of the Buick and stood on the wet sidewalk, we could see the lights of the Olympia marquee shining through the foggy evening, see the long rectangle of the huge red brick edifice that went back for what seemed like miles on McGraw, and see the throngs of girls, most of them in flared skirts and flared wool shortie jackets, waiting in the slow moving lines to get in. Norma, the oldest, shepherded me along as we joined more teenaged girls, hundreds of them, making their way to the stadium across the dark wet pavement of Grand River. I knew I was one of the youngest, and I felt like the luckiest girl alive.

Olympia Stadium was a perfect place to see the Detroit Red Wings play hockey. It wasn't much of a concert hall, at least not a normal concert hall like Masonic Temple, where Aunt Marie had taken me to see the opera. The seats rose up around the huge rectangular floor at a steep angle. The stage, with so many wires, was set up at the far end. We had balcony seats on the opposite end. I don't remember who played warm-up in this All-Star Show. I wouldn't have remembered at the time. It didn't matter because the time it took them to perform was only a torment. Elvis would be coming next.

The gold lamé suit. Elvis bounded out on stage in his gold lamé suit. I hadn't even considered what I would do. I probably had some private impossible fantasy going on. I probably thought I'd be keeping it to myself. None of it mattered. Along with a crowd of twelve thousand other girls with spit curls, crisp blouses or angora sweaters, I started to scream. Elvis was so far away he looked like a three-inch flashing metallic cartoon. It didn't matter. It was the way he moved. The unexpected ripples of wiggles that followed the patient moments of standing still. The screams came from deep inside me. The tears welled up and slid down my lightly made-up face. There was no stopping them. "Oh, my God! Oh, my God!"

A woman, the only adult I saw for rows and rows around, sat directly in front of me, with a girl and a boy about my age on each side of her. With the incline so steep I could see right into their laps. I'd noticed them from the beginning, and I felt sorry for the kids. The mother was an embarrassment. She sat there as though she were attending a school recital, clapping politely after every song, getting her kids to do the same, as though there were spaces between the songs. There were no spaces, no spaces whatsoever, between the songs. There was Elvis moving, moving fast and gyrating in synchronization to the jungle beat, or Elvis moving slowly, flipping back his raven hair, pausing, leaning into the mike, cupping it tenderly in a loving hand connected to a loving arm attached to a loving warm masculine slightly-muscled shoulder. Oh, there were no spaces between the songs. After about five songs the woman turned around and politely got my attention and said, "Could you wait until the end of the song to scream?"

I didn't know what to say. I pretended I didn't hear her, which was plausible, given the noise. I did feel a passing breeze of my old superstition. In a stadium full of twelve thousand screaming, sobbing, normal teenaged girls whose lives were being transformed forever, why did it happen to me that the only old fogey in the house sat right in front of me and requested that I be abnormal? Was she an agent of God or the devil or just my jinx? Besides, it wasn't possible. I did try to scream a little softer as Elvis ranged like a male lion in his flashy gold lamé suit with his guitar in hand around the center area of the stage, but only for a second. The screams were surging waves crashing up upon a shore, and I was powerless to stop them. I forgot all about the lady in front of me. Tears and more tears, a bucket full of tears, streamed down my face. I'd forgotten to bring a hanky, but there was no need to stop them as the concert grew even more intense.

And then it was over. Elvis was taken away, and twelve thousand girls (and a mere handful of boys) were left with nothing more to do than leave the stadium. I never felt such grief. As we filed out, I glanced at what everybody was wearing. Most of us wore nearly the same thing. I looked at the most attractive girls. They happened to be a bit tougher than the rest of us, and certainly a lot tougher than any of the girls at Holy Redeemer. They wore tight Levis and tight angora sweaters with little scarves around their necks. You could see their bra seams through their sweaters. They swaggered a little. They'd tweezed their eyebrows, and they weren't weeping quite as hard. They looked a little jauntier, freer and sexier than the girls I knew. They seemed to imitate the free easy way of Elvis.

Collectively, and then specifically, they looked a little more Southern. I could hear it when groups of them started to talk as the raw wet air hit us when we finally made it out the door, and when they pulled Parliaments from their purses and lit up as droves of us moved toward the bus stop. We girls crowded into a Clairmount bus, which at first was standing room only. After a few blocks, a large group of girls got off, and I moved to sit down. Just as I was doing so, the bus lurched and I sat down hard. One of those most attractive Southern girls turned to one of her friends and pointed at me with even wry irony. "Look at that ass fall."

I was crushed, although I didn't show it. Not only had I been wrenched from the most transcendent moment of my life—being in the same room, albeit a big room, with Elvis—but somebody was calling attention to the fact that I had a fat, ungraceful, unworthy, and singularly untranscendent posterior. She and her friends stayed on the bus after we got off at Vernor, probably going on down to Fort Street. I wished I didn't have such a big fat rump, wished I wasn't such an impossibly ugly girl who never knew what to do, wished I hadn't called attention to myself, wished I wasn't so young and earnest and awkward. And I wished I hadn't lost the only lifeline out of that reality, which was my connection to Elvis Aaron Presley, my Elvis, who was probably on the way to the airport or on a bus to the next city at this very moment.

The next afternoon when I got home from school, Mama brightly read me the story on the front page of the *Detroit News*. *Elvis Presley fans— 24,000 strong and all screaming—smashed the sound barrier twice yesterday at Olympia.*

I wasn't all that interested. I was still grieving in the sober light of the afternoon. I didn't know when, if ever, I'd see Elvis again. Somehow I'd grown keenly aware that all my fantasies were impossible lies. Elvis would never know me, never love me.

That didn't stop Mama, who seemed to be particularly amused. On she read, *The kids were whipped to a frenzy of anticipation by the preliminary rock 'n' roll variety show, but it was the main event—Elvis himself—that drove the teen-age audience to a peak performance in participation that was even more startling than the show itself…. His fans shrieked, sobbed, moaned and writhed in their seats, the noise reaching deafening crescendos with each intonation of the palpitating Presley voice. Only occasionally could his songs be heard and recognized. But sing, stomp, stagger and strum he did for a perspiring forty minutes. And when he got around to his closing number, "You Ain't Nothin' but a Houn' Dog," the ultimate in acoustical terrors was achieved. Hearing became a liability for uninitiated oldsters.*

Why were they writing about uninitiated oldsters? There was only one oldster I saw last night anyway, and that was that old bag in front of me. "Ma, that's enough," I said. "I don't want to hear any more."

Mama shut up for a moment, letting her amused eyes and upturned mouth readjust to the next page. It was a sunny Monday and the light, streaming in through the voile curtains, captured her profile. She continued to read, and most of what she read I already knew. Elvis wasn't going to ask for any special favors when he joined the Army. Elvis wasn't thinking of getting married. Elvis would be willing to go on TV with what the paper called his "crooning rival," Pat Boone. Elvis owned eight automobiles and was building a colonial-style Southern mansion. Elvis's suit cost $2,500. Well Mama was learning something from reading.

Finally, though, at the very end of the article, she struck a chord. *No one can quite explain his success—not even his most avid fans. An enraptured teenager, wearing an "Elvis for President" button, was asked—between sobs and screams—the question. "I don't know—and I don't care," she shrieked. "He's just wonderful. It's the way he does it.... I just can't explain it."*

Finally, somebody said it, I thought with a sigh. Elvis was wonderful. He was just wonderful. I looked at all the pictures on the back page. There was a girl who looked like me, although I knew that it wasn't. The reporter had interviewed girls at the matinee.

In March of 1958, I participated in the public grieving when all the teen magazines showed pensive Elvis in a barber chair with beautiful ebony locks strewn all over a striped barber gown. I, too, cooed about his patriotism when I saw the picture of him taking the Army Oath of Enlistment, and I, too, swore that I'd be true.

But somehow, the state of my bedroom gave away my infidelity. A week or so later I decided I'd had enough of the depressing wallpaper. If I'd learned how to paint a couple years before, I could paint again. And if I'd read *Tom Sawyer*, I could also trick my friends into a wallpaper peeling party, which I held during Easter vacation.

Before we started, I took down all seventy-eight pictures of Elvis, cut off any protruding Scotch tape, and put them in manila folders for safekeeping while I painted the room light green. When it came time to put the pictures back, I hung only four of them, this time with picture hooks, all glossy naked-chested framed pictures of Elvis, one on each wall. It looked less cluttered than it had before, and with the pictures rigidly centered in the middle of each wall, the two Elvises looking directly at another Elvis, it was certainly more formal and less haphazard. I examined my conscience about it because it seemed to me that fewer pictures, even if they were the nicest, seemed to mean less devotion. "Now, look at yourself, Mary. Do you love Elvis just as much?" "Yes I do. Of course I do," I answered. "It just looks better with only four." Still, in my heart of hearts I knew. I was cooling. I wasn't waiting. I had a cheating heart.

CHAPTER FOURTEEN
ANOTHER SIDE OF MAMA

During my junior high school years, Mama and I arrived at an undeclared truce regarding the house. Every Saturday, almost without fail, while she was in the basement washing, or in the yard hanging out the clothes, I cleaned the living room and dining room. Whatever clutter she left there that couldn't be crammed into the buffet drawers, or stacked on top of the china cabinet, I placed in Avon boxes. Then I carried them to the back bedroom, where I piled them on her bed where she couldn't fail to notice.

Her territory included the kitchen, her bedroom, the way-back room which she'd reclaimed, and the back hallway. The bathroom remained contested because of its generous size. I cleaned the tub, toilet and sink, and the floor around them, but she managed to stow many boxes of disparate objects in mounds on the opposite wall. I urged her to drape the mounds with attractive bedspreads—a blue brocade, and a yellow chenille. When she couldn't keep the mounds covered, I ran and repositioned the bedspreads when the doorbell rang, just in case any of our guests needed to use the bathroom. If the boxes were covered, I reasoned, someone might assume they contained something important.

The arrangement worked as well as could be expected, and, in retrospect at least, I see that the strange layout in the flat was perfect if one of its residents was a hoarder. It was relatively easy to hide the back rooms, especially when we closed the door off the dining room that led to the long crooked hallway. In the meantime I made dramatic furniture arrangements in the sparkling clean front room with the generous light pouring in through the large windows that framed the lovely park. Thus, Mama and I avoided many show-downs, and I could get on with my teenage life.

I grew to see another side of Mama—who seemed to be getting better, singing more often, telling more stories, finding more to do with others, and rendering her observations with funny wry comments. Mama definitely had her times when she felt secure and showed her best side.

In summers our flat was often unbearably hot, especially after Mama's handyman Ray had painted most of the windows shut. We couldn't generate a cross breeze, and, although everyone else owned a window fan by now, Mama wouldn't buy one. We sat out on the front porch glider, swinging and talking, often past midnight and into the wee hours of morning.

The heat inside the house stoked the intensity of our conversations on the porch. We no longer considered anything inside urgent enough to interrupt our nightly vigils. TV in rerun season, my books, and Mama's newspapers all melted away in the heat. The air sucked the breath out of us whenever either of us ventured from the porch to go to the bathroom or braved the heat in the kitchen for a drink of water. We both hurried back to the porch where it was cool, where the giant elm tree near the street, with its branches outspread, caught even the subtle breezes.

We viewed people's rituals on the sidewalk below. We could monitor the time on Monday and Thursday evenings by watching Mrs. Hofler tread home at nine-thirty, rain or shine, from each new movie showing at the Stratford Theater. We figured she held the best collection of dishes the Stratford gave away of anybody in the neighborhood. We could monitor the time every evening when her husband, Mr. Hofler, staggered home drunk at eleven, rain or shine. After midnight, Anita Gardner clicked by in her high heels as she stomped back from the Fort Street bus stop after working the afternoon shift as a waitress downtown at the Brass Rail. Mama always wondered, "How can she work in those shoes?" When we sat out on the porch, we watched Anita with her brisk no-nonsense stride. During the winter we heard her high heels from a warm bed of slumber. I awoke to notice it. "Ah, Anita is coming home. All is well." Then I went back to sleep.

As the evening progressed into night, the street and the dark park across the street fell still as the metal of the glider cooled. Our voices slowed and turned to murmurs, and, in this quiet, I heard every word Mama said. These were the times when Mama disclosed the things about herself she'd learned to hide from her sisters. These were the times when Mama shed her fears and uncertainties to reveal a Mama unafraid and smart, a rare, beautiful and essential Mama, one I could follow.

We had our own ritual. After dinner, whatever boring thing it was—the overdone round steak, the hamburgers, the pork chops, the Friday creamed tuna, the ubiquitous potatoes—and after she gave up on getting me to help with the dishes, she sent me up to Polo's Market on Vernor. When I returned with the pint block of ice cream, she'd already settled in on the glider.

I always bought only one pint. While many of our neighbors owned brand new dual-door refrigerators with separate freezers and compartments for beverages and condiments in the lower door, we nursed our second-hand pre-War fridge equipped with only one tiny compartment that froze two trays of ice cubes and nothing more. I usually bought the flavors she liked best—French vanilla or butter pecan. Whenever I bought a flavor I liked better—anything mixed up, textured and surprising—chocolate ripple, heavenly hash, or butterscotch swirl, she said the same thing, "Why did you buy that stuff? You know they make that hash out of all the flavors they don't sell." Her mouth turned down and her green eyes became doleful as though I'd broken a promise. I imagined her longing for that first bite of

French vanilla—it must be French vanilla, no other vanilla would do—all the while I'd been gone.

All ice cream was good, I reasoned. Butter pecan and French vanilla delighted her so much that I could be generous about it. If there was a Tigers game on, we tuned it in on my transistor radio. If there wasn't a game, we started talking right away. The routine was simple: I asked questions, and she answered.

On the porch at night Mama communicated a storehouse of knowledge she often hid in public out of modesty. She understood the workings of government, the history of the city, chemical and biological processes—from the making of steel to the growth of microbes in mayonnaise. Freely sharing it with me, Mama taught me the system behind the talent she didn't hide—her abundant vocabulary, apparent to everybody. She told me countless stories of her own life and the life of her family, answered thousands of my questions, and, in anticipation of my studying it in high school, taught me the rudiments of Latin.

On the porch Mama told me about her childhood before her family left their farm on Miller Road on the Rouge River, about hanging from a tire tied to a willow and jumping off to swim. Her family worked hard—she and the others starting to pull weeds when they were only three. Her German father hung a horsewhip in the barn, and he worked and worked her older brothers with the horsewhip as a threat.

She told me about her mother, how busy she was with the farm and ten kids. She didn't take any sass. "She'd throw a wet dishrag in your face if she even thought you were giving her any lip." I figured my grandmother couldn't have carried a dishrag with her everywhere. It wasn't like a horsewhip hung in the barn. Mama was remembering an act of rage against her. Her face in the streetlight let me know that it was true. She slowed down. A look of surprise crossed her face. And then a look of hurt.

I wanted her to tell me—to let it out, the hurt. But she didn't. I had never heard her say anything even vaguely negative about her mother. She continued on in a positive vein with the family story.

My grandmother drove the horse-drawn wagon to Western Market on Michigan Avenue every Saturday. If she didn't sell all her produce at the market, she drove up and down the streets, even Clark Street, to sell her beets, carrots and potatoes for less before she turned toward home. She always returned home with an empty wagon. Sometimes Mama accompanied her mother, and she remembered seeing Clark Park as a little girl. The park in those days, Mama said, was contained inside a ring of well-maintained shrubs and bushes that spanned most of the entire perimeter.

Mama recalled my Uncle Pete, one of the few younger than Mama, as a little boy crying every Saturday after my grandmother left for market. Every Saturday the older sisters locked him in the closet as punishment for crying, where he banged and screamed for hours until he fell asleep, draped against the door. When they opened the door, his little body rolled out into the room.

Mama talked about my grandfather selling the farm to a man who turned out to be an agent of Henry Ford's. Five other farms on Miller Road were sold to different men, and once the transactions were completed, the land was immediately turned over to Henry Ford. My grandfather's farm became the site of the Ford-Rouge plant.

Before the family moved to their new house in Wyandotte, Henry Ford arrived unexpectedly to inspect my grandparents' farmhouse. Henry Ford saw Mama, who was ten years old at the time, along with Aunt Marie and Aunt Kay, washing dishes. He reached into his pocket, pulled out three silver dollars, and handed one to each of the girls. "You are good girls," he said, approving their industry. Mama quoted wryly, and we lapsed off into a discussion of Henry Ford and his views on workers. She wasn't a big fan of Henry Ford.

The sturdy well-kept farmhouse of my grandfather remained standing to became the first infirmary for the Ford-Rouge plant. My grandfather got good money for the farm, although, Mama explained, he might have haggled on the price, had he known he was selling the land to build the great factory. Still, the money allowed my grandfather to build a huge brick house on the Detroit River in Wyandotte, invest the extra money, and retire at age forty-seven.

Mama talked about the first year they lived in the big house in Wyandotte. Her favorite older brother George died of typhoid in 1917, only days before Mama, too, was expected to die. She remembered hearing her mother tell her father, "Cod, I don't think she'll last the night." They called in another doctor at the last minute, Dr. Berdineau, who demanded they plunge her into a tub of ice water to bring down the fever. She remembered part of it, floating in and out of delirium. The fever broke. She lost a lot of hair and had to learn how to walk all over again.

I suspect having typhoid colored her outlook on life. Instead of telling the story as though she'd triumphed, she told it as though she'd cheated death. She seemed stuck in the misfortune, as though she was still in the room with death, as though her beloved brother George was calling out to her, "Verna, come with me." Mama had more than an acquaintanceship with death. They seemed to be on intimate terms.

She was a girl of eleven at the time, and she insisted the typhoid was the cause of her small breasts. She always felt sad about what she thought were her small breasts—"underdeveloped" she called them. "One time your father told me my breasts were beautiful anyway," she said, with a fleeting smile

Most of the time, though, when she talked about her body, she became sad, some struggle with shame seeming to go on in her head. "Marie and Delores, they have good-sized breasts," she said. No one in her childhood had encouraged her to love her body. And no one it seemed had ever pointed out that she was a lot prettier than the large-breasted sisters who kept up the steady stream of criticisms about her small breasts and big feet, about her slow ways and lack of grace. Something terrible had happened to Mama, probably something not so dramatic, but steady, steady like her younger brother being locked in the closet, and by the same older sisters. Without my father to shore her up, she couldn't see much to love about herself.

Mama told me stories about the river, about the North End of Wyandotte, about ice-skating on Ecorse Creek. One time Mama and four of her friends almost drowned when their wooden ice raft with blades and a sail suddenly picked up steam in a gust of wind. Heading down to the mouth of the creek toward the open water, she and the other kids jumped off just in time. They lost the raft that sailed into the deep waters and strong currents of the Detroit River. "We were probably out there too late in the season, anyway. You know you've got to watch the river. It thaws quicker downriver than it does up here."

Mama's father drowned in the river when she was only fifteen. He fell off a boat into the shallow waters in back of their house, came up and hit his head on the underside of the dock. The story sounded implausible. How could he hit his head so hard in only four feet of water? He'd been with two of his fishing buddies.

"Was he drunk?" I said.

She darted her eyes. "I don't think so."

I tried to check the story with some of her other sisters.

"Aunt Marie, had your father been drinking the night he got drowned?"

Aunt Marie cast a furious look in my face, raised her head, snorted, and clammed up. I think he was drunk, but I don't know how often he was drunk. I asked Aunt Mag a little more tactfully, but she also clammed up. I never asked any of the others.

I don't know if my grandfather was an habitual drinker. Years later, though, I realized a tragedy in his story. Mama had mentioned that the cause of the typhoid outbreak in the home that killed one and nearly killed another of his children was judged to be contamination from him digging his well too close to the river. He would have had something powerful to grieve about.

Mama liked to tell about how she was one of the smartest girls in her class at Saint Patrick's High School in Wyandotte. She was Sister Eunice's pet, and in her senior year in 1924, Sister Mary George had called her aside and suggested, "You might want to consider going to college." Mama, of course, knew college was out of the question. She was a girl. "Besides," she said, "I didn't want to wait that long to start earning money."

Instead she enrolled in comptometer training school and, once she finished, was hired right away at Cadillac in the Payroll Department where she earned a perfect record for all paydays. After inserting cash in twenty-dollar-bill increments into hundreds of pay envelopes, her accounts balanced on the first run every time. The operators were required to stay until their accounts balanced. Mama pranced out of the office early every afternoon before payday.

On so many of those long summer nights, when she wasn't telling me stories, or I wasn't trying to get her to see objects and constellations in between the branches and the leaves of the elm tree, Mama spoke to me about Latin.

"The nouns in Latin are different at the end, depending on how you use them in a sentence. There are different cases—nominative, genitive, dative, accusative and ablative." She started to explain, but then it got too difficult. "They'll tell you about them in high school."

"*Agricola, agricolae, agricolum*," she crooned. I loved it. It was like an incantation or a rune. I couldn't wait to study Latin.

She told me about a multitude of roots—how you could guess pretty accurately what so many English words meant by looking at the Latin. She taught me *uni* and *bi* and *tri* and *quad*. She taught me *dis* and *de* and *un* and *anti*. She taught me *ectomy* and *otomy* and *ology*. I loved the way the parts of the words kept reoccurring, from the *corpus* and *sanguine* of the Mass to the English words that I was always reading. "You'll have to learn the declensions and the grammar in high school."

"*Veni, vidi, vici,*" she said, remembering a speech she'd given in eleventh grade for Sister Eunice, laughing while rendering the punch line for me, which was the translation. "I came. I saw. I conquered." I could almost imagine Mama cast in the role of that smug Julius Caesar.

Mama's recitations, her songs in Latin, her remembrances of memorized lines from Plutarch and Virgil, were the tunes ringing back to a time when she was happy. She seemed to be trying to go back to herself as a vigorous young green-eyed, brown-haired girl who had been noticed and favored by somebody, somebody from outside her family, where she never curried favor. Her eyes softened. Her energy improved. I don't think she was very aware of me. I was an excellent audience for her reveries because of my good questions. She trusted me, and so was able to convey more about learning than lessons. She showed me her passion.

Mama's muse was the river, and we made constant pilgrimages to the river. We went down to the river on every happy and sad occasion, every time we needed to make a major decision, through every season, and often on our way to or from somewhere else.

Mama came alive near the river, became more animal-like, as the air raised the hair on her arms and as she inhaled the moisture in the air through slightly flared nostrils. She knew the rhythm of the river, having lived on its bank in Wyandotte. She knew all the access points, weaving around the factories to get down to the river—at Windmill Pointe on the Detroit east side border, on Belle Isle, at the Bob-lo boat dock downtown, on the Bridge, at the Boulevard Dock, at the parks in River Rouge, Ecorse and Wyandotte, at Elizabeth Park in Trenton where the river widens, at Gibraltar where it flows into Lake Erie and ceases to be. And she knew the Canadian side as well.

Mama set her feelings free near the river, her senses always charged by seeing, smelling, hearing and feeling it. She also embraced it with her brain. Mama knew the river was the lifeblood of Detroit's history, from Cadillac founding the trading post on the straits, from the battles and contested borders, to the sailing ships, the steamships and the freighters. "If you want to truly understand Detroit, you've got to look to the river. Everything we've done here has been because we've got the river." It put the smoke stacks and the factories and the expansion to the suburbs in perspective, just the here and now in a long continuing history.

Mama knew the Great Lakes freighters. They were like old friends. "There goes the John Ericsson," she would say, before we could read the name printed on the hull, as we sat on a bench and licked Good Humors down by the Boulevard Dock.

That was the closest and easiest place for us to get down to the river. It was cool there in the evening, with the sun setting downriver, winking behind the factories on Zug Island and the steel mill in Ecorse, turning the smokestacks and the sandstone pink. The Ambassador Bridge, connecting the U.S. to Canada just upriver, framed our skyline view of downtown. The cars high up on the bridge seemed to creep along in slow motion, and I always imagined that when they crossed that point at the top of the arc, with the small ragged U.S. flag and small ragged Canadian flag standing side by side, they'd be transformed into something else. The first time I walked over the bridge was with Daddy and Betty when I was five years old, while Mama drove the car, parked it, and waited for us on the Canadian side. We stood with one foot in the United States and one foot in Canada, and I noticed the current moving downstream in an in-and-out rhythm, with the exact borderline hidden in the braids of water.

Mama chose Belle Isle for special occasions. She couldn't let an Easter pass without visiting the Easter lilies and hyacinths at the Conservatory. Belle Isle was for ice skating in the winter, for canoeing in the summer. Downriver was for the height of summer, the Fourth of July carnival and parade in Ecorse, with my cousin Bobby and me atop a Ferris wheel seeing how the river started to spread out, seeing the downriver finger-shaped islands.

Gibraltar was for the fall and spring migrations of the birds. Mama moved so slowly it was hard to imagine her in the woods and marshes, yet to see the birds return and fly away, she made an exception. Mama delighted in every plant and flower in the woods and marshes and knew the names of many. It was so easy to tell when Mama was happy. Her face became beatific. Striking.

Mama, it turns out, was a poet of the senses. She had a more acute sense of smell than anyone I've ever known. When I was very young, she used to claim affectionately, "You can't hide from me. A mother can smell her child." I believed that she was like the other mammals. I even tested her, hiding in all sorts of places, the front closet, the clothes hamper, even venturing one time into the webs of old lady Dixon's dark fruit cellar. She always found me.

Mama had ears that deciphered nuances. She knew where to pitch an alto harmony to songs. Her skin responded in ecstasy when she felt things, the water, cutting through it with her Esther Williams side-stroke, her white teeth gleaming in the smile that spread to the edge of her white bathing cap. Her weakest sense was sight. Surely she couldn't see the clutter and the hideously mismatched colors in the rooms. Her strongest sense, though, was taste, and taste, taste, taste she did, so often begging me to taste. "Taste it, Mary. It's good."

Mama ate slowly, slower than anyone I knew, and after all the relatives were through with dessert and ready to clear the table, she continued to eat the last of the large quantities of food she'd piled on her original plate, still savoring, patiently chewing, enjoying every morsel. She couldn't be rushed, and she couldn't be stopped. She ate too much. In the slow-but-steady consistent way she ate, she slowly got too fat. Though her weight exacerbated the pain in her arthritic knees, she showed no inclination to give more than lip service to a diet.

Mama talked on the porch. She felt by the river. She showed the sharpness of her mind and senses, her remarkable capacity for bursts of joy, ecstatic moments that only those who'd been so suppressed could feel. On the porch and by the river it was as though the clouds rolled off. These were the clearings where she could be seen.

CHAPTER FIFTEEN
SOUTHERN BEAUTY

Liz Ayers and her handsome husband Hugh rented the downstairs flat after Jack and Dean Ramsey moved out in May 1956. They brought along their two blond daughters: three-year-old Suzie with curly hair and a quick mind, and Debbie, a plump-cheeked baby with straight bowl-cut hair just learning to crawl. Hugh had arrived in Detroit a few weeks before from Kingsport, Tennessee. When he got a job at Fleetwood, he sent for Liz and the babies. Lucky for me, and lucky for Mama, he noticed the "For Rent" sign in the window. This was in the summer of my eleventh year, the same summer I cleaned up the way-back room and started dreaming of Elvis.

Liz was a gentle friendly person. She was also young, graceful, sexy and cool—the antithesis of Mama. From the start she made time to talk and listen to me. She answered my many questions and seemed genuinely amused by me.

In the early weeks of my almost-daily visits downstairs, Liz, still sorting things, reminisced as she found a place to store her family picture album. As valedictorian of her high school class, she had spoken at the graduation. Hugh, her sweetheart since eighth grade, had been a star athlete. No one doubted they'd marry. "My parents wanted us to wait," Liz said. "But we decided to get married the week after graduation."

Liz flipped back a lock of her fine brown hair, flashed her green eyes, and broke into a smile that showed her white teeth. She chuckled a little. "There was a struggle with my parents, but I've got no regrets." A year and a few months later Suzie was born.

"Let me show you the album," she said.

We sat on her new beige-colored fricassee couch, which had arrived only the day before. Liz showed me her church-going mother and father who looked staid but a lot younger than Mama. Her old-timey grandmother and grandfather looked fierce. There were snapshots of her and Hugh as teenagers that were taken by another couple. One of them showed Liz, with her small waist and tulip hips, leaning against Hugh's shoulder. Hugh, a head taller, casually draped his arm around Liz. On the opposite page Liz had pasted reciprocal pictures of the other couple. They all looked so beautiful, so carefree, like they were having so much fun. Would I ever have a boyfriend? I hoped to be in a picture like that, too.

Several close-ups of Liz and Hugh were taken in a photo booth. Liz's round face rests against Hugh's narrow smooth-shaven, side-burned cheek. More of Hugh: standing 6' 2" in his football uniform and pads, standing in the foreground of the mountains, with his brown eyes and coal-black, slicked-back, pompadoured hair crowning his Scots-Irish Southern brow. One of Liz in cut-off short shorts, her rounded breasts filling her halter top. Another of Liz in an angora sweater filling a pointy Platex bra. Liz radiant in her simple white street-length dress at the small church wedding.

When Liz got to the baby pictures, three-year-old Suzie drew near and sat beside her. "Is that me?"

"Yes, that's you, Honey" Liz said. "You were a beautiful baby."

A snapshot taken in our own backyard in July shows me holding Suzie up on the seat of my Schwinn Cruiser, supporting the weight of the bike while allowing the little girl to pretend she is riding. My attitude is attentive, my arms holding the bike around the child. My head leans toward the child, but I direct a small shy smile toward the one who holds the camera. Suzie, perched on the high seat and clinging to the handlebars, gazes directly at the camera—a little fearfully, given the precariousness of her pose. Liz holds the camera, the new Brownie Hawkeye I'd successfully nagged Mama to claim for me with S&H green stamps. Another snapshot taken after shows Suzie and me in the same pose, but with chubby baby Debbie added in, sitting in the basket of the bicycle like a little Buddha. The snapshots reveal that I'd already gotten my hair cut to try to imitate Liz's DA. A hairdresser at Roger's Beauty Shop cut it too short and clearly didn't understand, even though I'd been able to utter the words: "I want a DA."

I prize the pictures because they catch me in that period of happiness and equilibrium. A jaunty irony inspires the poses that Liz and I created together—a three-year-old riding a full-sized girl's bike while carrying a chubby baby like a grocery bag in a front wire basket. Liz trusted me, sure I wouldn't let either of her children fall.

I studied Liz—what she wore, how she slicked back and sprayed her hair, and mostly how she casually bore herself in acceptance of her beauty. I recognized the easy sensuality in Liz's ways and wardrobe, sensuality totally vacant in our upstairs flat. Liz was sexy in her perfectly-broken-in Levis, and I wanted to be sexy too. I recognized what I wanted, but I didn't have the words for it.

I got Mama to buy me genuine Levis downtown at Hudson's, but they didn't look good on me. They didn't cling and ride low on my hips like they did on Liz. Mama insisted I get them too big. I scorched them with kettles of boiling water in the bathtub, but they wouldn't shrink, and they still didn't fit— still a little too long in the torso, a little too short in the legs. Uncomfortably scratchy, they chafed my legs. But wear them I did. I am decked out in them in another snapshot, one Mama took of me in August on the bridge at Elizabeth

Park. I wear the jeans, a jacket, white socks and scuffed-up saddle shoes. Along with a scarf around my neck, again in imitation of Liz.

In many respects Mama was getting better, coming out of the worst of her sadness, and I relied on her for many things, including excellent conversations about the world and wry observations about the relatives and neighbors. But I was getting better, too, starting to understand and gradually accept her intractable fears and limitations. I held great ambitions: first of which, to make our own home "normal." If I couldn't do that, with effort and study, I might still grow up to be normal. But normal was impossible without beauty and sensuality. I longed to be sensual, attractive and pretty.

I'd already developed a plan to become normal in other areas of life, observing Dean Ramsey's housekeeping and other parents' authority—I would learn and do the opposite of Mama. When it came to sensuality, though— would I become an attractive sensual woman?—I came up short. I wasn't sure there could be another way but Mama's. I hadn't seen any opposites. I didn't want to be like Mama.

Even though Mama's selling Avon brought knowledge of beauty products into our life, we never talked much about beauty. We never talked about the beauty of the body from the neck down. We talked about the ugliness of the body, the ugliness of its smells and upheavals and accidents, the body as a source of shame. All talk between us about the body, *my body*, as something beautiful, or as something that could be made attractive, was taboo, out of the question.

That fall and winter of seventh grade, with Elvis in my life, babysitting money in my coffers, and Liz in the flat downstairs, I started to quest for and buy many of my own clothes. I wanted one of the new shift dresses shown in line drawings in the newspaper ads. I learned from window shopping that the dress shops up on West Vernor in Saint Gabriel's Parish sold relatively cheap versions of the dresses, cheaper than the upscale dress shops on Fort Street.

With some of the more than $60 saved from the summer of babysitting the matryoshka dolls, I rode my bike up to West Vernor.

I could hardly bear looking in the store mirrors, seeing in the flesh that I didn't look like a model. I didn't look petite. I didn't look like some of the popular girls who seemed to be acquiring breasts and hips at a steady graceful even pace, as though they would spin into more and more dramatic versions of an egg timer. I was alarmed by the changes in my body, the pubic hair, the gargantuan hips and derriere, the towering height and the stretching feet. I could hardly keep up with my mortal embarrassment at the loud verdicts of shoe-store clerks. "Size eight." "Size nine." Before it was over, shoe clerks were suggesting, "Why don't we try a ten?"

Still, I got over my alarm at looking in the mirror when I tried on the pretty pink cotton shift that covered most of me. I looked sideways. I gazed at the dress through one mirror into the mirror behind me. It was what people were wearing. I liked the way the little bump on the back of my neck looked tender above the scooped neckline. It looked nice with my hair color. I liked it. I bought the dress plenty big for me, unaware that a shift is most flattering when it almost skims the hips.

Not only did the dress itself lift my spirits, but the buying of it put me in a state of elation. When I got home I modeled it for Mama. The dress was way too big, but Mama looked me over with a frown. She tugged at it, grabbing several inches of the fabric, a fast jerking tug of the cloth with her strong hands at my most vulnerable point, the thickest part of my ballooning hips. "That's too tight," she said. "You'll outgrow it."

My spirits fell.

I quickly learned that her response to almost everything I bought would be invariable: the brutal tug of the cloth at the hips, the refusal to appraise me in a loving way, the words: "That's too tight. You'll outgrow it." If it were a white sweater, she said I shouldn't have bought it, that I'd spill something on it. A pair of shoes? Too small. I never heard her once say that the dress, or skirt, or blouse, or sweater, or bathing suit, or that I looked pretty. She was preparing me to get used to a life of ugliness.

The "You'll-outgrow-its" echoed in my mind. It seemed she assumed, or maybe even wished, I'd grow overweight like my sister, overweight like Mama herself. I didn't know what I'd look like once I finished growing, so of course I worried. But I knew for certain that all chances for beauty would be lost if I ever became as fat and sluggish as Mama.

When I brought home a clutch purse because I'd seen the cool girls carrying them, Mama turned it over and over, regarding it as though it had come from outer space. "But it doesn't have a handle to carry it with. Is that what all the girls are carrying?" Her words seemed to rub in the fact that I had tried to steal "cool." Her face registered disdain. "A 'clutch' purse? Is that what the girls are calling it?" Her voice, which embraced so many different words, seemed to bracket the term "clutch purse" and judge it unworthy.

That hurt, too. That incredulity. That rigidity. I wanted affirmation of my choice. A purse didn't need to have a handle. She was just too old. At thirty-eight she was old when I was born, she was old to start. But worse than that, she was stuck in some ancient time, perhaps the time of her early marriage when she loved my father before either my sister or I were born. She didn't like anything new. She wished the world wasn't so modern, and I couldn't understand that. At one time she must have let ideas flood into her head, but now she was closed.

Sometimes Mama's responses enraged me, and then I fought against them in my mind with the fervency and passion of a Scarlet O'Hara. I thought, "Mama *wants* me to be fat. She wants me to be ugly so I won't ever leave her. Mama wants me *to think* I'm ugly so I won't ever leave her." Her consistently cruel insensitive comments seemed to prove it true, and then she fueled my ambition. "As God is my witness …," I thought, "As God is my witness, I not only won't be ugly, I'll be beautiful. And then she'll watch me dance away." But I didn't think I was beautiful. I didn't have enough self-confidence to dance away. Mama had consistency on her side.

At first it was accidental, since I often stopped in the downstairs flat before going upstairs anyhow. Liz answered the door and immediately spotted the brown paper bag I held, the bag that had gotten soft in the rain exposed in my bike basket. Her eyes lit up. "What did you buy?'

"I got a dress up on West Vernor."

"Come on in. Let me see it." Both beautiful blond daughters came up beside her, stood at the screen door and smiled, glad to see Mary at the door. By this time Debbie was walking.

"This is a nice fabric," Liz said. She fingered the ribbed cotton I'd pulled from the bag. "Why don't you go in the kids' room and try it on? I want to see."

I went into the room with the single bed and the crib and used it as a dressing room, flinging my clothes on the bed. I hurried. I didn't want to be apart from them. I slipped the zipperless shift over my head, smoothed it out, tucked the price tag inside at the back neckline, and walked through the door.

Liz looked me up and down, steadily. "Oh, that's nice!" she said.

I'm certain Mama never meant to hurt my self-esteem. Besides, with her it would have been a combination of feelings, all having to do with her, something about spending money, about loss, about worrying I'd outgrow the dress and she'd have to part with her own money to replace it.

Yet underlying her reactions, something raged—self-hatred that extended to me because she thought of me as an extension of herself. She could fix her beautiful face to an extent, put on lipstick and flash her pearly white teeth. Her greatest scorn, though, concerned the rest of her body. Hers was an active, punishing hatred like a horse-whipping or a scourging. Mama hated her body.

And me, I was a child cast into a raging torrent, uncertain, unguided, my body unique enough that I couldn't find my type. I didn't look like anybody else. My body began smelling the way Mama always warned me it would smell. Growing, growing, growing into what? Size ten shoes? A tall girl, taller than the boys? Hips I could never hide? Would I hate my body?

Liz affirmed me with her joy, with her faith that I would get to shore. I would be beautiful. The dress looked nice. Yes, Mary looked nice.

Liz kept the downstairs flat clean, but she wasn't as vigilant as Dean Ramsey, and that was one reason why she had time to talk with me. She and Hugh also bought furniture on time from Crown Furniture on Fort Street, and some of it was the exact same blond modern stuff Dean and Jack had installed in the flat three years before. When pieces of it arrived every other week or so, I was tactful enough not to point that out. The same black-panther ashtray sat on the blond coffee table in the living room instead of where Dean had placed hers on the bedroom dresser. Liz and I sat in the living room, on her beige couch with the modern stick legs, in front of the blond coffee table where Liz tapped a Salem ladylike-fashion into that sleek black-panther ashtray. Often, we each supported a little girl on our laps, as though we were going for a ride.

We were on a ride—a ride Down South through music. Across the room the strains of Eddy Arnold's honeyed baritone, or Webb Pierce's twang, or Johnny Cash's bass, or Ferlin Husky's heartache, or young Roy Orbison's tenor floated from the miraculous brand new hi-fi that sounded much better than what we had upstairs. All we had to do was listen, listen, sing along, be moved to tears or dance or laughter. I was surrounded by love—the music, joyful Liz, and the little girl Suzie asking me, "Do you like that song, Mary?"

I'd kept track of the mainstream pop songs for years. Mama and I sang the hits and learned the lyrics when they were drilled into us each week by *Your Hit Parade* stars: Snooky Lanson, Russell Arms, Gisele MacKenzie, and Dorothy Collins.

If the songs were hits for weeks, we were treated to weeks of different performances of the lyrics. I even remember Giselle or Dorothy, down on her hands and knees, trapped like a fly on fly paper, extending the strings of glue stuck from each finger by raising her arms and singing, *Let me go, oh let me go, oh let me go, Lover!*

I also knew the old Tin Pan Alley songs from Mama's time and before. I learned them when all my aunts and girl cousins sang them around Aunt Marie's piano. "Begin the Beguine" was witty, "Smoke Gets in Your Eyes" haunting. "Sweet Adeline," "Let the Rest of the World Go By," and "Shine on Harvest Moon" were old and corny, but they offered us the best opportunities for harmony until the Everly brothers came along. In our case it was sometimes four-part harmony, with Mama singing that clear sweet alto of hers to carry the lower voices along.

Liz opened the door to an entirely new kind of music, one hauntingly familiar though, one I recognized as hidden and primal. I'd never heard the whine of a pedal-steel guitar or the heartbeat of a great big double bass guitar until I heard it resonating from Liz's hi-fi and rolling along the floor or shaking all the windows of the house from upstairs, the only instrument at that distance you could hear. Of course, I'd heard fiddles before, but never in dialogue with the voice, never as punctuation to the music, never as the soul crying out and holding the body of the other instruments together. I'd heard Southern voices, in the neighborhood and Tennessee, and, although I'd forgotten it, the mild Southern voice of Daddy, the first male voice I knew. But I never imagined I could summon that Southern male voice in song whenever I wanted it. Faron Young cried out to me, *I miss you already and you're not even gone.* He sang about loss and the fragility of love after he'd been *untrue.* I didn't know any specific meaning for *untrue.* I'd heard the Jordanaires singing behind Elvis, but I never paid attention to the backup singing until I heard them singing like a Greek chorus behind Jim Reeves. Or heard the backup singers lilting behind Ferlin Husky and bringing Liz and me almost to tears when they echoed *Since you're gone.* Johnny Cash sang "I Walk the Line," as I counted off the bass guitar chords going oompa, oompa, oompa. We bounced the little girls on our knees.

"Do you like that one, Mary?" Suzie asked.

I studied Liz and Hugh as a couple. My great ambition of the years before—to be a saint—shifted toward a great ambition to be married. I'd supposed in a fuzzy way before that I could be both—a married saint with ten children, yet I couldn't find any married saints I wanted to emulate. Besides, I'd already learned that sainthood requires obsessive attention, and that leaves little time for romance. So I made the final adjustment: I'd be married—not a saint, but still a good Catholic.

I'd never really known a functioning marriage. I was consciously and keenly curious to learn how men and women got along, and painfully aware that I'd need to look outside my own family.

I couldn't have picked a more loving couple to study. In contrast to the last tenants, the Ramseys, who'd been entertaining because they were odd, Liz and Hugh were gods, as beautiful as the handsome loving couples on television who spoke in full sentences to each other and slept in twin beds. Liz and Hugh were more real, the love between them the real McCoy. It was clear from the way they looked at each other, the way they stood together, sat together, tickled and gently poked at each other, and ruffled each other's hair, that they would never sleep in twin beds.

They most impressed me when they were unaware. The casual male voice, the answering female voice, the male voice speaking in the domestic register that I yearned to hear. When I was down in the basement I overheard them talking casually from room to room. "Where did you put my brown belt?"

"It's right where you left it under the bed."

"I can't find it."

"Look around, honey."

I leaned up against the concrete laundry tub where I'd been standing, stricken with longing over the most insignificant exchanges, feeling them. If only someday I might have such a conversation. I knew that people took it for granted. I was afraid that I would ruin it. I'd be so grateful I'd cry.

At night I heard their radio after I punched off my own new blond plastic, bedside model bought with babysitting money. I could barely hear their radio playing softly from their big bedroom below me. It was the sound people made at night, not offensive, distant, but comforting, evidence that normal lives were being lived below, supporting me through my slumber. Like many of the new arrivals to the neighborhood from tobacco-growing states, Liz and Hugh smoked cigarettes and made it glamorous, loyal to particular brands, like Detroiters to their cars. Liz smoked Salems and Hugh smoked Camels, and on those early nights Mama and I could smell the smoke through the cold air return. The smell of the smoke from downstairs seemed natural to me, that and the sleepy radio, the embers of a nightly passion.

I studied the country song lyrics. How else was I to find out what men who weren't priests were like and what they wanted? What would make a man shed the mask I saw so often in the strangers I chanced to observe or meet? Would a man ever cry? What would bring him to tears? What would make him laugh? What would make him laugh the way I saw Hugh laughing with Liz?

I looked to the lyrics. Of course I listened to other songs. But the country songs were honest. They matched the moods and struggles of the adult women in the neighborhood I so eagerly listened to as they talked among themselves. It always surprised me to hear a man proclaiming his love for a woman and his understanding of the scheme of things. *What a darned good life*, Jimmie Rodgers sings, *when you've got a wife like honeycomb.*

The world of the songs was full of honky-tonks. It was fun to imagine getting dolled up, go out on Friday night, dance and flirt and deliberately spend money. What a novel idea. After all the years with Mama, I'd never imagined one could joyfully spend money. Johnny Horton sang about honky-tonk men who spent all their money in the honky-tonks and then staggered home to their good old loyal women. It seemed like a man thing, this going downtown on Friday or Saturday night. But then again, there were gals that Carl Perkins sang about who spent all their time two-stepping on the honky-tonk hardwood dance floors. Hank Williams still sang the best about honky-tonks. You might get the honky-tonk blues that made you just want to leave the city life altogether and flee back home to your daddy's farm. I imagined my uncles' farms, safe and simple places, down home.

Honky-tonks filled our world in Detroit along our strip of Vernor Highway. Men filled these bars, some men staring into bottles, getting drunk on weekdays, deliberately "drowning their sorrows" caused by women who left them alone. *There stands the glass that will ease all my pain and settle my brain. It's the first one of the day*—Webb Pierce explains it. *Just one more ... and then another* George Jones advocates. Men drank because women left them. Women left men because they drank. It was hard to see the road to redemption.

The world was full of heartache, but it was honeyed heartache, sweet slow pulsing heartache going down. People fell in love, often with the wrong person who didn't return the favor. Or with a person who returned the favor, but then fell out of love and went on to love somebody else. Sometimes people fell in love with the wrong person who loved them back but already belonged to someone else.

This world of song was full of honky-tonk women running wild, pathetically weak men who transgressed and transgressed again, but with perfect knowledge of the repercussions, who then loved to tell self-pitying tales of how it all went wrong. The world was full of heartache, but the fate of attraction and sexuality and music was the one rock bottom thing you could count on. You loved fully and completely. And if you lost, you kept your pride. So much pride.

These songs became the most important source for me for learning what to expect. And I eagerly learned the implied lessons for women. Be faithful, loyal, pleasing, and forgiving. Maybe then, with lots of luck, I too would find somebody to marry me, somebody to cling to me, somebody to stay with me forever.

Liz bought her country records at Lee's Record Shop down on Vernor, near the Dix Theater, on the other side of the park. In the meantime I bought the Elvis and the teenage and rockabilly stuff up on Fort Street. Sometimes we ended up buying the same records, and so I didn't need to bring mine down to play on Liz's hi-fi. We both appreciated listening to the records over and over again to hear different things, and we didn't stop until we could sing along with the backup women singers on Buddy Knox's "Party Doll," or croon along with Sonny James who glorified "Young Love."

Young love was the glorious antidote to old widowhood. Young love, Southern love, Southern beauty.

The 3-J Bar stood on the corner of Clark Street and Vernor Highway. From our house a person of legal drinking age, such as Hugh, could get himself safely drunk without even needing to cross a street. If he ventured across the street, the Park Café stood opposite. The Gold Seal Bar, the Carnival Bar, Boland's Tavern and the Hi-Way Bar lured him if he turned right to walk down Vernor toward Grand Boulevard. If he turned left, he'd pass Tom and Gerry's, the Green Front, the Dixie Belle, and the doorways of eight other beckoning bars before he ever made it the five blocks up the street to Holy Redeemer.

Almost all of these bars played loud country music on hi-fi juke boxes. Some of them featured live country bands on weekends and a maple dance floor. All of them, from what I heard, enticed revelers with their own dear unique personality and set of regular buddies to greet. In those days, there couldn't have been a better place in the world to practice the art of bar hopping than on our strip of Vernor Highway. I heard all about it, yet I was too young to join the party.

I'm not sure when Hugh progressed from bar-hopping on the weekends to serious nightly drinking. I know if he'd stayed down home in the country and lived in one of those staunch Baptist or Methodist small towns, he wouldn't have gotten the support he got from the nightlife in the bars along Vernor Highway. The trouble with whiskey in the neighborhood was that it was laced with fun. And Hugh succumbed.

*   *   *

One afternoon in the early spring I babysat for Suzie and Debbie after school while Liz kept an appointment with Doctor Kuhn, whose office stood across from Redeemer on Junction Avenue. After she came back, I entertained the kids a little longer when she ducked into her bedroom to answer a phone call from Hugh, calling from the payphone at work. When she emerged from the bedroom, tears glistened on her cheeks. "I just told Hugh I'm going to have another baby."

"Why are you crying?" I said.

"Oh, that's just the way it is." She smiled, one of her beautiful Liz smiles, and I figured it out. Tears were for good news as well as bad. Tears naturally welled up when a man told you he loved you, that everything would work out fine, that he was glad you were having another baby. Tears were for being close to a man.

Liz told an overjoyed Mama the next day. She also voiced her concerns to Mama. She worried about money, worried about how close the children were in age, worried about Hugh and whether he'd do better and spend less time in the bars. I don't think Liz wanted to get pregnant, but I also don't think she fought it the way women would later fight it. By then Liz talked about almost everything with me. But for things I couldn't understand, Liz also talked with Mama. Liz proved to be the sister I'd lost and the daughter Mama had lost. We were determined not to lose this one.

Even though getting the news of another kid made Hugh say the right thing, it didn't make him do right. The right thing must have been easy to say. After all, he loved Liz and the kids he had already, and of course he wanted everything to be OK. But he couldn't stop drinking.

The love that unraveled because of it is someone else's story. I watched it though, uncertain, like each of the players, of how it would turn out. I was certain that I would learn from all that happened to Liz, learn as she progressed through her pregnancy, learn as she fought to build the life she wanted with Hugh.

At first the story followed the song lyrics, *If you loved me half as much as I love you, you wouldn't worry me half as much as you do.* It seemed all about worrying and waiting—Liz waiting for the baby to be born, worrying about Hugh and wondering when he'd get home. I visited the downstairs flat practically every day. I listened to the lyrics and tried to make sense of them. What was the lesson for Liz?

"Four Walls," sung by Jim Reeves, is written from the point of view of a woman who waits for her man attracted to the bright lights like a moth to the flame. The woman passively waits for the knock on the door, even as the four walls close in on her and she has no way of predicting when the man will return. A night with you is heaven, the song explains. I figured a night with Hugh would be heaven, too.

Liz hurt greatly during the waiting—I saw it—as she set the table for four with two adult plates, got supper ready, glanced at her blue teapot wall clock, smoked a cigarette and stubbed it out, stirred a pot, and then ceased to be responsive to my patter, seeming not to be there. She finally fed the kids, watched them eat, wiped their faces and fingers, and released them from their chairs.

Mama had told me to always come upstairs when Hugh arrived, so as not to wear out my welcome. As it got later and later, it became awkward. Liz finally told me, "I guess you'd better go upstairs, Mary. Your mom's probably got supper ready."

And the closer it came to the birth of the baby, the bigger Liz's belly, the longer and more often Hugh stayed away.

During the last month before little Billy was born, Hugh spent almost every night in the bars. Liz was huge, and in those days a fully pregnant woman was considered unattractive. I could see the attitude affecting Liz, who knew she was beautiful, who usually showered the world with smiles, and who usually carried her graceful body like a queen. Now she wore Hugh's old shirts and old Levis cut off at the knees. One afternoon we regarded her profile in the full-length mirror of the living room closet. She lifted up Hugh's shirt to show her belly protruding over the waistband of Hugh's worn-out jeans. She was fat enough, but in a sudden playful moment, she stuck her belly out further, and it struck us both as wildly funny. We laughed so hard we cried, while Suzie, who had radar when it came to anything joyful, ran over to join us.

After Billy was born, it wasn't like the song lyrics anymore, and I was surprised. I don't know whether it was Liz's native intelligence or something else in her that fought against the pit she'd fallen into with Hugh. Liz wasn't content to wallow in her own tragedy. Now she seemed to be turning it over in her mind, without self-pity, and she started doing one rational thing after another. She must have talked to Hugh, because he stopped drinking and tried to make it better.

When Billy was about three months old, Liz took a job as a secretary downtown to help the family get out of debt. Hugh, now working afternoons, cared for the kids all day, and I came to relieve him after school before he left for his four o'clock shift. Hugh was good at taking care of the kids. Unlike so many other men in the neighborhood, he didn't mind cooking and changing diapers. When I arrived at three-thirty, Billy had been changed and all the kids had been talked to, played with, and fed.

I saw it work for a while, although I felt lonely with the kids in the flat without Liz. Liz and Hugh were paying their bills, and Liz came home one day to say she'd been promoted.

But then Hugh started drinking again, spending the money set aside for the installment payments, hitting the bars on Vernor Highway again.

And then the rocking chair he'd bought for Liz before the baby was born got repossessed.

In the end Mama and I lost Liz. I wasn't there the Monday Liz's parents drove up from Tennessee to get her and the kids. I was at school. She was gone, sending her love to me in a message through Mama. "Liz says she's sorry she's leaving like this. She says she's going to miss you."

"Why didn't she tell me she was leaving?" I said.

"She didn't know," Mama said. "She just decided over the weekend."

I was there to see Hugh stay on for a while, grieving, quiet, never venturing out except to work. I was there the Saturday morning Hugh came up to tell Mama he was heading south, back to Kingsport. "I'm going home, Mrs. Rhodes. I don't want to stay up here without my family. I just hope I can get Liz to take me back."

"Well, I'm sure you can get her back, Hugh," Mama said.

The next morning he packed and loaded all the furniture into a trailer hitched to his Chevy. We waved "Goodbye," telling him to give our love to Liz.

As he pulled away, he teased me like he always did. "Take care of that pretty red head."

I'd give the world to see Liz again, to know how the rest of her life unfolded. From her I learned how to regard my body in a loving way. From her I learned the way of love and sensuality between a man and a woman. I never doubted the deep love on both sides. I also learned the way of a woman's body, how it becomes rounder and rounder, extravagant and ripe.

CHAPTER SIXTEEN
GIRLFRIENDS

Everything about Redeemer's junior high school ranked higher with me than Redeemer's grade school, even the daily ritual of being dismissed. We didn't tromp out of school to the tune of a Sousa march as in grade school, keeping in line and then tumbling out into a cheering free-for-all as soon as we'd cleared the door. In junior high we simply waited for the bell, gathered our books and coats, and casually left without supervision through the junior-high-school door on Eldred Street. Sometimes we glanced in the cloak-room mirrors, adjusting spit curls, as we wore thin nylon head scarves folded into a triangle to tie around our heads. We adopted the Polish word for them, *babushkas*. We also assumed a different posture now, pressing the books and binders to our chests and encircling them in our arms like babies. The boys never held books that way. They gripped them in their hands, extended their arms and balanced them against their legs.

I'm not exactly sure when I noticed that Trina walked the same way home as I did. Sometime during the fall of seventh grade we both rounded the corner at Eldred, walked up Junction past the grade school, the old convent and the church, and then stepped up to the light at Junction and Vernor at the same time. As we stood at the red light together, I had only two choices: either drop back to avoid her, which would have been awkward, or greet her and start walking together. I think it was her easy smile when she glanced at me at the crossing that made me ask her, "Do you live down this way?"

"Yeah, I live on McKinstry." She lived north on McKinstry, almost to Toledo Street, while I lived south on Clark. When we arrived at the corner of Vernor and McKinstry, we propped our books on top of the shiny metal drop-box that Veteran's Cleaner had installed, and we talked for more than two hours over the traffic and whirlpools of grit thrown up by passing trucks. We promised to meet each other the next morning in the same spot and walk to school together. Since school started early with eight o'clock Mass, we'd naturally sit together. We'd already become friends.

Trina's family consisted of two parents, four brothers, and three sisters, and, like mine, her family presented its troubles. Yet we never found the time to talk or complain much about them. Her father, who stayed home on disability and only worked occasionally, was an alcoholic. We never talked about it or speculated about what that alcoholism would do to his children. Her mother worked long hours as a sales clerk at Hudson's. I felt sorry for her mom when I saw her come home visibly exhausted, but I never felt the need to share that thought with Trina. I had my family, my profound loneliness, my dead father, my absent sister, my eccentric mother. We were just friends and never once talked about how losing so much so soon might affect my future.

I loved Trina's house, and I started spending so much time there that I felt like one of the family. Her house was shabbier than ours, less substantially built, a one-story workman's cottage among a whole row of such cottages built at the turn of the twentieth-century with a side porch, three front windows, a crawl space under the house but with no basement. The rooms in Trina's house were cut up even worse than in our flat, or, more correctly, the large family necessitated that parlors and sitting rooms be converted to bedrooms. You had to walk through the boys' bedroom to get to the girls' bedroom, which was originally designed to be a parlor within a parlor.

What I loved about Trina's house was the wall-to-wall people, the way they never locked their front door, the way I just came in without knocking, the way whoever was in the living room—there was always at least one person in the living room—just looked up to see it was me without saying "Hello." I loved the smell of her two handsome older brothers who slept in on Saturday mornings, lumps under covers in their bedroom, as I walked through to get to Trina's and her sisters' room. I passed by the double bed to reverently contemplate each of their whiskering faces, aware that this is the way it would be: so this is what a sleeping man looks like. This is the hot smell of a sleeping man. I thrilled, knowing that I was part of it all. I'd sometimes wake up Trina, and her brothers would groan a little as they heard us whispering while walking through their room to get to the living room.

I loved Trina's smart younger brother Steven and her cute youngest brother Rob. They were children, and there was laughter and teasing. I loved the way nobody cared about rings on furniture, or crumbs on the floor, or the possibility of spilt milk. Mama couldn't focus well enough to deal with rings or crumbs, and she couldn't even contemplate the tragedy of mopping up spilt milk, and that's why she kept up a steady fret about the possibility of any of these things happening. All of that worry was suspended at Trina's house, where a pot of something always simmered on the stove, often something not too appetizing, stews of cheap cuts of meat. Any of the girls and older boys could move to stir it. Communication was conducted by way of gesture without a lot of words. I felt one among many, just a person of a low-key collective where I needed only to be low key to fit in.

I'm certain Trina enjoyed my house, where not even I, who lived there, could make it past the front door at the top of the stairs without being bombarded by the verbal onslaught of Mama: "Did you have a good day?" "Are you hungry? Sit down. I can make you something to eat." And then the list: "I've got some nice ground round steak. I can make you a hamburger." Trina liked Mama's attention and formal manners. She grew to love Mama, who could be kind and charming. I liked the privacy at Trina's, where you were never asked to be a companion for a lonely woman. We each got something we lacked at home in the other's house.

When the weather was bearable, though, we hardly spent time at either house. So many of our adventures in junior high school were about walking and talking. We walked all over the city, making an odd pair, with me getting taller and taller, and Trina staying short, until I'd tower over her by at least eight inches. In the summer we walked until all hours of the night. We walked down by the warehouses near the Ambassador Bridge with the wilderness of weeds and grasses, unkempt willows, and the summer evening quiet there with the chirping of crickets and the lapping of the water. We stopped at the park at the Boulevard Dock and ended up sitting on the swings with their rubber-belted seats that pressed our legs against each other, swinging slowly, slightly kicking at the dirt, just talking.

When we walked downtown we loved the bustle and the crowds, the shop windows, the way the buildings on streets we took—Lafayette, or Fort Street, or Bagley, or Michigan Avenue—got larger and more sophisticated, until you knew you had given up all neighborhoods. We often stopped to see Trina's mother, who worked in the Hudson's children's clothing department on the fourth floor, Trina talking in her family code, less words than at our house, but checking in on projects and whereabouts of the others.

Sometimes we walked across the Bridge to Canada, ending up drinking cokes in downtown Windsor, which was then a sleepy backward town that faced the mighty Detroit skyscrapers across the river.

We walked up Vernor Highway to Saint Gabriel's neighborhood, up Fort Street to All Saints', up Junction to Saint Hedwig's, down Vernor to Saint Anne's.

We walked up Jefferson past the Hungarian neighborhood in Delray and crossed the Rouge River, ending up at my aunt's house in River Rouge six miles away where my sister cooked us excellent spaghetti with mushrooms in the sauce, Betty's specialty by now. Fueled on spaghetti, we made the long walk home. Sometimes, no matter how long we'd walked and talked and how long it had taken us, we stood talking on the corner, too involved and never tired enough to just go home.

Walking was our way to exercise our independence from our families, a way to sense the ethnicity of the city, walking through the Polish neighborhoods at night, with the men standing, holding garden hoses, lost in private meditation, patiently watering. They acknowledged us, turning their hoses so we could pass across their span of wet pavement. We smelled the warm grass soaking up the water.

On Fort Street we saw handsome single Southern men, shaky bums, and couples dressed to the nines at midday, all piling into the D & C Show Bar the minute its doors swung open at noon. We tried to construct a story from our imperfect knowledge of the world to account for their interest, but we couldn't interpret all the cues. We did know to avert our eyes when we passed the notorious Rex Theatre, with its crew of furtive middle-aged men standing on the sidewalk out in front, smoking stubs of cigarettes and staring at us, coming and going, all the way down the block. Whatever movie was playing there was never listed on the marquis.

Downtown, we bought a copy of the *Philadelphia Sun* at the huge newsstand on the corner of Woodard and Campus Martius. We sat at the counter in Kinsell's Drug Store and fingered it as though it were a rare important document, reading the same weather report, the same ads and local interest stories as those happy dancing teenagers from South Philly we so admired on *American Bandstand*, when it first aired nationally in the fall of 1957.

All the while we walked, we talked. And yet I find it difficult to remember what we talked about. We never psychoanalyzed each other. We wouldn't have had the words. Yet we drew out each other's deepest thoughts. Trina possessed a stable kindness, along with a thoughtful intelligence that was exactly what I needed in a friend. I also find it hard to explain the consistency of our love and support for each other. We were young, had made no big mistakes, and believed most of the moral and ethical script we'd been handed. We even worked at it, so often I remember now talking about what would be the right thing to do.

Trina and I had our futures, but we also had our current problems. We weren't popular. But even that we bore with acceptance. We weren't going to suddenly become popular. Trina had a flair for detail. She could remember names and faces and wasn't affected by my habit of not really looking at people in the face. We each had long-term crushes on certain boys, and we shared our day's worth of observations of them from across the classroom. We observed the popular boys and girls, spent many hours talking about them, but even that we did without much bitterness. We studied people, their motivations, analyzing how the popular girls behaved, remembering how they handled situations. We were entertained and probably learned something we'd use later. But we didn't walk around with hatred or raging jealousy. I credit Trina with that.

In the shy way of Catholic girls, we supported each other as our bodies changed. Trina sitting in front of me in Sister Mary Owen's eighth grade class and standing up to answer. I noticed that it had happened to her, the same thing that had happened once or twice to practically all of us: a fresh wet darkness on the navy blue gabardine uniform. I followed close behind her while we walked to the lavatory where she would do as our mothers had instructed: rinse the stain in the coldest water. I shadowed her even closer on our way back to our seats—the skirt now clean but wetter.

Once when Trina was absent from school, sick, I believe, with bronchitis, I went to her house after school to see how she was doing. The house was cold and quiet, nobody but Trina around. She had a fever. She'd just discovered something when she passed by the mirror in her brothers' room, and she led me back to the same mirror to show me. "Look," she said with her clear blue eyes and her honey-blond hair, now set against her flaming red cheeks, "I'm really not that bad. I'm beautiful."

We each had our imperfections. Trina was overweight, but for me it was just Trina. I encouraged her to trim down, but we never spent long hours lamenting it. I demonstrated some of the same imperfections as I have now: quick to anger, often impatient, often obsessed with ideas and projects that could render me exhausting to listen to, splitting the hairs of other people's behavior in the search for absolute truth and justice. Trina understood me. She balanced my impatience with tolerance, not the avoidance of Mama that contributed so much to my annoyance. She followed my ideas and humored my obsessions, having faith that they would carry me into the new territories I constantly needed to explore. She seemed to know my soul was restless, and that only in death would I be still. We had faith, an unshakable faith that would one day carry Trina into a lucky good marriage.

In seventh and eighth grades we had a band of friends, girls like Diane Porter, Ann Kraft, Pat Malewski and Sharon Hillerich, girls who weren't too popular and who lived down our way from school. At the end of eighth grade, we were invited by Sharon Hillerich for a weekend at her family's cottage. "You're welcome to come," her mother told us. "But you'll have to bring all your own food and put it in a box." Trina and I got money from our parents and spent hours in the Banner Market on Vernor deciding which hotdogs, buns, and cereal to buy. It was the first time I'd made decisions about groceries on my own. Since Trina and I were told to bring *all* of our own food, we even settled on a bottle of ketchup. We shared everything.

Chapter Seventeen
Mortal Sin

In March of 1958, all 150 of the eighth graders, from all three homerooms, attended a Day of Recollection headed up by Reverend Father Walter Bracken of the Shrine of the Little Flower. Regular classes were suspended, and we met in morning and afternoon sessions in rooms in the auditorium building and the church instead of the school. It was a cold day, and Trina and I shivered as we scurried back and forth between sessions. Friends could walk together as long as they kept silent.

Now that we were growing up, facing new temptations and ready to grow more fervent in our faith, we attended religious retreats as part of our yearly routine. Most of the time they were conducted over a two- or three-day period by teams of Redemptorist priests known for their skills as motivational speakers. The retreat masters were also known for inducing the most thorough examinations of conscience in their audience, and for inspiring young adherents to heights of penitence and renewal. Sometimes they succeeded in getting members of their audience to declare vocations. In fact, following our Day of Recollection, three boys decided to join the seminary right after eighth grade.

For one of the morning sessions, the boys heard their lectures in a separate location from the girls. When they filed into the church for the general session afterward, with downcast eyes and serious red self-absorbed faces, they drew the attention of every girl in the pews around me. I suspected the other girls were pondering what I was pondering: Were these boys contemplating their own occasions of, or actual commissions of, mortal sins against purity? Of course, I couldn't ask anybody. We were in retreat mode, keeping silent. As the boys entered from the side door near the sanctuary, trooped past where we sat, moved to the center aisle, genuflected and turned, I'm sure we all wondered, "Who touched himself last night or thought bad thoughts?" As each boy passed, we had plenty of opportunity to review him. "Look at Larry. He looks like he's been crying a little." "What about Dennis? He looks worried." "Doesn't Mike's face look cute with those blushing cheeks?" We had to be careful that we didn't linger too long on these questions; to imagine any one of these boys grabbing his penis and fondling it was a bad enough thought to constitute our own mortal sin. "Please, dear God," I prayed. "Please, dear God, don't let me think bad thoughts."

I don't remember the name of the priest who talked to the girls about sexuality and purity in the afternoon, probably the same priest who shook up the boys in the morning. He was a Redemptorist, wearing the familiar black cassock with swinging rosary beads from the broad sash around his waist, and the super-sized crucifix centered on his chest, but close enough to his belly that he could tuck the foot of it into his sash.

This Redemptorist was of medium build, medium height, pale, brown-gray haired, a little tired-looking, and soft spoken and mild-mannered when introduced that morning. Once we had clanked down the auditorium seats, settled in and quieted down, and after Father Crane introduced him again and left the stage, he transmuted into a thunderous speaker with wide theatrical pacing and gestures. For the first time, color flushed his face, and his eyes, with their pronounced brows and Irish folded upper lids, became hard and sharp as a bird's.

Without introducing his topic, though we knew full well what it would be, he said, "If anything happens between a boy and a girl, you can mark my words, nine times out of ten, it's the girl who's to blame."

He paused to allow the effect of his words to register and then continued. "You know boys sometimes can't help themselves. They're carrying a burden. That's the way they're built."

He paused again and used the stage to strut back and forth while we thought about how boys were built. What must it be like to carry that weight around all day? Did it hurt? And how could we help them?

"It's your job as Catholic girls," he continued, "to help them by keeping them in line. And keep them out of the occasion of sin. Always." He looked out over the tops of our heads with eagle eyes. "Always."

He ran through our duties as Catholic girls and women, and there were plenty of them, from dressing modestly, which we already knew, to maneuvering through a date with only a goodnight kiss, to saying "No" to drive-in movies, to declining drink. Putting ourselves in the occasion of sin, for instance, by sitting with a boy in a parked car, or by letting him take us to any secluded place alone, were examples of what he'd been saying in the beginning. "If anything happens between a boy and girl in these situations," he said, "the girl is to blame." He paused again for effect. "Mark my words."

"And how should you young ladies treat your own bodies as Temples of the Holy Spirit?" He paused and started pacing back and forth, abruptly stopped and faced us. "A girl might stand in front of the mirror," he said. "She might even stand there naked, admiring her body. I'm sure you think her sin is vanity. Ah, yes, that too. But her bigger sin is against purity. God wishes for her to save herself for her husband's eyes in marriage, for her husband's gaze alone." Our Redemptorist paused another pregnant moment, eyeballed a spot on the back wall just above the heads of the audience, strutted back and forth again. I started to see his pattern—the way his voice lilted from loud to soft, from fast to slow, the way he used the stage and his eyes to reinforce his points. He could make his face animated, then weary, and his arms swung forward in conclusion.

He continued. "You think you have the freedom to think what you will. Now don't you? It's a free country." Pause. "You think you might fill your mind up with scenes of you and a boy and what you'd like to do." Snarl. "You may even hear romantic music. You say, 'I'm only thinking, Father.'" Pause, pace downstage, turn. "Ah, only thinking. Such thoughts are a mortal sin. Surely they're as much of a mortal sin as if you'd committed those impure acts in the flesh. Imagining impure acts is a mortal sin." Long pause, upstage pace, dramatic downstage turn. "And what of the girl who dwells on impure images—from the television set and from the magazines? She is committing a mortal sin."

The Redemptorist lectured on, pacing, gesturing, staring, and using the silences to make sure his words sunk in. And then, on one of his pacings, he moved far upstage so that he could slowly stroll downstage on the next declaration. "Now," he said, moving toward us, "we must turn to specificity, for I will not leave you with any of this unclear." He hit the midway point. "Clarity is just too important for your immortal souls." He stood so far downstage by now that he looked like he might topple into the girls in the first row.

He delivered the delicate information that followed in a mild conspiratorial hush. Yet all seventy-five of us could hear him. "Now girls, as we know, girls are built differently than boys. Boys are no mystery. They carry their burden on the outside. Girls are mysterious. Their burden is inside of them. You cannot see what is inside of you. It is hidden." His eyes spun upward for a second, perhaps in appreciation of the mystery. I saw him briefly lick his lips. "Still, your own hands can wander over your own body, wander to your developing breasts. They can also wander down to the seat of mystery. You might take your fingers and rub downwards or back and forth on the spot between the folds of skin. The spot is called a *clitoris* and the folds are called *labia*, labia in Latin means 'lip.' Yes, girls, like a boy, you can touch yourself with your hands in an immodest way and feel pleasure. Intense pleasure. Such pleasure, you must know, is a mortal sin!"

The priest had ventured into uncharted territory where none of the sisters had dared go. This was "specificity" we'd never heard before. All ears were trained on the Redemptorist, but many of us needed to turn our eyes a little downward, for modesty's sake.

Of course, I'd been paying devout attention, even as I also admired the Redemptorist's oratorical skills. I followed along. I was already fairly sure I hadn't touched myself in any impure way, had only fondled my breasts to see if the new tissue was firm or spongy, and I knew I hadn't stood in front of the mirror too long. I didn't look good in the mirror.

After an appropriate pause, he continued. I thought he'd be clarifying what he'd just said with a few afterthoughts. It didn't seem he could get more specific.

"And it is not the hands alone," he said. Pause. His eagle eyes flashed beneath the hawk-like brows. "A girl might rub herself against a table. And feel pleasure. She might rub one body part against another. She may do any number of things," he said. He paused again, tossing his arms out from his elbows, as though he needn't mention all the alternatives, might even be at a loss for specific words. And then he summed up. "The long and the short of it is this," he said. "If you ever feel a rushing in your loins, and especially if you feel release, you are committing a mortal sin against God and your own body, the Temple of the Holy Spirit, which should be a vessel of purity. Mark my words—it is a mortal sin!"

I wasn't prepared for my reaction. What he said tore at me with the force of the bitterest savage wind. What he said applied to *me* and it was undeniable, the long and the short of it. *A rushing in my loins... and then release. A rushing in my loins... and then release.* "That habit"—could it be a mortal sin? *A rushing in my loins...* "That habit"— it must have been a mortal sin.

A veil of dimness fell in front of my eyes. Lights flashed in my peripheral vision and then floated across the stage. The priest blurred. I couldn't see the stage. I couldn't hear him for the rushing in my ears. I couldn't catch my breath. If the boys blushed red after his talk in the morning, I knew I'd been struck white. I thought I'd faint in my seat.

All those years, all those years, through second grade, third grade, fourth grade, fifth grade, through all the shame and punishment, I had been committing mortal sins. "That habit" was a mortal sin. And nobody had told me.

No wonder Sister Florita hated me, had hurled me around and slapped me. No wonder Sister Callistus had cried. But I didn't know. I was sure I didn't know. Why didn't they tell me? Why didn't they just tell me?

In this moment of utter despair, my saving grace was that the lecture wasn't over. The Redemptorist went on a few more minutes to talk about something else, but I couldn't concentrate enough to hear. If we'd been asked to stand, I would have fallen.

Later, when we did stand, I could hardly get my feet to work. My body trembled and my legs shook. I made ready for the tears.

I knew I had to go to Confession. But not today. Even though, as the last activity of the retreat before reassembling in front of the church for closing hymns and final prayers, we were already on our way to Confession. I knew I could not go today. The other girls in line would have to wait too long. I'd be in the confessional longer than anyone else. Today was impossible. Besides, I needed time for the magnitude of the multiple mortal sins over years to sink in. I'd never be able to count them.

I waited, weak-kneed, in my pew while the others crawled over me, lining up in the pews opposite the confessionals. I would go on Saturday at the regular time when the priests heard general parish Confessions, at a time when the chances of anybody in my class being there would be unlikely. In resolving to go on Saturday, I had three days and nights to worry over it. I knew I couldn't count the sins, so I counted the years. I didn't know what to do about the fact that I hadn't known it was a sin. I examined my conscience in every conceivable way. I studied a booklet my sister had left, *The Catholic Girl Examines Her Conscience*. I'd looked at it before and agonized over whether I'd *failed to check vigorously impulses and daydreams of unruly love and affections* with regard to Elvis. The booklet also exhorted, *Have I touched myself or others in an impure manner?* I hadn't touched myself. I reread all the possibilities. It didn't list what I had done.

I recalled everything that had been said to me by the adults who must have known what I was doing was a mortal sin. I recalled and realized they'd said nothing. They'd been sad. They'd been alarmed. They'd been outraged. They'd been driven to tears. They'd shown by their words and actions their disgust with me. It made so much sense to me now.

To make it easier to choose the best priest to hear my Confession, on Friday night I reviewed several possible candidates who might be there the following day. In order to think it through rationally I had to suppress my feelings.

One priest was hard of hearing. Though the kids joked about how lucky it was to get him, he was out of the question for what I had to say aloud.

There were easy priests—Fathers Flanagan, O'Connell and Connelly. I didn't want an easy priest. For the first time in my life I had something that I knew would need to be talked about. This wasn't going to be an ordinary Confession.

There were indifferent priests, ones like Father Quinn, who always seemed bored, a little jittery, waiting through the time without a cigarette. In this case, an indifferent priest was not a good choice either.

There was one mean priest to avoid. I'd forgotten his name, but I knew I'd recognize it if I saw it on the name plaque on the door of the confessional.

On the way up to church, I contemplated options: I would leave and come back if I saw even one kid I knew. We always monitored how long each other stayed in the booth. I would leave and come back if only loud or easy or hard priests were hearing Confessions. I would leave if I couldn't get anyone besides the Pastor, Father Crane. I didn't want anybody with too much power to hear my Confession.

Now that I finally knew the crimes against Heaven I'd committed, I was almost certain that the problem of Mary Rhodes must have been discussed at length among the authorities. Why wouldn't it be? A girl who committed mortal sins every day in class and having the audacity to go to Communion every day as well? The blood trapped behind my cheeks, the tears dammed up in my eyes threatened to explode whenever I took in the magnitude of it for even a split second.

Confessions were heard in two stints on Saturday, from three-thirty to five-thirty in the afternoon, and from seven-thirty to nine-thirty in the evening, usually with four or five priests available at those times. During Lent, though, when the least devout of the parish made their yearly Easter Duty, more priests heard Confessions. Theoretically, ten of the twelve priests living at the rectory could be hearing Confessions simultaneously in the confessionals that ringed the outer walls of the church.

Even though it was Lent, when I got to church that Saturday afternoon, only five priests were hearing Confessions. A red light above the door of the middle booth signaled that a priest was on duty at that confessional, and a wooden name plaque hanging on the door announced his name. A green light above the doors of the booths on either side of the priest meant "vacant," a red light meant "occupied." The lights worked like this: the priest turned on the switch when he entered his booth; when a penitent knelt down on the kneeler in either side booth, it tripped a switch underneath. The weight of our knees made the light on the outside of the booth turn red.

I systematically reconnoitered the church on both sides, walking up the left aisle, making the turn to take in Saint Joseph's altar, turning to cross in front of Our Lady's altar, and genuflecting in front of the main altar to continue to the right. Priests at five confessionals, two on the left side, and three on the right. Two or three people waited in the pews outside each confessional, absolutely no one I knew among the people waiting. All good signs. Several of the priests hearing Confession were ones with whom I was totally unfamiliar. I eliminated a Polish priest, probably somebody who'd come over from Saint Hedwig's, Father Zamanski or something, who'd be hearing Confession in English and in Polish. Sometimes the Polish priests were just as good as the others, but the old ones, who favored rather loud Polish, presented too much of a problem.

After making one more circle, I decided on Father Spitzer. I'd seen him say Mass a few times on Sunday, not too old, and yet not too young. He'd never come to visit any of our classrooms, so I figured the chances were good he wouldn't recognize me. His confessional stood in a good spot on the north side of the church. The stained glass window next to the confessional would not cast enough light for him to see me, no matter which side of his booth I entered. I went around to the center aisle, genuflected again, and slid into the line that formed in the pew opposite his booth. I recognized one of the women in the pew, as one of those who haunted the church on weekdays. She, who prayed fervently on her crystal-colored Rosary, would go before me. I hoped her sins, which might match the fussy look on her face, would bore Father Spitzer, and thus prepare him for a real sinner such as I.

I planned to monitor the time it took for the middle-aged man going before the devout woman. I hoped he might take a long time. I figured that if Father Spitzer had to take a long time with an adult who had complicated sins to confess, he might develop some patience to listen to mine.

Once I knelt in the pew to wait my turn, I promptly went numb. Time didn't matter. I knew I'd find a way to say it, but only if I made myself numb. I also knew I'd go through with it, no matter how tough it would be. I'd had too much rehearsal through my reading about heroic people, men and women, boys and girls, not to know that what was coming up was one of those moments that took the highest kind of courage that I'd face squarely and pass through. To turn back, to run, to hedge, to lie—all out of the question. Still, to get through it, I'd have to be numb. It would be just too shameful if I allowed myself to feel.

I jumped when my turn came. I had planned it right. The crystal-colored Rosary woman was already situated in the right-hand booth. Nobody waited in line after me, so the chances of being overheard were greatly reduced, nil if no one came after I went into the left side of the confessional. I rose from the pew and acknowledged the middle-aged gentleman exiting the left booth. He didn't look shamed, and he didn't look smug. That might be another good sign about Father Spitzer. I entered, closed the door, and knelt down on the oak kneeler, resting my arms on the smooth oak arm rest that allowed me to guide my weight until my forehead leaned into the screen. I waited, trying to determine how much I could hear of the Confession in the opposite booth. I could hear voices, the woman's and Father Spitzer's, but thankfully I couldn't hear the words. If someone knelt down in the booth opposite me, and if I modulated my voice, and if, more importantly, Father Spitzer moderated his voice, a new penitent might not hear. I waited. But my state of mind—numb—could not register the time that passed.

I heard Father Spitzer close the screen on the other side of the confessional. Soon after, he slid the screen on my side open, the signal that I was to begin.

"Bless me, Father, for I have sinned," I said. "It has been one week since my last Confession." That was as much of the formula as I could use. It didn't seem appropriate to simply go on as usual and list the sin, and then the number of times I committed it. This Confession was like none that I had ever made. "Father, I have something special to confess," I said.

"Go on," he said. I detected something encouraging in his voice. And from the part of him I could see beyond the open screen, I thought I saw him shift in his seat to get set to pay attention. Maybe I'd done what I knew I'd needed to do, got him to understand this would be no ordinary Confession for a girl my age, prepare him for it so it wouldn't shock him as much, wouldn't hurt him as much, and he wouldn't hurt me as much. No one, no one from history, not even from the most profligate of the later repentant saints, no one I'd ever heard of, could have committed as many mortal sins as I had at my tender age.

"Father," I said. "Yesterday the Father at the retreat said something that made me realize I'd been committing mortal sins since the time when I was six." It was lucky for me that Father Spitzer knew the context. He didn't regularly deal with any of the students in school, but he would have known that the Redemptorist speaker was staying at the rectory. He would have known there had been a Day of Recollection for eighth graders.

"What was the nature of your sins?" he said.

"They were sins against purity, Father. I didn't know I was committing a sin. I didn't touch myself with my hands. But the Father at the retreat made me know that it was still a sin."

"Did anybody ever tell you that you were committing a sin?" he said.

"No, Father. Nobody told me. I was committing sins almost every day, but nobody told me."

"Well, if you didn't know it was a sin, then you committed no sin," Father Spitzer said. "Now you know it's a sin, so you won't do it?"

"Yes, Father."

"Good," he said. "And so now you know. But before you knew you didn't commit any sins. Is there anything else?"

"No, Father," I said.

"Now pray to be strong," he said, "I want you to say ten Hail Marys." He then asked me to make a good Act of Contrition, and I did.

I left the booth and blinked at the light in the church. I went to the kneelers at the altar to say the Hail Marys. I reviewed what I had told him. I determined I had told him all. I wasn't required to tell him I had committed the sins in school. But he'd been clear. They weren't sins because I didn't know. And he didn't ask me to say the Hail Marys as a penance. He asked me to say them to be strong from now on. His voice had been compassionate. His voice had been gentle. His voice had been certain in its determination. Because I didn't know, I hadn't committed any sin.

I started walking home on Vernor rather than Christiancy. All the windows in the stores were decorated for Easter. It was cold, about to drizzle. I passed Clark and kept walking. I needed to walk. I walked down to the Boulevard, and then over to the Ambassador Bridge to Canada. I paid the dime to walk over the Bridge in the drizzle. I kept walking until I stood among the trees on the campus of Assumption College in Windsor.

Along the way, I contemplated the question that would plague me on and off for a long, long time. If they knew it was a sin, why didn't they just tell me? They wouldn't have had to slap me even once, or cry, or worry, or carry me as a burden. Didn't they know I would have gladly faced death rather than commit a mortal sin? How could I have known that my comfort was a mortal sin?

CHAPTER EIGHTEEN
TRACKED

"This is an important test," Sister Mary Owen said to our class of eighth graders for the last time. "How you do on it will determine the courses you take in high school. Let's pray we all do well." It was May 1958.

We said a "Hail Mary" to help bring out our talents. We made sure once again that we had two sharpened number-two pencils, then we were told, "This is your last opportunity to visit the lavatory. Remember, lunchtime will be postponed until you have finished the placement test."

We lined up to make the trek across the dewy morning schoolyard to the high school with Sister Mary Owen and her jolly face and staunch stride leading the charge. Boys followed the girls. A few of them with sullen little moustaches brought up the rear, defiantly out of line.

No one could describe the schoolyard as a beautiful space—no trees, benches, fountains, or playground equipment except for the basketball hoops that hung from the power plant building next to the convent. The asphalt was old, showing patches and seams and sprinkles of grit and glass and gravel. Some of it, in fact, wasn't asphalt at all, but old rough dried concrete with little lake rocks bubbling above the surface. When it rained, the water ran across the pavement from the power plant and out to Junction Avenue. Not high enough to be a hill, but still a slope, bald in places, a big gray space, it grew hot in sunshine and oily in rain.

The schoolyard, like lots of things at Redeemer, served different functions, depending on the weekly cycle. It was the schoolyard on weekdays, with the yelling kids, the nuns on patrol, the girls playing jump rope games, boys playing ball games, and the priests on the side nearest the church pacing, smoking, and reciting their breviaries.

On Sundays it would be clogged with shiny big-winged cars parked in rows mere inches from each other. When Father Forbes had been pastor a couple years earlier, from the pulpit each Sunday at ten o'clock High Mass he used to deliver long harangues about the way he wanted the cars to enter, park and exit so that no one would be late to Mass. One time, while I wasn't paying much attention, I heard him say, "Now, you wouldn't want me to puncture your tires, would you?" I came to attention when the adults around me tensed up their shoulders, frowned and rolled their eyes. After Mass they stood around outside the church, gossiping. "He's gone too far this time."

Still, he had a point. They needed a system with seven Masses in the upper church and three in the lower church, all happening before the last Mass at twelve-thirty. Even Mama, who preferred to drive, walked to church when the weather was fair rather than brave the congested parking lot.

The schoolyard made me proud to be a part of Holy Redeemer School and Holy Redeemer Parish. Maybe it was because the rectangular space represented the epicenter of the Redeemer complex, with imposing buildings surrounding it: the church, the old convent used for charity cases, the grade school, the junior high, the real convent where the nuns lived in mystery, the physical plant with its puffing smokestack set a little in front of the convent, the driveway, the high school, the tunnel leading to the gymnasium and the auditorium, the other tunnel passing the back windows of the rectory, and then the church again. It didn't quite look like it, but Sister Mary Owen told us, "The schoolyard should give you a little idea, at least, of Vatican Square." It was a place where you could feel proud because from it you could see or imagine how the parish would take care of you from the cradle to the grave. Redeemer was a little city that would always be there.

I was doing pretty well in eighth grade, getting mostly "B"s, with "A"s in reading, English, and spelling. I had Trina and some other friends, and I looked forward to high school, with challenging classes, walking to them by myself all day, instead of waiting for teachers to come to us. I'd have a locker, a space I could organize, and I'd join some clubs, probably the chorus. I was looking forward to this placement test. I did well on tests.

The high school doors swung open, and we all squeezed through the doorway, entering as quietly as we could, as Sister Mary Owen had directed. The girls were routed toward the library.

The high school library was all new to us. The setup was unusual for a test, not rows of desks, but five rectangular tables with chairs in an open space, enough tables for all twenty-eight of Sister Mary Owen's homeroom girls to find a seat and a fairly generous space for elbows and pencils. By the time Trina and I had oriented ourselves to make a choice, most of the places had been claimed. One odd table not in the group of four, the one farthest away from the teacher's desk and off to the right side, proved an exception. We went for it. We sat there with one other girl until Sister Mary Owen approached with Teresa Rivera, holding her by her hand. She guided her into the seat kitty corner to me—the seat closest to the other tables and blocking my sight line to the teacher's desk. Sister Mary Owen quietly left the room when Sister Stella Mary, a tallish nun I'd never seen before, came forward and introduced herself, "Welcome, girls. I am Sister Stella Mary and I will administer this test."

Teresa Rivera shook with agitation. "Do you have a pencil? I need a pencil. I don't have a pencil." I guess she'd come late, which was one reason why Sister Mary Owen had given her special attention. Trina and I gave her one of our extra pencils and put the other extra one in between us on the table so it would be handy in case either of us needed it.

It was no wonder Teresa was a nervous wreck. She'd come from Puerto Rico only a little more than a year before, appearing in the middle of the year in seventh grade. Whenever she was confused, her voluminous anxious talk in English was impossible to understand. She stumbled painfully when asked to read out loud in class. She was the only person in real life I'd met who sounded like Desi Arnaz, with her difficulty with English consonants. She was the only girl from Puerto Rico I'd ever met.

Sister Stella Mary intoned the familiar words, "Read the directions on page one of your test. Do not turn the page until you have been directed to do so. You will have twenty minutes for this section of the test."

"What's she saying? What she want us to do?" Teresa's eyes were pleading, even as we tried to ignore her. "What she saying? What we supposed to do?" "What she want us to do?" Teresa's eyes were beyond pleading. They were demanding.

The bad luck of having Teresa at our table wasn't her accent, but her anxious, agitated, constant talking. She responded to everything said by any teacher in any situation with desperate over talk. "What she saying? What she saying?" And she didn't have the slightest idea of how to behave while taking a test.

"You're supposed to read the directions," I said.

"And then what are we to do?" The pupils of her big brown eyes were pin pricks. Didn't she know, I thought, that in this country tests like these are serious business, calling for the highest standards of independence? Any talking, any explaining, any collaboration is cheating. I was patriotic at the time, and I'm sure my smug displeasure showed. Maybe she thought about it as a cooperative situation. Why were we trying to ignore her? We were all girls together. I think she wanted us to stop and help her, and that's why she got fussier and louder and, along with blocking my view, managed to keep me from hearing what Sister Stella Mary had to say. She kept up a steady stream of fidgeting, coughing, and asking furtive questions to all of us at the table— during every set of directions for every section of the test.

Consequently for me, most sections of the test were a disaster. On one section, I answered the questions on the first page and then patiently sat waiting for the directions to turn to the next page, wondering, again a little smugly, why the others weren't done, thinking Sister Stella Mary had said, "You may *not* turn the page until you have been directed." That wasn't it. We were supposed to go on. "Stop. Turn your booklets to page twenty-two and wait for the next set of directions."

"What she saying?" asked Teresa.

There were whole pages of the test I didn't take. And Teresa, I'm sure, fidgeting across from me, did worse.

I knew immediately I'd blown it. I felt badly, but had no idea how I might approach Sister Mary Owen, even though Sister Mary Owen was the kindest teacher I'd had so far. I was still afraid of talking to nuns, and I didn't know what to say. I didn't want to tattle. After a couple of days, I just stopped thinking about it all together. It would probably all work out in the end. By now I had a reputation for being pretty smart with good grades. One test wouldn't matter.

It didn't ruin my summer, which I spent getting up at noon, watching old movies on Bill Kennedy's program on Channel Nine in the afternoon, reading about all the American wars, particularly the American Revolution, contemplating whether, with my father's background, I would apply to join the Daughters of the American Revolution as well as the Daughters of the Confederacy. In the evenings, and often into the wee hours, I spent the time walking, walking, walking with Trina. In July we met a tall, handsome and friendly Canadian boy on his way to sell illegal fireworks in Detroit. He looked so beautiful in the sunset, and I hoped that same light shown on me.

The ninth graders reported to school in late August, the Tuesday before Labor Day, for a special half-day orientation session.

Trina and I arranged our usual meeting in front of Veteran's Cleaners. It was a great day, our first day of high school. It would be an easy day, no real academic work, and for the little business we had, we weren't required to wear our uniforms.

Upon arriving in the high school lobby, we were told the good news— of the four ninth grade homeroom teachers for the girls, Trina and I were assigned the same one, Sister Victoria. We almost jumped in jubilation. After getting to our homeroom, we greeted the other friends who'd landed with us.

Sister Victoria was OK, although quieter and more timid, it seemed, than Sister Mary Owen, who exuded self-confidence. Still she delivered an impressive introductory speech, stressing the importance of homeroom spirit. "You'll be going to different classes throughout the day, but these faces are the first you'll see in the morning and the last you'll see in the afternoon." We looked around, and it all seemed good. We would walk all over the school to our classes, quietly, past the hallway monitors, but all on our own.

There was little other business except for passing out our class assignments.

Sister Victoria held a stack of papers, each one folded and stapled so you couldn't see the front. "Do not open your sheet until each girl has received her own," she said, and so we waited.

From the back of each she called individual names and, helped by Janet Mooney, passed them all out. When instructed to open them, we removed the staple.

Immediately I saw something was wrong. I didn't see when I was supposed to go to Latin. I heard the other girls already starting to compare notes. Something was wrong with my schedule. I couldn't find when I had Latin.

I looked at Trina, who sat next to me, and we looked at each other's schedule. Trina didn't have a time for Latin either. Her schedule was exactly the same as mine—English and Speech in the morning, Mass at eleven-thirty, lunch, and then Religion, Science, and Math in the afternoon. I'm not sure how long it took the reality of the situation to occur to me: *Maybe we've been put in the dumb group.* I looked around for Teresa Rivera, but she'd been assigned to another homeroom. As the idea grew, the room started swirling around. Trina and I had both been placed in the dumb group. I looked at her reddening face.

In the meantime, the other girls were merrily comparing notes, leaning out of their desks, signaling across the room, and turning around to talk to those in back of them.

"I got Latin at 10 o'clock." "Me too." "I haven't got Latin until after lunch." "Do you have French *and* Latin?" "So you got English right after Latin? Me too."

They were sorting it out, finding out where their friends were placed, and, from Sister Victoria's point of view, getting too boisterous, so she made quiet-down gestures with her hands.

We couldn't hide it indefinitely. Donna Byk, a friend of both me and Trina, finally drew us in. "What do you have? When are you taking Latin? Hey, how come your schedule doesn't have Latin?"

I might have gone up and asked Sister Victoria. I don't remember. If I did I would have gotten the reserved confirmation that this was no mistake. "You haven't been assigned to take Latin." There would have been no direct words about it, but the message would have been clear.

Students in Holy Redeemer High School, under Mother Mary Patrick as principal, were tracked into four ability groups. The "honors" group consisted of a girls' class and a boys' class of about fifteen students each the first year, winnowed down to a class of boys and girls together the second year. These students took two years of French and four years of Latin. At least two thirds of the students belonged to the "normal" group, with boys and girls enrolled in separate classes, each taking four years of Latin. The girls' "dumb" group, to which Trina and I had been assigned, like the boys' "dumb" group, did not take Latin. The first year we were given Speech as the elective. The girls would be urged to go into secretarial arts, the boys into vocational training. A fourth slower group, consisting of no more than a dozen or so boys and girls, didn't take Speech, but a class called "Reading Skills." I learned after school that Teresa Rivera was assigned to this group.

We took it personally. I'm not sure how much I associated the placement test with our fate. Unlike Trina, who had forgotten about it entirely, I always remembered the experience and could pinpoint the start of my being "dumb." Soon, though, the public shame, and our conditioned response to accept the voice of authority, started us on the course of blaming ourselves. I was dumb. Trina was dumb, too. The more we accepted it, the worse we did in school.

The worst thing to me was that I wasn't going to take Latin. But that wasn't all. The regular classes that everybody took the first year—Religion, English and Algebra, along with the ones they'd take in subsequent years, were also tracked. That meant that while the honors group had Sister John Mary and would be reading Shakespeare and writing long essays, I would sit in English with Mrs. Lewis, reading very little, writing nothing, doing punctuation and grammar drills all year about stuff I already knew. Mrs. Lewis would stand in the front of the room and regale us on the responses we were making while filling in the blanks. "I'm teaching my heart out," she said. "And most of you are still not getting it right."

There's a reason why the first days of school in September are half days. Those are the sentencing days, and then you have the weekend or the holiday to get used to it before you must serve the sentence. "Mama, they don't think I'm smart enough to take Latin. I'm not going to be taking Latin." I told her as soon as I knew. She didn't intervene. She didn't even react. And neither did Trina's mom or dad. Parents in the parish did not question the nuns' authority.

In October in tenth grade, when I was cutting across the schoolyard, I ran into Sister Mary Owen, my former eighth grade teacher, and we stopped to have a conversation. "How do you like Latin?" she said.

"Oh, I'm not taking Latin, Sister," I said. "They put me in the group that couldn't take it. They didn't think I could handle it." As usual, the reasons, the explanations, the excuses, just seemed to trail off, though It didn't sting any less than it had the year before.

Sister Mary Owen didn't say anything for a few seconds. I saw a puzzled frown cross her broad face. When she recovered, she said clearly, "Well, that shouldn't be." We went on, talking a little of other things—the chorus, the Booster Club, and, yes, last winter I'd made purple and gold pom-poms, attended all the games, and cheered wildly for the winning basketball team. I didn't tell her I fell in love with Jack Clement, a star forward.

A week or so after that meeting I was called to the principal's office. "I've called you in because your classes are going to be changed," Mother Mary Patrick said. Tall and energetic, she always spoke with absolute certainty and authority. She scared me to death, but she wasn't unpredictable or crazy.

They had it all worked out. "Yes, all your teachers already know about it." I'd be taken out of slower Biology, Geometry, and Religion, and placed in normal versions of these classes. Since the schedule couldn't fit me in normal English, I was placed in honors English for the rest of the year with Sister John Mary.

"Will I be allowed to take Latin?" I said.

No, too late for Latin. "We don't want you to drop back to take Latin I with the freshmen now that you're a sophomore."

And so I would never take Latin. Instead, I took Spanish with Miss Val Verde.

It was a strange intervention. The next day I changed the entire routine I'd been given in September. I memorized a different sequence of classes, in different rooms. The only bad thing about it was saying goodbye to Trina, who hadn't been rescued like me. "Don't worry, Mary," she said. "We'll still be in homeroom together, and we'll still walk home after school." She would have to wait another year before she, too, was rescued.

It was like being pulled from a swamp where I'd been sinking and being set down on a breezy hill. The new Biology class was already a chapter ahead of the old Biology class in the same book, and with the same teacher, but I found it easy to catch up, because now Biology was so much more exciting. For a month I contemplated how that could be. How could a textbook I thought so dull instantly become so interesting? "Kingdom, Phylum, Class, Order, Family, Genus, Species." I loved the way they got more and more specific in such an orderly way. "*Ameba, protozoa, coelenterata,....*" I memorized the categories, noticing the Latin and loving its ring in my ears. I loved the recursiveness of the processes, the stamens and pistels, the taking in of carbon dioxide and the giving out of oxygen. The plants providing the oxygen desperately needed by the animals; the animals exhaling luscious carbon dioxide needed by the plants. A fair trade.

I took home three Petri dishes and did an experiment recommended by Sister Mary Sebastian. I did nothing to one, kissed another with lipstick on, and kissed the last without lipstick. I had my own hypothesis about Sister Mary Sebastian's hypothesis. The conclusion would no doubt be: "Don't kiss. It's germy. Even worse with lipstick."

Still, I eagerly went along with the experiment. I put the Petri dishes on the heat register to culture for three days. It didn't work out because our old coal furnace, the last one left in the neighborhood, melted all the Petri dishes in one of its typical sudden heat sprees. It didn't matter. I reported on it to the class anyway, holding up the hideously misshapen melted plastic dishes, stressing the failure of the laboratory conditions. When I held them up in front of the class, the girls in normal Biology laughed. The Petri dishes looked like Salavador Dali clocks. I took advantage of the opportunity. I exaggerated the performance, held them up again, dangled them from different angles, and glowed in the laughter. It was the first time I tried to be entertaining. A few years later, when I joined the theater group in college, I would discover that entertaining people was my passion.

Later in Biology, I completed a science project, quite lame in retrospect, on Mendel's theory. I made a cardboard poster showing the probability of eye color over several generations of dominant and recessive genes. Sister Mary Sebastian talked to us like we could learn it. The kids around seemed to think they could learn it. I fell in love with it and learned it, until I was the best in the class, and everybody knew it. I would be a biologist when I got out of school.

It was the same story with Geometry and Religion, although not quite as dramatic. Honors English with Sister John Mary was the only big challenge.

When I started attending the class they were in the middle of studying "Sir Gawain and the Green Knight," and the assignment Sister John Mary gave at the end of the session was to draw the castle as it was described. I had to read the whole poem up to that point to catch up. And then I had to draw the castle, with rings and a moat around it, studying over and over again just what was written in the poem, drawing without artistic ability. I did it once, tore it up, did it again, tore it up, did it again and decided that was it.

All the while I kept thinking of the other students. These were honors students. Some were the kids who'd been on the honor roll all through grade school—the well-washed happy kids who never got in trouble and who'd always done well and been favored in school. They caused me embarrassment when I remembered myself. They scared me when I wondered how much they remembered. I had to assume nothing.

There were others besides the kids who'd been in my homerooms in grade school, others from other teachers' rooms. And new kids who'd joined us from other grade schools. Diana Kujawa, a shy girl from Saint Hedwig's, was probably the smartest kid in the class. Somehow, she was someone with whom I could talk. The honors students were so sure of themselves. Everything they did was bound to be better.

I tore up the last attempt, and did it over again, this time, like every time before, trying to render a better drawing of what I'd envisioned on the first close reading of the poem. When I got to school the next day, Sister John Mary asked us to get out our drawings. Mine was just as good as everybody else's. Most of us had rendered a fairly faithful if slightly different representation. I noted that none of the honors students seemed to behave as though they'd had much trouble. They simply took out their drawings and showed them. I had enough sense to do the same.

Maybe the only difference between an honors student and me was that I had to work harder. I kept up with them all year, even as they talked of all the other classes they had in common, Latin and French, honors everything else, and the clubs and activities they were in or being encouraged to join—the Latin club; the French club; the forensic team; the Optimist Club; the Genetian drama club; the math club; the science club; the *Sentinel*, which was the school newspaper; the quiz-show team; Student Council, and others. In tenth grade they had already bonded into a close-knit intellectual learning community based on being nurtured by their teachers and seeing each other all day every day. By our senior year, they ran the school. I kept my loyalty to the friends I'd made in the slow group—many sensitive silent humble girls whose good will and generosity were consistent, whose minds were unknown.

Though I hadn't quite overcome my self-consciousness and the suspicion I was an imposter in the honors group, I got a "B" in honors English, up from the "C" I'd gotten in English the year before. In eleventh grade they assigned me to normal English to fit the rest of my schedule.

The change to normal classes boosted my self-esteem. My grades between ninth and tenth grade improved dramatically, and in junior and senior years they continued to climb. Without the intervention of Sister Mary Owen, I wouldn't have even thought about going to college. My life would have been far more limited and proscribed. Yet without being assigned to the "dumb" group, I wouldn't have experienced firsthand the effect of tracking and self-fulfilling prophecies.

In July 2007, I retrieved my high school record from the Detroit Archdiocese Archive. The chance to confront my grade school record motivated my inquiries, and I suspected an elaborate file on me might still exist, spanning third, fourth and fifth grades. Perhaps I might find speculation about what they thought was wrong with me, perhaps one teacher's note to another warning her to look out for me. Perhaps too I might find that someone had had some compassion and insight. Certainly I'd find notes from when they met with Mama.

After I finally worked up my nerve and inquired about where to find the record, I learned that grade school records from that long ago had been discarded. The Archdiocese Archive would hold the high school record, but it would be little more than a transcript. I didn't expect to find anything I didn't already know, yet I paid the three dollars and applied for the record anyway.

When the record arrived in the mail I saw for the first time the simple reason why I'd been assigned to the dumb group in high school. Crystal clear and succinct, it was a test score. On the second page of the transcript, I read: "Test name: Placement; test date: 5-58; result: I.Q. 93." My I.Q. was 93! A "normal" I.Q. ranges between 100 and 110. I was definitely below normal. I don't know Trina's score.

By the time I graduated from Holy Redeemer High School in 1962, I was restless and bitter. I couldn't wait to get away from it, as far away as I could, however I could. I didn't ever want to go back to it. I didn't want to think about it for many years. I'd had to do everything the honors students did to prepare for college completely on my own.

That we were given an excellent education nonetheless was the irony that stoked my bitterness. I'd have had little reason to be bitter if I hadn't missed out on opportunities I could see right before my nose. I couldn't appreciate that for a long time. It took me many years to come back. But once back to it, I realized that it was the I.H.M. sisters at Holy Redeemer who inspired me in the first place. Smart women were mentoring girls to be smart. That was a profound gift to have been given—in that neighborhood, and at that pre-feminist time.

Still, I miss taking Latin.

CHAPTER NINETEEN
A CHANCE TO WIN A NEW MERCURY

Every year the freshman, sophomore, junior and senior classes in the high school competed with each other to see who could sell the most Holy Redeemer Fall Festival tickets. Awards were also given to individuals who sold the most tickets for this huge fund-raising event which along with Sunday collections sustained the parish. Trina and I never won any awards, but over the years we developed some secret methods that insured a distinguished sales record.

Our winning combination rested first on selling the tickets together. Individually, I doubt we could have interrupted strangers on the street. Together, we somehow achieved the one-two punch of confidence that allowed us to sell a remarkable number of chances to win the new Mercury, along with assorted second and third prizes—bicycles, televisions, washers, dryers, electric ranges, cash prizes, and lots of Thanksgiving turkeys. The Holy Redeemer Fall Festival was conveniently celebrated the weekend before Thanksgiving in November.

The secret to our success depended on our derring-do in negotiating the city. After numerous disappointments, we soon realized the senselessness of trying to sell them within the parish, trudging up and down Vernor Highway, where probably scores of other kids had gone before. "I already bought five dollars' worth," was not a response we wanted to hear. It made the most sense to hop on a bus, or walk, strategically, to other neighborhoods.

I remember one episode though when we were still attempting to sell in the neighborhood. We walked into Sam's Barber Shop between Morrell and Junction on Vernor Highway and politely asked each of the three men getting a haircut if he'd like to buy some Holy Redeemer Fall Festival tickets. Two of the customers politely declined, but the third, a reddish-haired Irish-looking man in his thirties, must have had a grudge against Redeemer, the first of the many bitter renegade Catholics I'd meet in the coming decades. "Why should I buy a ticket?" he asked. "The Church never did anything for me." His voice sounded educated, but not polite.

Even though I was maturing, I hadn't quite lost my evangelism. The effect of Sisters Florita, Callistus, Frederick Marie, Althea and Mary Owen, as well as all of the messages coming from the *Holy Redeemer Weekly* and the *Michigan Catholic*, were not about to give way without a fight. Here was an opportunity and a palpable duty to Defend the Faith. "The Church has done something for all of us," I said.

"Well, tell me then. Or, better still, get Father Crane to come over here and talk to me about it. I'll be here for an hour. If he comes over here and talks to me, I'll buy ten dollars' worth." He paused to regard my face as I thought it over. After a few seconds, he continued, "I can assure you he isn't going to come around."

During this pause I considered walking back the half block to fetch Father Crane from the rectory. Here was an opportunity for him to talk to an angry man who had obviously fallen away. Father Crane coming over to the barbershop no doubt would show the man that, even though he was a lost sheep, he was worth the effort to bring him back into the fold. But I just couldn't do it. I couldn't imagine ever speaking to Father Crane. I had never spoken to a priest—except in the confessional. It was unthinkable, a girl like me addressing a priest. The only words I had ever said to a priest outside of Confession were, "Yes, Father," and "No, Father." Reluctantly, I let the idea go, but I kept the challenging image of that renegade Catholic.

Trina and I had better luck in other neighborhoods, where we learned to also be selective. If it made little sense to work our own strip of Vernor Highway, it also made little sense to go to West Vernor and try to sell them in Saint Gabriel's Parish, or trek down Fort Street to All Saints. These parishes bordered ours, and competition for a sense of identity was high. I knew I'd never buy a ticket to a Saint Gabriel's puny little *fête*. Why should I? My loyalty was to Holy Redeemer.

Our unlikely goldmine neighborhood for selling Fall Festival tickets turned out to be Skid Row on Michigan Avenue. The bums bought Fall Festival tickets, and they didn't seem offended when the odd pair of one too-tall girl and one too-short girl approached them on the street. They never walked briskly by, pretending like they didn't hear us. Many of the bums had already perfected the art of street begging and held a modicum of empathy for other beggars being ignored or rebuffed with a brusque refusal. Besides, they had time on their hands.

"Excuse me, Sir. Would you like to buy a Holy Redeemer Fall Festival ticket?"

A whiskered old gentleman in tattered work pants with furiously shaking hands needed only to contemplate it an instant. "Ah, Holy Redeemer. How much are they, now?"

It was the Holy Redeemer that roped them in. After all, many of them still living in flop houses on Michigan Avenue, still living in Holy Trinity Parish, had relatives who'd ridden on the great Irish wave that spread itself under the viaduct near the train station, swelling into the new parish founded by the Holy Trinity Irish, our own Holy Redeemer. The bums had a soft spot for Holy Redeemer.

"They're fifty cents each, or three for a dollar."

"I'll buy one of them," said a grizzled old codger with the sun glinting off his whiskers in the bright November sunshine. He fumbled in his tattered pants pocket, came up with his change, examined it in the light, and picked out two quarters.

"What is your name and address, Sir? I've got to put it down on the stub so they can notify you in case you win." I knew his hands were shaking so much he'd never be able to fill out his own ticket, and so I filled it out for him.

That was when our Skid Row customers usually got impatient. The address of the flop house may not have been memorized, although several times resourceful customers gave me their full name for the stub and pointed out a particular bar for me to write down on the address line. "They'll let me know if I win." Usually, though, by this point in the transaction, customers fidgeted. It was taking too long. Perhaps they were starting to regret their impulse to support Redeemer. As quickly as I could, I copied down their names and whatever address information I could gather on the stub, tore off the ticket, handed it to them, and wished them good luck. I really wanted them to win. A fifty-cent investment was considerable for them, and what a pity none of my Skid Row customers ever won, not even a bicycle or a turkey.

We sold in various other conveniently located neighborhoods, trying in the Wayne State University neighborhood because of its proximity to one of our regular destinations, the main branch of Detroit Public Library. One day I approached a pleasant-looking black man, probably a student, in his twenties.

"Excuse me, Sir. Would you like to buy a Holy Redeemer Fall Festival ticket?"

"What can I win?" he said.

The grand prize was always the same, since the priests and members of the Saint Alphonsus Guard negotiated annually through their connections with the bigwigs at Ford.

"You can win a new 1960 Mercury Monterey with four doors, white wall tires, and back up lights."

"What else can I win?" He looked both Trina and me up and down, amused, I think, by the earnest pair who so easily rattled off the spiel. Besides, he was softening for the sell. I thought I detected a glimmer of native-Detroiter excitement in his face, hearing about the new car.

"You can win a thousand gallons of gasoline, or a Frigidaire washer and dryer, and there's two seventeen-inch portable TVs you can win," I said.

"I'll take five dollars' worth," he said.

I tore off the fifteen tickets, and explained how he'd have to put his name, address and telephone number on the stubs so he could be notified in case he won. I handed him the stubs and clipboard I'd brought along for backing. We'd learned to bring something flat to write on.

When I took the stubs back I glanced at the information and was struck by his last name. "Rhodes," it read. What a coincidence.

"Rhodes," I said. "That's my last name. I wonder if we're related!"

The gentleman broadly smiled, took a step backward, and produced a long drawn out, "Yeahhh."

In a flash, I knew exactly what he meant by that exaggerated "yeah." Maybe my Tennessean great great grandfather had owned his great great grandmother. Through my embarrassment—I'm sure my face reddened— he kept smiling and wished us a good day.

I continued down the street complaining to Trina about what I should have said. What would have been the right thing to say? What should I have said? I didn't regret mentioning the possible connection through our shared name. It was an exuberant leap, and I wouldn't have been ashamed at all to claim the pleasant, intelligent (and quite handsome) man as kin. It was what I should have said afterward. "Should I have told him I was sorry about whites owning blacks?" Too heavy for the occasion. "Should I have told him I understood the history?" Unnecessary. "Should I have had the sense to keep my big mouth shut in the first place?" Maybe. "Did I hurt his feelings?" I hoped not.

Although I tried, I couldn't figure out what it was like to be him. This kind young man and his generous attitude would come to me several times during the next decade. We were on the same right side—but we just didn't quite know how to talk about it yet.

CHAPTER TWENTY
1960 AWAKENINGS

One Saturday in February, Trina and I stood in the biting wind in front of Hudson's department store, waiting for the Woodward bus. The plan was to do some research at Detroit's main library, borrow a few books, and stop at one of the joints around Wayne State University for a hot chocolate and an order of fries.

A huge snow had fallen the day before. The buses and cars padded along the snow-caked pavement, making pink-brown tracks that rubbed the salt into the snow but stopped short of melting it. The sound satisfied me— quieter and slower than the hiss the traffic would make once the salt melted the snow.

On the Woodward bus, we were lucky to get a seat above the floor heater that blew warmth up to our frozen faces. The bus took on more people at each of the next three stops. We'd settled in a little, at least had gotten out a hanky to blow our noses, when we noticed the marquis of the Palms Theatre after we passed Grand Circus Park: *On the Beach*. We had no idea what the movie was about, but under the circumstances, the gift of a Saturday free of constraints, it sounded intriguing. Trina liked Ava Gardner, and we both liked Gregory Peck. We nodded at each other, Trina pulled the rope, and at the next corner we got off the bus. We often did that—decided at the last minute to change our Saturday plans.

I supposed the film would carry us off to the tropics with warm sand, gentle surf and sexy scenes. We had no idea we'd be viewing a love affair between two people in the aftermath of World War III, a couple waiting along with all the other human beings left for the multiple radiation clouds to reach them in Australia, the rest of the human species already lost. We didn't expect we'd be watching various minor characters picking their poisons, planning the day and hour when they'd ingest the death-inducing pills which the government distributed to save them from the slower retching death by radiation. Or, like one of the supporting actors, Fred Astaire, choosing to die in his beloved race car, the engine on, rags blocking any air that might seep inside the garage door. I'd heard the haunting Australian song "Waltzing Matilda" before, but not as an anthem of annihilation. By the time we stumbled out of the theater, tears still pouring down our cheeks, night had fallen, the traffic hissed, and the snow underfoot squeaked cold.

In the scant two hours it took to view the movie, my course toward pacifism had been paved. I often wonder if others of my generation, who later protested against war in general, and the Vietnam War in particular, could trace their attitudes as easily to *On the Beach*. Many say the 1960s didn't start until November 1963, after Kennedy's assassination, after Dallas. For me, they started right on schedule, in the winter of 1960.

On the Beach shook the steely edifice of American patriotism I'd built up after the Russians launched the first *sputnik* in October 1957. In the aftermath of *sputnik* I memorized the lyrics to America's patriotic songs and misted over to the strains of any one of them, holding my arm against my heart and pledging from the halls of Montezuma to the shores of Tripoli to give 'em hell and die if need be for my country. The patriotism itself supported the hatred and fear of the Communists I'd been taught in school. It all ran together—the arms race, the competition to be first in outer space, the Catholic Church against the Soviet and Chinese atheists' intent on conquering the world, stamping out Christ and Our Lady, and stripping us of our freedom and the superior American way of life. I wouldn't say I lost my jingoistic attitude about America all at once, but at least after seeing *On the Beach*, I could see that such an attitude, if unexamined and unchecked, might lead to doom.

In winter 1960, in tenth grade, as part of an effort to build homeroom spirit, Miss Val Verde asked each person to prepare a short speech. We listened to one or two each day until everyone had taken a turn.

Diana Kujawa, the brilliant honors student, would go on to graduate second in the class. I liked Diana. She wasn't unreasonably snooty or unreasonably pretty. In fact, she was quite eccentric. Based on a simple elegant syllogism, her five-minute speech argued that not all Polish people are "dumb Polacks," a common enough belief of most of us at the time. She began by cracking two or three dumb-Polack jokes, which got us laughing and served to introduce her straw-man major premise. We believed in the idea of dumb Polack, at least in jest. Then all she had to do was counter the argument in her minor premises. Minor premise one: Copernicus wasn't dumb. Minor premise two: John Sobieski wasn't dumb. Minor premise three: Frédéric Chopin wasn't dumb. Minor premise four: Madame Curie wasn't dumb. Therefore, we'd better think again—not all Polish people are dumb Polacks.

When she placed a long-playing record on the school's turntable and cued it to a Chopin nocturne, she, quite simply, changed my life. I'd never heard anything so beautiful. Something happened to the classroom, which I can still vividly see at that moment, Diane leaning into her turntable, as the beautiful piano music, full of sadness, anger, delicacy and hope, flooded through it. Diane finished her section on Chopin, went on to Curie, and rendered her conclusion just as the bell rang. We applauded the speech, gathered our books, and trooped out of the room.

The next day after school I flew downtown on the Baker bus, and then out Woodward on the Woodward bus to the main branch of Detroit Public Library. I climbed the familiar marble stairs, cast glances at the familiar ornate ceiling, and topped the stairs to look straight into the familiar mural of a giant, eyes cast upward, holding a few men and women, a horse, a carriage, and a horseless carriage in the palm of his outstretched right hand. The Music and Performing Arts Department on the third floor of the library housed bins and bins of long-playing records of classical music. Next to the bins were sound-proof booths with turntables.

The librarian told me how the numbering system worked, which made browsing easier than searching through the catalog. I looked for and found Chopin. I didn't know the difference between a nocturne, an etude, a polonaise, a mazurka or a scherzo. It didn't matter. I played an album of Chopin, noted which other albums also contained the same short piano pieces I'd just fallen in love with, and checked out two albums to bring home.

For the next month I devoured Chopin, listening to the records over and over, locating him in a directory of composers, and reading a book about his life. The details of Chopin's life validated what I'd already figured out from listening to the music. For instance, I could hear what Chopin thought about the November 1830 uprising in Poland through the outraged *Etude in C Minor*. It was no wonder they called it the "Revolutionary Etude." All the music soothed my passionate adolescent heart. All the stories fed my longing for romance and tragedy, for a fit of fatal consumptive coughing. The trials and tribulations of Chopin slid into the context of the nineteenth-century European history I already knew. My passion for the new classical music was obsessive, private, cathartic, often bringing me to tears.

Before long I started to bring home recordings of other composers. Nearly every week I maxed out the lending limit of six records. Chopin led me to other piano music composers, Ravel and Debussy, and then eastward to Dvorak, and then to Tchaikovsky. The records of orchestral music I brought home, with crescendos and percussion, and even an occasional canon shot, lent themselves to being played louder.

"Turn that down!" Mama was nearly frantic, her eyes darting hither and yon. "Turn that damned thing down! What are the neighbors going to think?"

That was the rub. I already suspected what the neighbors might think. Scornful curiosity: "What is that junk she's listening to?" Scornful judgment: "Who does she think she is?" Scorn for the music, born of insecurity: "That crap doesn't even have a melody." Scorn for the uppity girl. "Who does she think she is?" My burgeoning middle class taste was making me an outsider on the block. I felt like it might be wise to hide.

Mama could be a drag, but she worked full time now, leaving me alone with my music. I had no trouble changing my usual after-school TV ritual, abandoning *American Bandstand*, followed by the British *Adventures of Robin Hood* with cute Richard Greene from Windsor's Channel Nine. I learned to

modulate the volume and studied the lode of European music, weaving up
and down and back and forth across the continent of Europe, going back to
the eighteenth century, coming up to the twentieth, reading biographies and
books of music history. I got out Daddy's old 78s and played them, waiting
while the old record player slowed and strained before its tone arm released
the next record in the stack to fall on the one just played—*plop*. If I thought
the downstairs tenants—Margaret and Bill Jackson from Georgia, with their
grown career-Girl-Scout daughter Joannie—weren't home, I danced. I turned
the music up a little louder and danced, waving my body back and forth,
letting my fingertips be the last in graceful motion, stepping lightly, sometimes
even jumping, imagining I was taking wing and caught in the currents of
melody that reached back from the dining room to stream into the dark
hallway. By the time I graduated from high school, I'd acquired a taste for and
recognition of music that ranged from before Bach to after Bartok. Although,
like all of my self-guided sprees of learning, there were gaps.

During the height of my infatuation with the music, I pulled a fold-out
postcard application from a magazine that came to the house. I wanted to
join the Columbia Record Club. Mama practically had a heart attack when I
made the mistake of casually quoting from the ad as I studied it at the dining
room table.

"You're not thinking of joining," she said. "Don't you know it's a come-
on? They're going to send you records and records you don't want, and I'll
end up paying for them."

There it was again, her unwarranted terror, her refusal to acknowledge
my competence.

I assured her in fairly surly terms that I was no dummy. I'd already read
the rules and already knew the trick was vigilance. I'd need to send back the
notice that came in the mail before they sent me the Selection of the Month
if I didn't want it.

"But what if the response card gets lost in the mail? I'm not paying if
you run up a bill," she said.

"Fine." She couldn't stop me in the end. I was a teenager with my own
funds. My culture was my own. I marked the Classical category on the
Columbia application, mulled and mulled, and eventually chose five wonderful
recordings to start my collection of Beethoven, Ravel, Chopin, Rimsky-
Korsakov, and Tchaikovsky. I belonged for two years and never once received
a record I didn't want.

In April 1960, Adolf Eichmann was caught in Buenos Aires. The
capture exposed me for the first time to the knowledge of what the Nazis
had done to the Jews of Europe during World War II. Beginning with a
Signet paperback I bought at Cook's Drug Store for fifty cents entitled *The
Case against Adolph Eichmann*, I started reading everything I could about the
historical facts that had eluded me, while also trying to understand why they'd

done so. The knowledge shocked me, as I began earning a reputation at school for knowing a lot about history, including World War II. My longing for tragedy had even carried me into military strategy, Hitler's Eastern Front campaigns and suicidal decision to dig in at Stalingrad. And still I hadn't learned a thing about the mass exterminations of the Jews. Had there been a conscious effort on someone's part to block it out of history? I didn't remember it being talked about in school or written about in textbooks. Still, I probably could have learned about it—I was doing almost all of my reading in library books now and not in textbooks. Maybe I simply missed it as I let one book suggest the next and learned about the War almost serendipitously.

The word "Holocaust" applied to the mass extermination didn't come into being until later. I think that was good. Not being able to name it, we had to think harder to explain it. And then, how could we? By the time I started eleventh grade in the fall, I was working hard to comprehend the incomprehensible.

I didn't talk to many kids about it. Maybe others in school were taking it just as hard as I was. I don't know. The unfolding of the atrocities caused me so much angst. I took it personally. So many questions. So many uncomfortable coincidences, some profound—to me at least. It rocked my world to think that Eichmann was still signing orders dated the very day I was born in November of 1944, was still dispatching thousands to their deaths. And in the drama of Germany in the weeks and months that followed, Eichmann was busily cleaning up, tidying up, and moving to hide the evidence. It was grisly. Fifteen years had passed. Why hadn't I known about it yet? Why did it take this notable Nazi Adolph Eichmann being caught to start a conversation that in my mind should have been talked about steadily for fifteen years? Why hadn't I learned about it as readily as I'd learned about the battles?

Meanwhile, Mama fondly pointed out the virtues of the German people. After all, her heritage was German, even if distant, all vestiges of the language besides the lullabies discarded by her family during World War I. Still, Mama had so much good to say about Germans, from the food to the music to the feats of efficient engineering to the patient problem solving. Why on earth was she not tempering her idle, rather sentimental remarks with the undeniable dirty facts of history? Knowledge of the world was never a taboo subject between us, and in our house native curiosity and strategies for finding out always trumped ignorance.

"Mama, why didn't you tell me?"

"Well, I don't know," she said. "I never believed it. I heard about it after the War. I heard there were those camps, but I don't think the German people could do such a thing." We didn't have the other phrase we'd eventually learn—"Holocaust denier."

She made me furious, those green eyes darting in the same way they did when she denied family facts, trying to create a pretty fiction out of a heap of more than dirty laundry. It was as though the Nazi evil was a family secret. Mama wasn't stupid, but Mama was a denier, and she'd always been a denier. It enraged me that she tried to bypass historical facts that had come to light in the same way she tried to deny her own insufficiencies.

I felt betrayed. On that level it was personal. How many hours, how many days, had she and I spent on the front porch glider having her tell me all about the War when I asked her—where she was, what she was doing, what she perceived, how she reacted on all the important dates, from Pearl Harbor to V-J Day, what Detroit was like during those times when we were the "Arsenal of Democracy." The rationing, the blackouts, the Liberty Bonds, the salvaging, the double, triple shifts in the factories and the churning out of tanks, planes and ammunition. All of it, she told me freely. The people she had known who fought, some who didn't come back, one who did but wasn't good for anything any more but to stay in the Veteran's Hospital. She pointed him out when we drove by that monstrous edifice on Outer Drive. "Jack Gary is still there. I don't think he's ever coming home." I wondered what he might be doing in there at the moment—eating lunch from a tray, walking the wards, cowering on the floor with a brown army blanket wrapped around his head, on the far side of the bed where no one could see him, taking cover. Mama wasn't much for military strategy, but she knew the rudiments—and some surprisingly astute criticism about the arrogance of Douglas MacArthur. Still, she never once mentioned anything about Hitler and the Jews.

"But what do you mean you don't think the German people could have done it? It's right here. It's undeniable. How could you be so naïve?" I held the book open with one hand and waved a picture of piled corpses in front of her face. I hadn't progressed enough in my thinking to qualify my accusations. In fact, the German people had not been of one mind: many among them had mounted plenty of courageous resistance to Hitler.

"The German people are good," she said, and from the way she said it, I knew she was digging in. She didn't want to know, and so she wasn't going to know. She was hopeless. I pushed at her directly a few more times, but it wasn't going to work.

Maybe Mama just couldn't believe it. Maybe believing it would make her despair. She could hardly imagine the less extreme versions of intolerance she saw around her every day. She couldn't believe racism existed in America since it went against her moral grain. "I believe there's good and bad in everyone," she said and detached herself from the conversations among the neighbors and relatives who regaled against Negros or Jews.

Mama lived her code. I never saw her flinch from speaking directly and with respect to any black person, or Jewish person, or any other person she met. She was readily capable of stereotyping; in fact, stereotyping proved a helpful method of dealing with the different ethnicities that coexisted in the ethnically aligned city. "You know those Italians are hot-headed." Stereotyping, often with humorous appreciation, was one thing, but racial hierarchy was another. It offended her inherent sense of the underdog. She knew so well from her family what it was like to be an underdog.

I thought about it further and started to feel compassion for her. She denied it because to accept it was to despair. That despair, I figured out, was exactly what I was facing. How was I going to believe it, and of course I couldn't help but believe it, looking at the photographs, seeing the corpses piled in heaps, the walking skeletons, the children with sunken faces, the lampshades made of human hide, the crematoriums. How could I believe it, believe that the Germans, any civilized society or people, could systematically and efficiently set out and carry out the murder of another people, striving to kill every woman, man and child? I could believe it, but I couldn't understand it. I invested all of my energy in trying to understand.

I was strident, challenging the denial or ignorance of the older generation as strongly as I could. Not everybody reacted to it as I did. One day in the summer when I arrived at Trina's house with the book I was reading about the butchering, I ran into Trina's father among several of her brothers and sisters in the living room. I lectured, pointing out the pictures in the book. Trina's father cut in. "They should have made lampshades out of all of them."

No one in the room responded. When I asked Trina about it later, outraged as I was, she almost shrugged. "I don't listen to him. He doesn't know what he's talking about."

I was amazed at her seeming indifference, but when I pondered it further I saw her wisdom. No one was going to raise the consciousness of Trina's father, and a long discussion would have only meant more anti-Semitic expressions of his feelings.

My angst after Eichmann was captured involved the fact that knowledge of the mass exterminations had slipped by me. But there was more to it. It seemed that the extermination of Jews by the Nazis presented an evil so profound that to study it, to understand it in at least a small measure, to find a way not to despair, was necessary to my survival. I was soon reading Jean Paul Sartre, who shows that anti-Semitism and hate arise out of insecurity, and brilliantly writes about living afterwards, our actions earning us a measure of authenticity. After Sartre, I read Albert Camus' novels, attempting, I think, to soften my sense of despair by carrying it into the realm of reduced expectations—the absurd and our simple caring for each other. If it was already 1960, I was only ten or so years behind these writers who would have a profound influence on me.

I extended my personal campaign to keep from slipping into despair. I read, I read more, I read even more, from transcripts of the trials at Nuremburg to *Mein Kampf*, to histories pointing out the genesis of Nazi racism, even, as Wilhelm Reich theorized, in the Bavarian Catholicism so similar to that of my mother's family. I barely understand a word of Reich's long treatise, *The Mass Psychology of Fascism*, but my Aunt Mag, I reasoned with a sickening shudder, would have made a good Nazi. It wasn't difficult to support my claim with evidence. She was a long-time devotee of Father Coughlin, the priest who in the 1930s had spit out weekly anti-Semitic venom on the radio, and he still wrote little pamphlets and worked as the pastor of the Shrine of the Little Flower in Royal Oak. I read about the patterns of racism and denial, about the failure to do anything to stop it, about the disease that affected America as well.

I also needed to walk among Jewish people. It was hard to explain. Maybe it was the appreciation of the culture I'd gotten from reading John Hersey's *The Wall* about the Warsaw Ghetto. It didn't matter if I'd be walking among American Jewish people with the good luck of having parents and grandparents who left Europe long before the War, long before the Nazis ever came to power. I read and I prayed and I walked and felt a palpable gratitude that a people so tortured would not vanish.

Few Jewish people lived around Holy Redeemer. With the exception of a couple of shopkeepers, who I wasn't sure were Jewish, the only Jewish person I'd ever known was Dr. Himmelhoch, who'd been a gun-collecting friend of Daddy's before he became our pediatrician. We'd been out to his house years earlier after he'd gone into semi-retirement and attached an office to his house near Seven Mile Road and Livernois. I knew the neighborhood was Jewish. Mama had driven west on Seven Mile Road, pointing it out to me, showing me the Stars of David on the markets, stopping to buy some pastries at one of the Jewish bakeries.

I started taking the Livernois bus to Seven Mile Road and transferred to the Seven Mile Road bus to the Jewish neighborhood between Wyoming and Schaeffer, getting off opposite the Jewish religious store, Borenstein's Bookstore. I usually went alone, although later Trina went there with me.

I felt compelled to study the displays in the windows of the bookstore. I looked at the menorahs and the prayer shawls, and so many objects whose purposes I didn't know. I looked through the glass to see the clerks wearing yarmulkes. I walked past the kosher meat markets and bakeries and grocery stores and saw the Mogen David displayed over those business doors. I had to see it displayed casually, meaning something else, meaning the food was kosher, to get the memory of it being worn as a badge of shame adjusted in my mind. I had to walk by the synagogues. I had to see an occasional yarmulke on an observant boy or man, although I rarely saw a person in the dress of a strict orthodox Jew. (I didn't know at the time that a more orthodox neighborhood was actually closer to me on Dexter Avenue.) I took delight in every person I passed. I knew they were Jewish. They looked Jewish; at least they looked like what I recognized as Jewish. They didn't know, but I was almost moved to tears of joy by them. Their walking freely, laughing, talking, self-absorbed or absorbed in someone else, was the only salve that helped to heal the wounds that my knowledge carved in my soul. These living Jews were proof a culture would flourish, that it wasn't dead.

I knew it was a long shot. It wasn't Israel. Most of these people had been as safe and sound as we had been during the War. But it was symbolic, and it was my way of dealing with it. It was my secret way of bearing what I unexpectedly discovered. Genocide, one people wiping out all traces of another, can happen. In America, some Indian tribes were totally lost. I needed to see survivors. And of course none of the people I passed on the street had any inkling that the adolescent girl casting subtle looks at them was experiencing an epiphany, seeing our shared existence as survivors. I too had suffered discrimination and I too was a survivor.

On Labor Day of 1960, John Fitzgerald Kennedy kicked off his campaign for the Presidency in Detroit in Cadillac Square. Coming before the Detroit crowd on Labor Day to kick off the Democratic Party's Presidential campaign followed a tradition set by Harry Truman. Trina and I walked downtown to hear the speech and attend the rally. It was a pleasant late summer morning, and we never seemed to get over the joy we experienced hiking all by ourselves over distances, getting somewhere important on our own steam.

I can't remember what we talked about on the way. Trina and I were political. All our teachers had encouraged us to be aware of national and world events, and we'd been reading the newspaper practically every day for at least a year. We were also political in the same way most working-class Catholics going into that election were political. The chance for a Catholic president was nothing less than a miracle—the anticipation cut across all generations—even as Kennedy took the heat for being Catholic elsewhere in the Midwest and the South. In Holy Redeemer Parish the prospect of an Irish-Catholic president put the majority of the parish into tremors of delirium. We even thought we detected a little smirk on the faces of the nuns talking about it. We definitely could see their habits swaying, which meant when they talked about it they couldn't stand still.

Until we saw Kennedy in person and heard him speak, we hadn't associated him with our generation. At forty-three he was a good deal older, the age of many of our classmates' parents, an older man. Of course we were aware our generation was in ascendancy. High principled and optimistic in challenging times, we saw no limits. We were young enough to consider the turning of the decade as a new slate, the end of a dull decade and the start of a promising time. After all, we were born in the 1940s, we'd come to consciousness and been schooled in the 1950s, and now we were ready to participate in the 1960s.

Trina and I arrived downtown early, and in the swirling throng that soon filled every inch of Cadillac Square, we maintained a good place, no more than forty feet from the speakers' platform situated on the steps of Old City Hall, whose days were numbered, considered old-fashioned and slated to be torn down. The pigeon-stained statues of famous Detroiters that stood half-hidden in its alcoves on the facade of the building looked particularly forlorn as they kept us company during the wait. By the time the speeches started at ten-thirty, about 60,000 people had swarmed into the Square from all directions, the majority simply breaking away from the Labor Day Parade marching down Woodward Avenue. Blocks of men and women with matching local union shirts, blocks of men and women waving matching local union banners, phalanxes of solidarity forever, flooded into the Square. Detroit, the staunchest biggest union town in North America—Kennedy would pitch his speech to the labor audience on Labor Day.

A few speeches preceded Kennedy's. Mayor Miriani, who was not a Democrat, welcomed everybody to the city. Al Barbour, the head of the AFL-CIO, Senator McNamara, Lieutenant-Governor Swainson, and other Democrats running for office spoke next. Walter Reuther, the head of the United Auto Workers, made a longer speech, ending in the endorsement of Kennedy. When Reuther, a greatly respected figure, voiced the first word of his speech, the wildly cheering crowd immediately fell silent and stood still. His speech didn't last long, and soon Governor Soapy Williams was introducing the Democratic Senator from Massachusetts, John Fitzgerald Kennedy.

"I have come today from Alaska, America's last frontier, to Michigan to state the case for America's new frontier." Goose pimples crawled up the sides of my stomach and settled in my nipples. Such verbal eloquence. The metaphor, already dear to my heart—I saw myself as a daughter of the Appalachian frontier. Medical care for the aged, a minimum wage of a dollar and a quarter. America would be first in the world and first in the fight for peace.

The sandy red-haired senator looked younger than any of our classmates' parents. He spoke clearly, relentlessly, beating out the measures of the cadence of his speech with his right hand. "I take my case to the American people because I am confident that the American people want to bring an end to racial discrimination everywhere—in the schools, in the homes, in the churches, in the lunch counters. I want every American free to stand up for his rights, even if sometimes he has to sit down for them." He talked about collective bargaining, about workers' rights, about economics, about the balance of power with the Russian and Chinese Communists.

He gave the germ of what would become his most quoted line from his inaugural address. "The new frontier," he said, "is not what I promise I'm going to do for you. The new frontier is what I ask you to do for our country. Give me your help, your hands, your voice, and this country can move again." The crowd cheered, and the birds flew up. I looked over at Trina, whose eyes were shining like mine.

With the speech over, Kennedy and his entourage moved to walk back to the Sheraton-Cadillac Hotel, where they had stayed the night. Most of the crowd was scattering, but Trina and I followed the Kennedy entourage, watching the brightly colored banners of the campaign workers and supporters, watching the line of "Kennedy Girls" in straw hats, white blouses, blue skirts, high-heeled shoes, and a banner saying "KENNEDY" across

their bosoms. Kennedy, as he talked to reporters, shook hands with well
wishers, stood out apart.

When the crowd turned the corner, just in front of the hotel, it shifted,
and Trina and I, who had been far in the rear, were suddenly thrust into the
front. As John Kennedy walked into the hotel, waving and grinning from ear
to ear, he passed no more than six feet from us. We were six feet away from
the soon-to-be President of the United States. None of the television speeches
of Kennedy, none of the newsreel footage, none of the portraits, matched
with any precision the mobility of Kennedy in person. A new day was dawning,
and I would have followed him anywhere.

Chapter Twenty-One
Out of the Neighborhood

By my senior year I was well known, at least among the girls, as a brainy rebel. I didn't like being tall, but I saw a certain symmetry in the way I stood up and asked questions and my stature. I may have been insufferable to some, but I clearly remember being admired by others for my pointed questions and keeping our teachers on their toes. Others appreciated my sense of humor.

Of course, we all took roles. I felt safe as a brain because I'd honed the requisite skills. I lacked the self-esteem or social skills to be popular. I didn't hold enough honors-group status to be powerful. With the exception of one real boyfriend, another brainy rebel like myself, I didn't have the confidence to step into the light where I'd be noticed by boys.

Also, I didn't exhibit the submissiveness or reserved good manners to be loved by the nuns. Some residual fear, a little like that of a dog beaten as a puppy, kept me out of reach, for better or for worse, of any of my nun teachers. I'm sure they could see it in my eyes. Yes, there was a little of the cur in me, distrustful and suspicious, covered by a capacity from all my reading to articulate and challenge ideas.

Sister Mary Kevin, my senior homeroom teacher who also taught history, was an extraordinarily smart woman whom I adored. A spirited red-faced, tiny woman from England, she spoke with an accent that was best heard when she was excited. As a history teacher, she often became impassioned.

One day I accidentally challenged Sister Mary Kevin about the Virgin Birth, a doctrine I failed to understand, especially after studying biology. I knew that the Angel Gabriel came to announce to Mary that she would give birth to the Savior, but I assumed that biologically Joseph had to have impregnated Mary. After all, I'd come to appreciate the propensity of God to think in male and female terms across the range of creation. Call them seeds or eggs, call it sperm or pollen.

Sister Mary Kevin had posed a question to us: "Which is better, the vocational life or the married life?" I think she wanted us to say both were blessed, but a religious life, involving a calling from God to a vocation, was at least slightly, if not substantially, better.

I raised my hand and stood. "Well, the married life can't be less, Sister. After all, Our Lady was a married woman."

Sister Mary Kevin's eyes performed a double take followed by a long pause. Even some of the other girls looked around. "What do you mean 'Our Lady was a married woman'?"

"She was married to Joseph," I said. "Our Lord was our Savior, the Son of God, but Joseph was His human father. Mary was a married woman."

Sister Mary Kevin was probably dumbfounded that a fundamental Catholic doctrine had eluded one of her brightest students. She had a habit of looking a little absent when she was thinking hard, responding patiently and thoughtfully to challenging questions. Although it seems incomprehensible, what really had eluded me was the literal meaning of the word "virgin." Of course, I prayed to the *Virgin* Mary, Mary *Virgin* of *Virgins*, Mary our Blessed *Virgin* Mother. Of course, I had admired virgin martyrs such as Agnes and Saint Maria Goretti. I knew "virgin" meant chaste and innocent, but I didn't know it actually meant a woman or girl who'd never had sex. After all, we girls at Holy Redeemer didn't say we were going to remain virgins until marriage. We said we were going to remain pure. "Pure" meant a girl with an intact hymen who'd never had sex.

"But don't you believe in the Virgin Birth?" Sister Mary Kevin said. "Mary was chosen by God. She wasn't impregnated by Joseph. She didn't have sexual intercourse with Joseph. She remained a virgin."

"That's preposterous, Sister," I said. "Why? How could she have a baby without sex?"

"It was a miracle," Sister Mary Kevin said. "That's why Gabriel came to her at the Annunciation to tell her she was with child."

"But that doesn't make sense," I said. "God doesn't work that way. There's nothing wrong with sex if it's within marriage. Our Lady was married to Joseph. God wanted her to be a model to other married women. She was a mother."

Sister Mary Kevin's face turned beet red. "It's a doctrine of the Church," she insisted, "and you have no business disputing it." It wasn't like her, falling back on authority like that. She usually responded to my challenges with dialogue, calling on her store of knowledge.

The bell rang. Time to rotate to our next class. After school I browsed numerous books of doctrine at the holy store. Of course her explanation of the Virgin Birth was correct, and once again I'd failed to grasp the Church's absolute teachings—or somehow followed my own reasoning to avoid them—because of vague language. The Virgin Birth was Church doctrine. Still, it seemed fishy. And not particularly reverent. I figured you could love God better when you noticed and accepted the way His mind worked, that He kept doing the same thing over and over again, like any artist. He liked the symmetry of requiring all species to couple, from the flowers to the birds to the bees to the wooly mammoths. Why, if He so loved the world, would He introduce His Only Begotten Son in such a totally unnatural manner? I was starting to question Articles of Faith.

In the middle of twelfth grade, I quit Sodality, the club of girls who did good works. I couldn't stand those after-school meetings where the pious girls sat around comparing evidence of their holiness. "I volunteered at Saint Pat's last week, and it was very rewarding." "Oh, I find the Home Visitors of Mary to be even more rewarding. Have you gone there?"

I'd only joined Sodality to supplement my involvement in the chorus after I'd lost interest in the Booster Club. To maintain my membership in the National Honor Society, I needed two activities, and I didn't feel secure enough as a Johnny-come-lately to join in the activities controlled by the honors students. I was losing interest in being holy. Unable to face the nun who was the Sodality moderator, I told Sister Mary Kevin in homeroom that I wanted to quit.

"If you quit, you'll relinquish your membership in the National Honor Society," she said.

"I don't care, Sister," I said. It was an act of rebellion.

"It's up to you," she said.

A little after Christmas in twelfth grade, Trina and I had a falling out. It also involved Pat Malewski, who'd been a close mutual friend since eighth grade. In years of reminiscing, neither Trina nor I remembered exactly what our disagreement was about. Finally Pat suggested that she remembers being jealous over my managing to attract a boyfriend. Jealousy was understandable. With the segregated classes and the high school caste system, most of the girls didn't mix with most of the boys, a situation yielding bumper crops of perfectly-normal adolescent-girl wallflowers. I'm not sure that jealousy was all it was about. I certainly didn't consider it as a reason at the time.

It pained me greatly to watch Pat and Trina become best friends and taunt me in twelfth-grade English class. Trina, who'd finally been placed in normal classes in her junior year, sat next to me, while Pat sat in front of me, so I was forced to endure their friendly banter. In late April we were asked to pass our term papers to the front of the room. When I did, Pat made a show of turning around and reading and sniffing at my title. I'd written on Japanese *koto* music. Listening to records for hours at the library had led me into territories that still surprise me. The first sentence of the paper, *The Japanese have distinguished themselves in the art of borrowing*, is still familiar to me, for I worked on that sentence and others an entire weekend, turning a clunky introductory paragraph into something a little more graceful. Pat's snub hit the mark and hurt. I was acutely aware that my interests made me an outsider in the neighborhood, and that people might think of me as a snob. In fact, I wondered whether my middle-class interests and aspirations toward college may have caused the rift.

When the rupture between me and Trina insured we would not support each other in the last transition, only bitterness was left for me. This falling-out shook my ability to trust. Trina had been a friend with whom I'd shared everything for years. Somehow, even with the betrayals of my life, my father and my sister leaving, Mama letting me down at times, I behaved with Trina as though nothing would ever come between us. I had no wariness about the repercussions of being out of sorts one day or saying the wrong thing the next.

Trina and I could disagree and maintain our separate interests. She joined Junior Achievement in tenth grade and volunteered to do a lot of work in Dearborn, while I wallowed in books, books, books, music and politics. In eleventh grade, I joined the Model United Nations where I planned strategies with Bob, that senior who became my first boyfriend. The separate interests between me and Trina provided more to talk about, more gossip about mutual friends and acquaintances. The trust I felt in Trina seemed absolute. I never imagined our friendship would end.

I kept other friends, a band of five girls, organized principally by me. They were girls on the fringe, the ones who never attend class reunions. As the year wound down, I became more anxious to get away from the neighborhood and Redeemer. I would be ruthless in my wish to get away, temporarily suspending my friendships with everybody immediately after graduation.

On the night of the prom, May 2, 1962, I organized all five of the girls to go hear Eugene Ormandy and the Philadelphia Orchestra at Masonic Temple. It was an act of total defiance—a kind of "stick-it-up-your-ass" gesture, fostered in part by the slim odds against most of the girls in the class being asked to the prom by any of the boys. With the boys and girls in separate classes and separate home rooms on separate floors, they just didn't see enough of each other to mix.

Even the nuns felt compelled to do something about the girls who would not receive invitations. They organized a mixer the month before and invited boys from Boys Catholic Central to come to Redeemer with the expressed mission of rescuing at least some of us girls whose hopes would be dashed. I boycotted the mixer and complained long and loudly to anybody who would listen about how hypocritical and desperate it was. What was the prom if you were so desperate you needed to rely on a strange boy's pity? My anger was a cover, one I used to hide my feelings from even myself. In reality I would have gone in a minute if I hadn't recently broken up with brainy Bob. I may even have attended the mixer if I hadn't had my hillbilly pride.

My solution, though, organizing the excursion to go hear the Philadelphia Orchestra, proved a classy alternative. I borrowed Mama's second-hand 1955 Chevy for the occasion and picked up the girls, none of whom wore prom dresses. Instead, we all wore dressy sheaths, rhinestone earrings, white gloves and high heel shoes. We took our programs from the ushers and hobbled up the steep balcony stairs of Masonic Temple—serious, sophisticated and formal. We glanced at each other to observe we were all there, all sitting pretty, and waited for the music to start.

The orchestra played a Wagner overture, Tchaikovsky's Fifth Symphony, and, after intermission, symphonic excerpts from *Lulu* by Berg. I saved the program. On the way home, Carolyn Thomas, the only black student at Redeemer, remarked, "I'm not sure I liked that music." The others reacted somewhere in between. Me, I liked the music, but even more I liked the ceremony of the occasion. I was proud of myself. The next day, we all had something important besides the prom to buzz about in home room. I looked around at the others, the ones who neither came with us, nor went to the prom, a disproportionate number of them from the dumb group.

When news of who got which scholarships circulated around the school in early May, I was stricken with jealousy, almost blind with alienation. I couldn't be a good sport about it, and acknowledge that the winners did better on their SATs and applications, because I'd never applied.

No matter how many times I nagged, I couldn't convince Mama to fill out and submit the financial section of the scholarship application. The form asked for marital status, income from employment, income from investments, a rough calculation of the cost of assets such as the house and car. She considered the questions invasive and outrageous. I couldn't win this battle because I didn't know how to fight it.

"Ma, everybody's parents have to fill out this form if they're going to try for a scholarship."

"I don't believe it. They wouldn't ask this information out of everybody. I don't want them knowing about my finances. I'm not filling it out."

It was one of those dart-eyed times, and she was absolutely set in her way. I didn't know the next step to talk her into it. She was doggedly suspicious. My SAT scores were in the middle nineties, high but not exalted enough to achieve recognition as a National Merit Scholar. Still they might have allowed me to compete for other scholarships that calculated financial status of the parents into the equation. I wasn't sure of any of it, and so I didn't know how to argue with Mama. I might have mentioned, that for as well off as Mama thought we were, for as much as she saved, she wasn't acquiring more wealth than the typical middle-class salary-earning *fathers* of the students with whom I'd be in competition. I probably had a chance.

Like many parents in the neighborhood, Mama didn't think it was a good idea for her daughter to go to college. Yet, in March of my senior year, I applied to two schools: the University of Detroit and Loyola in Chicago. Both schools were Catholic, both run by Jesuits. I was accepted by both but knew I'd never be able to afford moving to Chicago. Around the time the acceptances came in, she started her last-ditch campaign to talk me out of going. "Won't you at least go up to the bank and fill out a job application?"

She wanted me to work in a bank, preferably her bank, the Detroit Bank and Trust branch across from the church at the corner of Vernor and Junction. It's hard to describe just how much of a dream of hers that was. She loved money. Not simply because of what it represented. She loved money. Literally. When she saw it her eyes sparkled the same way they did when she faced a half pint of French vanilla ice cream or stared at the turbulent turquoise river. She liked to look at money. She liked to count it. She liked to turn the bills so the presidents all faced the same way. She loved stacking it in order, tapping it again and again on the table. She loved putting pennies into paper fifty-penny rolls. She loved licking her finger to count the big stacks. For her a kind of paradise on earth could be grasped, with legitimate cause to smell and fondle stacks of money, by working in the bank. It didn't matter how much time she'd spent observing me through childhood and adolescence, she could only put me in her shoes. I too would be happy working with all that money. And she could keep me close to home.

"I am not working in the bank, Mama," I said.

"But why don't you at least go up and fill out an application? You might like it."

"I'm not working in the bank. I'm going to college."

"But what good is that going to do you?"

She was a tough case, and so obtuse that I couldn't share my intellectual dreams. I had dreams of becoming a successful biologist or chemist, but they were ill-formed.

"How much is the tuition?" she said. "It costs a lot of money."

The tuition at University of Detroit at the time was twenty-four dollars a credit hour. I remember precisely because of Mama's and my negotiations. The tuition at Wayne State, the large public university in Detroit, was less than half as much. I briefly considered whether that would work on Mama, even though the nuns had told us we might lose our faith if we went to Wayne, the hotbed of communism.

The glimmer of a cheaper price interested Mama a little, but then she returned to the same argument. "But what good will it do you?"

"Well, at U of D," I said, "maybe I can find a good husband." The argument came to me in that moment of expediency. Her mouth got thoughtful. I knew immediately that I'd hit on something. I was convincing her. She was considering.

I went on to describe the odds. With the many engineering students, the odds were good. "You know, Mama, there's nine boys for every girl."

"Are there?" she said.

"Yeah, and they're all Catholic."

We agreed that Mama would pay my tuition, and I'd pay for everything else: clothes, books, transportation, and any food not consumed at home. I'd work the summers and, of course, live at home. Living elsewhere was an expense that was out of the question.

On the morning of high school graduation we wore white dresses. Mine was brocaded cotton with lace around the skirt and a tight bodice with spaghetti straps. We were to put on our white robes over the dresses in the girls' lavatory. I was in a fog—of grief, of anger, of not knowing what I felt. I had walked up to school alone. I had my little band of girls, but they all came from different directions. I walked into the familiar lavatory on the first floor, keenly aware that I would never walk into it again. I knew I'd never come back, never. The only agenda was to put on the robe, zip it up, stand in front of the mirror to comb my hair and bobby pin the mortarboard hat. Pat Malewski and Trina walked into the lavatory as I stood at the mirror meeting the challenge of attaching the hat to my bubble curls. Not seeing me, they giggled and talked about the upcoming ceremony. When Pat saw me, she gave me the look, the recognition, and then the sidewise and upward turn of the head, not even a nod or "Hello." I can't remember whether Trina acknowledged me or not. Perhaps I snubbed Trina, taking the initiative from Pat. They had each other. My heart broke with this last straw. I bore it because there was nothing else to do.

When we marched down the aisle of the church, Jerry Kohl, as valedictorian, led, followed by Diana Kujawa as salutatorian, then nine other boys and girls with gold stoles. Nancy Bogan and I, followed by Jim Coury and Bill Peterman, came next. We wore red stoles. We didn't belong to the National Honors Society, but they couldn't take away our grades and class standing. I wore my stole proudly, a badge of red rebellion. We were the last students with stoles. After us, the rest of the boys marched in blue robes, followed by the girls in white robes.

When we'd progressed a third of the way down the long aisle, I heard a middle-aged woman say to her husband, "Look at them. They've got *red* stoles." Her voice oozed, implying that we were even better than the gold stoles.

I kept the red stole crumpled up in a box, where it eventually turned pink with age.

On the hot sticky Tuesday in June, two days after graduation, I got dressed up in what the nuns called "business attire" and took the bus to the Cunningham Drugs headquarters on Twelfth Street, and immediately I came back with a summer job working at the soda fountain, assigned to the Vernor-Junction Cunningham's in the neighborhood.

It was strange serving some of the same kids whom I'd been afraid of or jealous of through all the years of high school. The tables had turned, literally, as I dispensed whatever they wanted, from the fairly-good French fries, to the suspect chili, to the safe cherry Cokes. For a few, I wondered whether I'd spit in their soup if they ordered it. They never ordered it, yet I knew immediately I would not. There was no need. We were now free of the past. And I was going to college.

I worked at our neighborhood Cunningham's through June, but then I started subbing at several Cunninghams,' and that gave me a summer of vivid memories of neighborhoods across the city. The Cunningham's at Oakman Boulevard and Michigan in Dearborn featured mice that came begging whenever I washed the dishes in the nasty water that pruned up my hands. At the same Cunningham's, they made tuna salad on Thursday evenings to cater to the Catholics who couldn't eat meat on Friday. They kept what they didn't sell all week, often in a tray refrigerated only by daily cycles of fresh ice. I wanted to gag when a couple of middle-aged women with veiled hats ordered it for lunch on Thursday.

Another ethical dilemma. Should I tell them? But this time that voice in my head that used to constantly pray had ceased. The voice that invoked at every turn, "Please, dear Lord, let me do the right thing," was dead. I experienced an epiphany of power: I was on my own. Whether I steered them away from the tuna or not was my decision, and not God's. I decided, making a calculated estimation—what the hell. I didn't like the way they looked. But it probably wouldn't kill them anyway. I scooped up a generous portion and ladled it out onto their already-toasted bread.

One time I got a precious taste of the capacity of a church congregation for generosity. I was told to report to the Cunningham's on Warren and Burnette for a week, starting when they opened at 8:30 AM on Sunday morning. I didn't think much about it as Mama drove me over in the car. I'd get the coffee made, drink a cup of it, figure out where things were, and go from there. I started the coffee, but then the double doors suddenly swung open and at least twenty well-dressed black women in big floral pastel hats accompanied by a similar number of well-dressed black men in light-colored suits and natty ties filed in. I looked around and they had filled every stool on the entire length of the long, long soda fountain.

They'd just gotten out of the early service at the Baptist Church down the street, and going to Cunningham's afterwards, I guess, was a ritual. They didn't just want coffee, or an English muffin or an order of toast or two. They wanted the full range of Cunningham's breakfast soda-fountain offerings—bacon and eggs, pancakes, hash browns, poached eggs, boiled eggs, pies and pastries and French toast. I hadn't even had time to figure out where most of the ingredients were located.

I cantered around in a heat, getting the griddle going, flipping open bins, scratching my head, and cracking eggs. They waited patiently. The entire counter filled with customers, some who'd ordered pancakes twenty, thirty minutes before, sat there in wondrous good cheer. Their soulful black faces and mild smiles opened a world of compassion as I paced up and down that counter. I finally got all the orders cooked and served. And when the customers started getting up and leaving, I found I'd made more tips than I'd ever made, tips sometimes larger than the bill, tips not for being good, but for trying. I never forgot it.

I wasn't much of a soda jerk, but I loved watching the people—seeing the way they sidled up, the way their faces changed as they got ready to transact with me, the way their eyes on the menu told me how hungry they were, the way they wore their work costumes or their ethnicities on their sleeves. At most of the stores, the soda fountain was a long stage I hurried back and forth upon, and I noticed that some of the men were watching me. It seemed a safe way to be admired.

*   *   *

As summer progressed and money from my cashed paychecks accumulated, I started studying what I'd need in the way of a college wardrobe, and I started visiting the upscale shops on Fort Street, gazing at myself in the dressing room mirrors of Winkleman's. I was tall and slender, with delicate wrists and ankles, nice hands, a small waist, and good legs. I might even have assessed myself beautiful, had I not twisted the expression: "not really *that* ugly," which I moderated to "not bad." I loved the clothes, and I knew my body was now pleasing enough to nurture. I'd treat it kindly. I started collecting a coordinated assortment of "coed" clothes—bright wool box-pleated plaid skirts, pastel blouses, and long cardigan sweaters. Anticipating the turning of the leaves, my color choices ran to green and gold, with splotches of red and brown. I stockpiled my coed clothes in a separate area of the closet—waiting for fall.

Toward the end of the summer I received a fat letter from the University of Detroit, announcing the program for orientation week, along with an assignment to procure and read Joseph Conrad's *Heart of Darkness*, a novel to be read in preparation for the English placement test. I'd cleaned up the way-back room again, this time making it a place where I could read and study, this time accomplishing the task with less resistance from Mama. I was surer now, more honest, and I told her exactly what I'd toss—the piles of print, the broken objects, the worthless and absurd. But I was also less exact as I deflated the piles and re-boxed them, not bothering to sort them to make them logical or clean. The disorder, I discovered, helped to calm Mama down. I found a storage space big enough for her treasures in the basement and told her, "You can get to this junk whenever you want to." She couldn't stop me, and she knew it.

On an August day, I sat in Mama's maroon easy chair that I'd brought back to the way-back room and lost track of time, my mind engrossed in the Conrad novel. I looked up through the open window to see the familiar red sun setting and then returned my eyes to the book. I looked up again, the sky redder, the familiar breeze at sunset stirring the curtain, the waning of light coinciding with the closing of a chapter. I was in total harmony—a girl sitting in a clean space reading a thrilling exotic book, a girl going to college with a closet full of beautiful coed clothes. I'd come to a milestone, and I was ready to go on.

Mama's attitude about my going to college improved that summer, starting with the day of graduation. I remember hearing her friend Laura Schuler congratulating her. "You should be proud of yourself, Verna. Just think! You were a widow and raised a girl who's going to college all on your own."

An Epilogue
The Way-Back Room Revisited

It didn't take long, as the 1960s decade progressed, to shift my view of Mama and her position on housework.

First it was sitting with my witty theatre-group colleagues at U of D in the green room, where we hung out before, after, and sometimes during our classes. We did a lot of talking about everything here. We were rebels, thinking for ourselves, adopting the ennui of Beatniks, critical of the values of the 1950s culture. My friends would sometimes speak of their mothers.

"She's so neurotic, she waxes the kitchen floor every week and strips it once a month."

"When she's not cleaning the cupboards, she's dusting the window ledges, and scrubbing down the basement floors." When they spoke of their mothers, they never mentioned hours of talking or excursions down to the river.

They spoke archly of what their mothers served them up for lunch and dinner—the canned green beans and spinach, Velveeta and Spam sandwiches on Wonder Bread, frozen pot pies and TV dinners—all things Mama refused to allow into the house. They thought my tales of Mama's eccentricity exotic, and they laughed when I mentioned that Mama did allow Franco-American spaghetti, but hopelessly diluted it every time, rinsing the can with water that she poured into the pan along with the spaghetti, because she didn't want to waste even the slightest vapor. "You've got to get all the goodness out," she would say.

As the decade grew, and we pulled more and more away from the 1950's consumerism and wastefulness, we started to see that the roles of women might be more than keeping a clean house and doing what they were told. And so Mama's refusal to participate in the 1950's culture could be seen in a new light. The late 1960's counterculture offered a fresh interpretation of Mama's "deviant" behavior. She became an interesting and admirable character, for she'd been a 1950s nonconformist.

In 1972, I bought a feminist poster showing a woman with a Mona Lisa smile holding up a broom she'd just broken in two. *Fuck Housework!* the poster announced in old English lettering. I hung it on my bathroom door as a subtle tribute to Mama, and I eagerly anticipated her reaction to it.

"Why do you have that poster with *that* word on it?" she said. "You know your children are going to be reading soon."

"What word, Mama?"

"You know the one I'm talking about."

"Oh, that poster's a tribute to you. You were a woman who dared to say fuck housework."

"Well, I don't use language like that."

She didn't use language like that, and she never got used to that splendid word that perfectly conveyed the hip and emancipating 1960s vulgarity I'd adopted. More importantly, though, she never accepted her hero status as the woman who dared to defy housework. To do so, she'd need to analyze her behavior, a scary thought for her.

But it was more complicated than that. First off, Mama wouldn't have wanted to be a 1950s-style housewife. Mama's values regarding the home were forged in the decades before the War, from a frugal time of *making do*. If her neurosis got the better of her and set her to extremes, she nonetheless valued finding usefulness in objects, improvising solutions from available materials, and keeping reminders of the past. These values I could whole-heartedly embrace. The final complication was simple. Mama didn't defy housework. She would have loved to have kept a clean and orderly house. Paralyzed by her neurotic fears of change and letting things go, she just couldn't do it.

I didn't understand the psychological condition, and wouldn't until much later, when the media brought to the public's attention the psychological disorder, *hoarding*. By the time I grew up, though, I knew Mama had suffered enough, and accepted that she couldn't change. She bungled the job of housework, and bungled it grandly. How much easier her life would have been, how much less would she have felt compelled to torture herself, if only she'd accepted that she wasn't going to suddenly wake up and get to it. How good it would have been for her soul if she could have said, "Fuck housework!" Even if she needed to say it more politely.

At University of Detroit I did find a good Catholic boy to marry, a boy whose mind and heart, like mine, embraced the unfolding of the 1960s culture, politics and art. The first Sunday after our wedding at Holy Redeemer we left the Church together. We didn't plan it. I'm not even sure we talked about it. Neither of us stirred from bed, neither of us contemplated the mortal sin it was, missing Mass on Sunday, failing to keep the Holy Day of Obligation. We seemed to be through with the Church. Like so many of our generation who had endured the rigidity of the American Church in the 1950's, and the rigors and rules in parochial schools, we simply reached the point at the onset of adulthood when we'd had enough.

Dan and I had our children baptized, the first child who came six months after our wedding, the second who came a year later. We simply bowed to the inquiries from both sides of the family, "When is the Baptism going to be?" Even then we weren't ready to talk about it. Getting the children baptized was a way to keep our privacy. Our leaving was final, but it wasn't dramatic, not like James Joyce's young hero Steven Dedalus in *Portrait of the Artist as a Young Man*, a book that had profoundly influenced us, as it did so many of our friends at U of D.

So many of the harrowing experiences of the lapsed Catholics of my generation were about authority and sex. In an ironic way my quarrel wasn't so much about authority and sex, but about authority and shame. We followed the 1960s decade to its radicalized end when my husband suddenly decided he no longer wanted to be married, possibly his ultimate act of rebellion.

I hadn't strayed as far from the Church as I'd wanted. I become a single parent in a disguised cloud of shame. It mixed together—grief at the loss of a man I loved and being ashamed, a flashback to that humiliation of my childhood. I tried, even valiantly, not to pass the shame down to my children. Still, that shame led me to cut myself off. I stopped attending any of Mama's extended family celebrations. Nonetheless, I rejected the idea of going back to the Church, of getting an annulment.

As time went on, I'd see my childhood terrors at the hands of the nuns balanced by the pleasure all the saints, statues, stories and songs my childhood devotion had given me. Today I feel no need to go back. I am a cultural Catholic—if there can be such a thing.

As for Mama, she never changed, and her hoarding grew steadily worse. What changed was my attitude, transformed by freedom and my own competence. I didn't hoard. I didn't shirk housework. I'd learned to do it efficiently and well from the several women I'd studied so carefully as a child. I even made an art out of creating beautiful rooms—a compensation for all those dreary rooms of childhood.

I could now appreciate the up-side of Mama's hoarding. The way-back room, with its mounds of junk, came to be a haven, the epicenter of home for me—the way-back room no longer a tomb to get buried alive in, but the site of an archeological dig.

Even as Mama kissed my children hello, took their coats, and asked them if they were hungry, reciting the familiar litany of everything she had in the house to eat, I was already feeling for the key ring on top of the bookcase in the hall. As I hurried to the way-back room, I heard her interviewing them in that respectful way of hers, speaking to them as though they were little adults. Had Mama been able to, she probably would have stopped me from heading toward the way-back room. I don't think she ever understood or appreciated my attraction.

I thrilled to insert the key into the deadbolt and turn it to the right, while turning the shaft of the missing doorknob to the left. I delighted in opening the door to see what was new, especially as her hoarding accelerated and she collected items from friends and relatives who had died, or moved to Florida, or downsized to apartments and retirement homes. Ah, she was winning at pinochle card parties—lots of prizes, crocheted toilet-paper covers, new calendars for years half gone, lots of plastic floral bouquets, ball point pen sets, salad bowls and tongs, battery-powered backscratchers and playing card sorters, more useful if she were willing to buy a battery.

She now swam at the Y, taking advantage of the "sea" change, when around 1970 the Western YMCA finally opened its two main portals, one labeled *Men's Entrance*, and the other labeled *Boys' Entrance*, to the girls and women of the neighborhood. Here was her gym bag with that white bathing cap. A pile of screws and a broken handle—she must have gotten Mr. Patterson, the latest of her unreliable handymen, to fix the back screen door. I examined the newest half-filled Avon boxes to gather evidence of how a life was being lived—like an archeologist finding potshards among the barley grains and chicken bones. I stood in the tiny path with the six-foot high mountains of boxes on either side, listening to the distant backyard birds, letting the disparate objects unhook my thoughts as a meditation. I deeply breathed in the dust and gave my cares away. I was home.

I also picked up the shorthand I needed to catch up with Mama. It was like I never left. "Hey, Ma, when did Mr. Patterson fix that door?"

"Oh, you mean the one downstairs? Well, he came last week, but he didn't get it done. He said he was going to come back to make it work, but he hasn't called."

"Did you pay him?" I'd never forgotten the lesson learned from the painter Mr. Gowan.

I enjoyed seeing what in the way-back room I could nag her out of. So many pretty things I could use. Things I could rescue. Here was a lace tablecloth among the rubble, brought in from the disassembly of the house of Mrs. Melvin up the street, or Eleanor Wright, Mama's friend who exchanged her big four bedroom home for an apartment, or Aunt Edith who died with no daughters. Fine linens, lace curtains and crystal lamps. Chipped cups, linen napkins, napkin rings. Silverware. Their receipts for light bills. Their family pictures. Their humble, rather boring, letters they received talking about the weather somewhere else. The evidence that they had bought tires for their cars or hired Aufderheide Brothers carpenters to caulk and putty their windows in 1953. Official papers in Old English letters with official seals certifying they'd paid off their mortgages.

During the 1970s Mama was appointed executor to several childless people's estates. She made a perfect candidate: excellent at math, scrupulously honest, curious and interested in the job, and, when it came to accounting, willing and able to promptly follow through. What remained that couldn't be sold or given away ended up in the way-back room. Even I had to admit that the pictures, receipts, and important legal papers begged to be saved. Print is a memorial.

"Mama, can I have this tablecloth?"

She looked up from the stove where she was frying up her famous cheeseburgers for the kids. She cooked the thick patties of ground round steak until they were dry and tasteless after being pressed down again and again with her heavy-handed spatula before she finally placed the thick uneven slices of sharp cheddar cheese on top and sandwiched them between slices of Koepplinger's whole wheat bread lathered with Miracle Whip. There was nothing like them, and the kids acquired a taste, probably because of the garnish of Grandma love.

"What have you got there?" she said.

I held it up.

"Oh, that's one of Eleanor's. I want that. You can't have it." Mama was still stingy.

"Ah, Ma. You're not going to do anything with it. I can use it."

Then we'd start a long round of wheedling and negotiation. It was a game we played. The strength of her resolve was an index of her health and her wits about her. I knew that if she ever became generous, it would mean the Mama I knew and loved was dying. I also knew that sometimes begging, begging, begging one day would soften her up for when I begged again the next time or the next. I managed to get the tablecloth, and the globe and unabridged dictionary Daddy had bought for us. After begging and finally putting my foot down in an ugly confrontation, I got the Hopalong Cassidy thermos Daddy had bought for me when I was five years old. "After all, it's mine," I said. "He bought it for me."

A couple years later I found Daddy's lunchbox balanced on a pile of books in the way-back room. It, along with an entire shelf of Daddy's things, had been hidden in the back bedroom closet. But when Mama had Mr. Patterson paint that bedroom, those jealously guarded things ended up strewn around the way-back room. I took it home.

Before disguising it in a plastic grocery bag from the kitchen, I meditated about taking it. I needed to take something of my father's from the house without permission. What might it mean to my mental health, what might it do to the lifetime of unresolved grief, if I took something of Daddy's without permission, without pretending to someone else that I didn't consider it important, without having to wrench it from another?

It didn't do wonders. One symbolic lunchbox could never undo the damage. But it felt good to take it. And good to see the stamped silver-colored metal nameplate *Rhodes* inserted into a slot on its smooth black side, the only thing I ever stole. What little else I got, I begged for. Mama didn't give love easily. She made me work for it.

Mama never missed the lunchbox, although a few months later I told her about it. It was then when I confronted her—about Daddy and me. We'd never had a history, like in some families, of filial hierarchy, of what a daughter dared to say or not say. I easily confronted Mama about her behavior: defied her, disobeyed her, pointed out when she was being irrational. However, I still had difficulty confronting her about my deepest feelings. I'd learned so early that if I expressed them they'd be denied. I took the risk anyway. "Why did you keep me from Daddy's memory? Why didn't you let me know he was also mine?"

The eyes darted. She kept trying to change the subject, ending with the weak, "But you were only a child."

"I was six years old. I needed him more than either you or Betty."

"Well, you were too young to remember."

"Then you should have told me about him. Told me about how he loved me."

"You knew he loved you. Of course he loved you."

"How could I have known that if you say I was too young to remember?"

"Well, I did the best I could. You know it wasn't easy, losing my husband like that."

I pushed the subject on her over the next several months, and in the end gave up. She wouldn't listen. She couldn't see how I had grieved, couldn't come out of herself.

As the word somehow got around the family that I was confronting Mama, I was approached by my Aunt Mag, Mama's oldest sister, the family matriarch. "Your father knew he was going to die in the hospital. He told me the only thing he couldn't resolve was what would happen to you without him. He kept saying over and over again, 'What will happen to Mary Frances?'"

I don't know whether she was telling the truth. She'd used my middle name, the one they used in the extended family to distinguish me from my cousin Mary Magdalene. Daddy would have called me Mary.

But that's not the only reason I questioned her veracity. If what she said were true, I reasoned, if Daddy, in that in-and-out rhythm of those last horrible morphine weeks, had talked of me, expressed his concern, wouldn't someone have told me that as a child? Mama? It would have made so much difference. It would have connected me to him and helped assuage the grief— for someone to have said, "To the end your father was thinking about you. He didn't want to leave you. He loved you."

Mama had sometimes spoken of Daddy's words in his dying week— always about him reconciling their religious differences—between the Catholic and the Methodist. "Mama, your way was better," he said. He did call his wife Mama, the way of speaking of a Southern man.

———

I'd confronted Mama about Daddy, but I couldn't confront her about "that habit." What did the school psychologist at Maybury say about it? Dr. Himmelhoch, Sisters Elizabeth Ann, Florita and Callistus: what did they all say? Why didn't she talk to me about it? She saw my devotion to Our Lady and the saints, my dresser transformed into an altar. Had it never occurred to her that her devout daughter would have stopped immediately had she known "that habit" was considered a mortal sin? Did Mama too believe "that habit" was a mortal sin?

I thought of confronting her, even to get answers to my questions, but I was already fairly certain that she'd make it mostly about herself and her own burden, the extra widow's burden she'd had to bear because of me. During the months I confronted her about Daddy, she shot back one time, "Well, you were no easy child to handle." From her arching tone and direct gaze, I knew she was referring to it.

To have confronted her on the issue would have violated my privacy and exposed me to another round of embarrassment. I wasn't going to get any belated comfort. More likely, she'd try to make me feel guilty. And that was the irony of it: I'd never felt guilty. I'd suffered profound misery and humiliation, but never guilt.

I had already sorted it out. I knew my self esteem was severely damaged. My capacity to trust in large social situations was damaged. My sexuality had not been damaged. I'd been spared some of the horrors that people I knew had had to face—other girls as children and adolescents. They were less naïve than I, knew full well that what they were doing was masturbation, and knew that according to the Church's teachings, masturbation was a mortal sin. They did it anyway, and they felt excruciating guilt. When I knew it was a mortal sin, I'd been spared the guilt. Father Spitzer had done right by me when I made that eighth-grade Confession, and I never questioned his word: "You didn't know," he said. "Therefore you committed no sin." It was one of those ironies of the pre-Vatican II Church. I hadn't sinned, but I grew used to being punished for good measure.

In December of 1972 Mama got a forlorn letter from the Redemptorist Fathers of Holy Redeemer Parish, asking parishioners to come back to church or pray for those who hadn't. The letter mentions that in 1945 the Redeemer community numbered 4,500 families, with 10,000 attending Mass on Sunday. The statistics in 1972 had fallen to an estimated 3,530 families, with only 3,000 in attendance at Sunday Mass. The parish was struggling, and it seemed the prophesies of Father Forbes, who'd spoken out so forcefully in the 1950s against the tide of leaving, were coming true.

But then a remarkable thing happened. During the 1970s and 1980s, Mexican-Americans who'd populated the tiny "Mexicantown" enclave around Bagley Street in Sainte Anne's Parish now spilled into Holy Redeemer Parish to join the relatively few who'd moved there earlier, displacing many of the Southern Protestants, who moved away. Again, our side of the parish, and Clark Street in particular, led the surge of the new migration, with a few Mexican-American families having settled there in the late 1950s. The Mexicans were joined by other Latino groups—Puerto Ricans, Cubans, Guatemalans, Hondurans, Chileans, Spaniards, and others, all, traditionally at least, Catholic.

Mama got to witness the transformation, see Redeemer's parking lot crowded again on Sunday, see it difficult again to find a seat at High Mass on Easter. In celebration, in the late 1970s, she enrolled in Spanish classes at

Western High School. Each Tuesday and Thursday morning she set off across the park, lugging her textbook, *Usted y Yo*, in a pretty sequined canvas bag. "*Buenos dias, Señora Villarruel*," she said, if she happened to run into our next door neighbor.

"Good morning, Mrs. Rhodes," Molly said. "You can speak English."

The neighborhood continued to grow. If Redeemer became a poorer parish, it still continued to thrive with people, and Father Forbes came to rest easy in his grave. The old hillbilly honky-tonks came to show little evidence of what they'd been. They became Mexican restaurants, and the whole neighborhood came to be known as "Mexicantown." Today, music blares from car stereos as cars crawl up and down Vernor Highway—often the *norteño* music of northern Mexico so reminiscent of the Polish polkas we heard in the neighborhood long ago.

When my daughter Lara was fifteen, and Mama was seventy-five, another critical time to clean the way-back room developed. Mama had just gotten out of the hospital, and so many boxes blocked the twisted hall I feared she'd stumble in the night and hurt herself. There wasn't any room to shove them into the way-back room. My daughter wanted summer employment, and between the two of them, with me goading them on, they negotiated a deal. My daughter would stay for a week, earn some money, and get a big cleaning job done. She would start in the hallway and then progress to the way-back room.

Five days into the job my daughter phoned. "Get down here, Ma. She won't let me throw anything out, and she's driving me nuts."

Mama had pretty much steered my daughter completely away from the job by spending the days offering her rounds and rounds of food, even though Lara had explained she was on a diet. If it wasn't that, Mama called her out to the living room to talk, or insisted they take her second-hand Ford LTD out for a spin and down to the Boulevard Dock to watch the freighters on the river, or take her around to visit relatives.

"When am I going to get started, Grandma?" Lara said.

"There'll be time, Honey. Your mom's not coming 'til Saturday."

"But, Grandma, I'm supposed to be working. I'm supposed to be cleaning up the way-back room."

I laughed all the way to Detroit, ninety miles away. Lara had told me on the phone, "I can't throw the stuff out myself because I don't feel like I have the authority." She was right, of course, and it had fallen to me to take that authority. Again my talent to insist on throwing things out over the resistance of the one they belonged to. A ruthless person was needed, and that was me.

And so, along with Lara's competent help, we stayed for a few more days and cleaned the way-back room again. This time, of course, we found it impossible to strip it of junk and put it to another use. It would need to stay a storage room. Too many jewels in the junk: more pinochle prizes, more fine linens, more furniture and keepsakes, party dresses and board games. Still, we deflated the mountains by removing the worthless stock reports, old newspapers, coupons, flyers, and broken brooms, making innumerable trips to the dumpsters in the alley. We categorized the treasures and lined them up in relative order in different stacks along different walls. We made wide paths and swept the floor.

Mama didn't protest too much about our cleaning the room. She was getting tired.

Monnie Webb and Al Konczal moved into the downstairs flat in 1984. Mama almost refused to rent to them because they weren't married. I heard about it in our weekly phone conversations. "How are they?" I said.

"They seem OK, but you know they're not married. That doesn't look good for the neighborhood."

A few weeks later, "Are they still OK?" I said.

"They seem to be. But you know they're still not married."

"Ma, they're probably not going to get married. That's the way a lot of people live nowadays."

Monnie and Al weren't married, but they proved to be attractive in one important respect: since both of them, in their early fifties, collected disability, the State of Michigan directly paid Mama the rent.

I finally saw Monnie and Al, walking toward us from across the park on Scotten, as Mama and I stepped down from the downstairs porch on a sunny day. They got bigger and bigger as they circumnavigated the latest "improvement" the City had made to the park: a concrete stage and a grassy hill designed to rise like an amphitheater dumped on top of the lagoon, the lagoon that had paved the lake, the lake that had trained the natural springs all hidden now underground. The only memory of the buried water: the hill, like the lagoon and the lake, is kidney-shaped.

While I gazed at Monnie and Al as they came closer, I decided they looked about as odd as any of the many odd couples who'd lived downstairs: Al a head taller, thinner, a deep rose to Monnie's milky white yellow. Monnie, a Southerner, and Al, a Pole, braided the disparate threads of traditional white ethnic diversity in the neighborhood—one tinged with deepening poverty. They passed muster and could now join the distinguished list of entertaining tenants. I didn't think to view them as Angels of Death.

The next month when I went to see Mama, every freshly cut blade of grass in the front and back yards waved in tandem. All the weeds had been killed, along with all the stray varieties of quack, crab, and fine fescue grasses that had been a part of the lawn from my earliest recollection. Two truck tires, painted white, had been sunk into the ground on each side of the walkway in the backyard, and in their rings grew bouquets of petunias.

"What happened?" I asked Mama.

"Al's been helping out with the grass. Doesn't it look beautiful?"

I had to admit it did; yet something about the situation worried me. I chalked up some of my displeasure to my nostalgia. I always liked that little tuft of resistant fescue in the side yard. As a toddler, I used to run my fingers over it while waiting for my sister to come home from school.

Some of my uneasiness though was caused by Mama's lack of resistance. I couldn't see her consenting to the truck tire flowerbeds. Knowing her, I figured she'd think of them as tacky. They were, in fact, tacky, but when I asked her about them, she didn't complain. "Oh, Al put those in." That wasn't like her. Mama could always be counted on to resist change.

As the year progressed, Mama started to change. On one visit, I noticed some of the antique furniture had disappeared from the basement.

"What happened in the basement?" I said.

"Al had to move things around to fix my water heater."

"Where's my bike?" The fat-wheeled maroon deluxe Schwinn Cruiser in almost mint condition had stood in the landing in front of the grade door for at least thirty years. The bike was a beaut, with extras such as a front basket, a battery-powered front-fender headlight, a chrome horn, a small rearview mirror, a locking mechanism in the frame with a real key, and a back rack extending over the shiny chrome rear fender. Daddy had bought it for my sister in 1950, and it had been handed down to me. I'd already calculated that it was valuable, although I liked coming home and looking at it where it stood. It reminded me of the freedom I'd felt, maneuvering it for so many miles through so many Detroit neighborhoods, during the years I was striking out on my own. The keepsake with its flat white-walled snazzy tires grounded me in all my further travels and comforted me.

"Oh, he must have put it in the basement when he took out the trash."

"It's not there, Mama."

"It must be in the garage, then."

Why didn't I intervene right then, sound the alarm, demand to know where the antiques were going, or simply take over? I'm not sure. It was her house, her tenants, her life without me, and I was living ninety miles away. I was all grown up now, no longer in charge of taking care of Mama, and I selfishly enjoyed the freedom. I also doubted whether she'd back me up if I intervened.

I did try to get Mama to confront Monnie and Al, tell them she was saving her antiques for her daughters. I pushed and pushed her to assert herself, and then gave up, unable to face the fact that the Mama I knew and loved was dying.

Six months later, I talked with Mama on the phone and listened to her weekly glowing recitations of all the good things Monnie and Al had done for her, things I was unable to do for her. As she moved to chronicle Monnie and Al's troubles with the welfare department, she casually said, "And Al cleaned out that third garage for me." She was speaking of the stall she'd filled with the boxes she rescued from the trash the first time I cleaned the way-back room when I was eleven years old.

"He what! That door was padlocked."

"Oh, he just broke it so he could clean it out for me."

"What did he do with the stuff?"

"He said there was nothing in there but boxes."

My stomach churned and my heart raced. It was too late. Gone was my chance to revisit my eleven-year-old decisions about the way-back room. The boxes and boxes of old man Dixon's gleanings were gone. The notes he carefully dictated to his secretary-mistress, on the "Catholic menace," on his hero Cal Coolidge, on the dog-president Roosevelt—all of it was lost. The sepia pictures of the boats on the river against the turn-of-the-twentieth-century city skyline—lost. The different proofs of publicity posters for his beloved city, Detroit, "Where Life Is Worth Living"—lost. The snippets of poetry old man Dixon's secretary wrote and read him in the way-back room, even as his poor wife labored in the kitchen below—lost. I'd kept enough of Mr. Dixon's artifacts when I cleaned out the way-back room the first time to know that what was left in the garage was a significant lode—if not valuable, at least critically interesting—of the mind of a nineteenth-century arrogant man who happened to love our city as I did. Now Mama was breezily telling me it was gone.

It got worse. Within a few months, Mama stopped locking the door at the top of the stairs. When I called, she often interrupted our phone conversation to say hello to Monnie. "But didn't you have to go open the door?" I said.

"Oh, no, Monnie just comes in. She's standing right here. Do you want to say 'Hi'?"

Each time I came home something more was different. The piles of stuff in the way-back room were shrinking—almost down to four feet from six feet the last time. The stacks of boxes of small treasures my daughter and I had categorized and stacked so carefully along the walls were diminishing. Besides, when I looked at the full Avon boxes on the top layer, they seemed to contain nothing but truly worthless stuff to discard. That, of course, was not the "normal" way of things. I became alarmed when I spotted a couple *Holy Redeemer Weeklies* from 1954. These had to have come from the boxes I discarded in 1956 that had been left in the garage.

I couldn't imagine that Mama would let anyone into the way-back room. She was mortally ashamed of it. That was her final secret.

"Did you let Al into the way-back room?"

"You know I don't let anybody into the way-back room."

"Why are the piles of junk going down?"

"Well, he did help me for a couple days."

"Were you back there with him?"

"Yes. I watched him and told him he could take some things to the garbage." The bright way she constructed that fiction, her directing him to discard, as though she were a normal housewife, told me she was lying. She hadn't watched him, and she would never tell anyone to throw something out. Besides, I could always tell when she was lying. There was nothing much I could do.

I went out to the third garage stall, now unlocked again without its padlock, with one of the alley doors coming off its hinges. I saw the Dixons' antiques were gone. I saw that the remaining boxes had been sorted, with only old newspapers and stock reports in them, but most of them were gone. Rats had been in. I saw plenty of their damp forlorn droppings.

I contemplated again the loss of old man Dixon's artifacts, things I thought would ultimately be mine when I got to them. I knew they would strengthen my connection to that man who, for all his arrogance, had taught me through his things to see a longer and more loving view of my city. Those pictures of the Belle Isle canals and bridges, with their exuberant nineteenth-century arches, those pictures of steamships and bandstands, of water, when excursion boats took revelers all the way to Cleveland, all the way to Put-In-Bay. I'd learned to appreciate the gone ones—my father and my old man landlord—in the artifacts that I could bring to light. Mr. Dixon knew it was and would be the City of the Straits, a miracle of lakes squeezed into a channel of profoundly spiritual energy. I stood in the empty stall and grieved. Grieved through an anger I would not resolve. Mama had rescued the valuable artifacts on that day the garbage truck came lumbering up the alley in that summer when I was eleven. She knew better than I did. Knew better than most of the twentieth-century planners who continually tried to erase the past by tearing things down. She'd rescued the artifacts. But now she'd lost them, allowed herself to be robbed of them. Allowed me to be robbed.

After Mama died, and even before I moved back into the house in 1996, my daughter Lara and I cleaned the way-back room for the final time. And then I did away with it in a single inexpensive stroke.

I hired a good carpenter to cut an archway into the wall of the way-back room, almost exactly the size of the one between the living room and dining room, with matching early-twentieth century molding. He fashioned a built-in bookcase out of the narrow doorway that had been the entrance, and installed a new beveled glass French door closer to the stairway as the new back entrance to the flat.

The way-back room, the spookiest room at the end of the dark twisted hallway, beyond the back entrance door and dark stairway, ceased to be. The way-back room, the hermetic, muffled, constipated repository of all brought into the house, the black end to the elegant light that poured in through the big front-room windows, was no more. No longer did I grope in the dark at the end of the twisted hallway. I stood in the prisms of light that poured in through the large leaded-glass window, and I could view tree branches full of friendly backyard birds. With the elegant archway, the room became an open sunroom or a parlor. Sometimes it needed the space heater, but never again would the room suffer so thoroughly in the grip of cold. With the Oriental rug on the clean pine floor, with the comfortable couches, stereo and TV, we could no longer call it the way-back room.

ACKNOWLEDGEMENTS

During the long process of writing this book I have been supported by numerous people and institutions. It began when I was awarded a summer research grant from Madonna University in 2003 to help defray expenses at *Anam Cara*, a writers' retreat in West Cork, Ireland. There I wrote drafts of a few chapters as fast as memory could carry me into creative prose.

Through a Distinguished Professorship in the Humanities from Madonna University, I spent the month of August, 2007, in Assisi, Italy, at the Arts Workshop International, where I worked with Dinitia Smith and Maxine Hong Kingston. A sabbatical followed in Fall of 2007, then another summer research grant, which allowed me to spend time at Wellspring House in Massachusetts. In addition to financial support from Madonna University, I have been inspired by the unshakable faith and encouragement of my colleague and friend Kathleen O'Dowd, Dean of Arts and Humanities.

I could not have written a memoir of much detail without access to various archives, and I am grateful for the Burton Archives of Detroit Public Library most of all. I also thank Sister Elizabeth Fleckenstein, former Principal of Holy Redeemer Grade School, and Donna Westley of the Immaculate Heart of Mary Archives. Sister Mary Jo Maher, Sister John Mary Baker, and Sister Stephanie Mueller shared remembrances of our days at Holy Redeemer School under the leadership of Mother Mary Patrick. Sister Mary Jo encouraged me to maintain my own perspective in the memoir.

Holy Redeemer's former Pastor, Monsignor Donald Hanchon, permitted me to review years of the parish newspaper, the *Holy Redeemer Weekly*. Geraldina Hernandez, Redeemer parish receptionist, assisted me with the task. The new Pastor, Father Dennis Walsh, gave me permission to include a 1955 *Weekly* ad with my photographs. Ziggy Gonzalez, Deb Sumner, and Anthony Benavides compared memories of Clark Park and the neighborhood. Bernadine Andrzejewski, Christine Cox, Mike Komiensky, Diane Meshinski, and Patricia Thayer compared memories of Holy Redeemer High School.

Friends and relatives provided me with distance and solitude—and escape. My son, Michael Minock, spent a week with me at his *stuga* in Sweden, his presence underpinning one of the funny chapters. My daughter, Lara Minock, and son-in-law Ken McMurdy, provided me a New Jersey space to write. My granddaughters, Meara and Josephine McMurdy, consistently and enthusiastically supported my project. Rick and Kathy Silva, Katie O'Dowd, and Mick and Lynne Reid lent me cottages and houses. Michael Koehler allowed me to escape the renovation of a house, as he worked on it during most of the year of 2008.

My gang of Springfed Arts poets, from Mary Jo Firth-Gillet's long-running Advanced Poetry Workshop, allowed me to come home each week to poetry.

I have been lucky enough to get critical and encouraging readers at several stages of the project: Dinitia Smith and Maxine Hong Kingston read drafts of chapters. Karen Dimanche Davis, Larry Gabriel, and Ruth Ray read the first full draft of the manuscript. The late Stephanie Matthews, my friend and fellow poet, read draft and revised chapters. Nancy Solak, my first copyeditor, helped me untangle many an awkward sentence and steadfastly worked with me when I created self-imposed deadlines, needing to believe the manuscript was almost "done."

I am deeply grateful to Kathryn Wildfong, Acquisitions Editor at Wayne State University Press, for her patient talk and astute suggestions. Ann Russell deserves special credit for reading the manuscript twice.

During the time when I was on the home stretch, M. L. Liebler and Katherine Oldmixon read parts of the manuscript. Carolyn Walker, Mary Schmitt, and the late Margo Lagattuta read the entire manuscript and offered their support and suggestions. Larry Smith's sharp editing let me know that he and Bottom Dog Press were the right editor and press for me. Robin Ward, of Madonna University's Art Department gave expert help with graphics.

Finally, I wish to thank the many people who populate my pages, and who provided me with the stories I tell. I have changed the names of some individuals to protect their privacy, choosing surnames that still identify their ethnicity. There are no composite characters in the narrative, and, save for the usual lapses and constructions of recovered dialogue and memory, I have attempted to be faithful to the way it was. I hope my narrative inspires them to remember it their way. And let me know.

ABOUT THE AUTHOR

Mary Minock is a long-term poet and academic writer, and *The Way-Back Room* represents her first excursion into memoir. Mary grew up in the 1950s and 1960s in the dense Southwest Detroit parish of Holy Redeemer during a time of remarkable changes. Eventually she left Detroit and went on to live in Columbus, Ohio, Ann Arbor and East Lansing, Michigan, and New York City, and returned to Ann Arbor. She came back to Detroit in 1996, fixed up her childhood home, lived there for a decade, and then moved three blocks away to help restore another stately home. She is an avid Detroit booster, looking at it over the long haul and seeing the city's continuity. From her strategic location near the Detroit River, she travels to the suburbs to work, and across the river to play—where she sings and plays tin whistle with a group of Celtic musicians in Windsor, Ontario. She also catches up with her son and daughter and granddaughters—scattered from New Jersey to Stockholm, Sweden.

Mary has taught at the University of Michigan, New York Institute of Technology, and Wayne State University. For more than a decade now, she has taught poetry and literature, as well as creative and academic writing at Madonna University in Livonia, Michigan, where she is a Professor of Language and Literature.

Her collection of poetry is entitled *Love in the Upstairs Flat* (Mellon, 1995), and recent poetry appears in *Driftwood Review, The MacGuffin, MARGIE, Mid-America, Patterson Literary Review*, and in the Detroit anthology *Abandon Automobile*. Recent awards include: the Gwendolyn Brooks Award from the Society for the Study of Midwest Literature, a Ginsberg Poetry Award, and Finalist status in the *Atlanta Review* and *Nimrod* prizes. In 2007 and 2011, she won Springfed Arts Awards in prose for earlier versions of chapters from *The Way-Back Room*.

RECENT BOOKS BY BOTTOM DOG PRESS

Learning using multiple analogies 267
Leeds Modelling System 126, 180–1
LEX 265
Lisp learning 143–4
Lisp tutor 16, 57, 73, 75, 142, 166–7,
    184–5, 302, 391, 394
LMS, *see* Leeds Modelling System
Logo 157, 166–7

Machine learning 58, 70, 164, 175–7,
    179–96, 337
Macsyma advisor 64, 66, 215, 227
Mal-rule 75–6, 87, 126, 158, 180–3,
    368–9
Managing multiple constraints 282–3
Mathematical education 30–43
Mathematical games 275
Mathematical microworlds 270–2
Memory organization package 147
Memory processes 144–6
Meno tutor 15, 17–26, 326
Mental model 49, 69–70, 77–87, 293
Menus 325
Meta-cognition 33
Meta-knowledge 58
Meta-rules 298
Metaphor based system 318
Method 70–7
Micro-PROUST 386
Micro-theory 124–37
Micro-theory evaluation quotient 130–2,
    135–7
Micro-theory system 124–37
Micro-theory systems and statistics
    126–7
Microworld 270–2
Minimal device space 83
Misconception 61–2, 158, 230, 260–1
Mis-generalization 182–3
Mistake 75–6
Modelling student's knowledge 293–8
MOLGEN 289
Multiple constraints 278–9
Multiple models 261
Multiple representations 12–13, 35–6
Multiple viewpoints 103–7
Multiple views 284–9
MUMATH 43

MYCROFT 362

Natural language interface 115, 119
Natural language program 395–9
NOAH 213–16
Notecards 283
Notepad 283
Novice programming 374–5, 391–409
Novices and experts 41

Occasion-driven teaching 329
ODETTE 390
Odysseus 66
On-line help system 338–60
On-line monitoring 228, 311–12
Operational account 83–7
Operational knowledge 333–4
Overlay 111, 172, 291

PAM 228–9, 232–3
Percentage of hits 129, 135
Personal construct theory 205
Personalized task representation 203–4
Perturbation modelling 172
PIXIE 181–3, 186
Plan-difference rules 383
Plan generation 212
Plan hierarchy 216–24
Plan methods 321
Planning 308, 343
Planning and intelligent tutoring
    212–13
Plan recognition 212–29, 308, 312,
    347–50
POISE 213–14, 228–30, 232, 302
Practical constraints 44
Pragmatics of programming 90–5
Problem description notation 379–80
Problem solving 32–41, 58
Problem space 79–80
Procedural knowledge 10–11
Production system 70–4, 125–6, 265–7
Program checking 361–73
Programming as translating 95–102
Programming plans 381, 392–3
Prototypical knowledge 295–6
Prototyping 251–2
PROUST 67, 363, 374–91, 393